ADVANCE PRAISE

"*New Bones Abolition* is a reminder that state repression is indiscriminate when it comes to gender—or generation. The NYPD strangled Eric Garner but his daughter Erica refused to accept defeat. Thank you Dr. Joy James for making sure that the floodlights of history will be aimed in the proper direction."

—**Kalonji Jama Changa**, cofounder of Black Power Media, organizer and founder of FTP Movement, and coproducer of *Organizing is the New Cool*

"*New Bones Abolition* offers a series of dialectical engagements with the captive conditions of a racist society alongside an incisive assessment of movement gains, losses, and betrayals. Utilizing the Captive Maternal analytic, Joy James brilliantly maps the continuum from coerced or conflicted caregiving to war resistance against the physical, emotional, and psychological outcomes that are produced under a predatory democracy. We must grow new bones to recoup our generative and reproductive labor from those who enslave and imprison us—new bones that move beyond the rhetorical to materially confront imperialist violence and premature death. James' thoughtful and urgent work leaves us with a renewed commitment to the unfinished struggle for Black liberation."

—**Jalessah T. Jackson**, founder of the Decolonial Feminist Collective and Access Reproductive Care Southeast Interim Executive Director

"From caretaking for those on the frontlines to war resistance against deathly policing and imperialism, Joy James details the myriad forms in which a 'new bones' abolition might learn from the life of Erica Garner and others. A beautiful love letter to those radicalized by trauma, and a clarion call to join them in the struggle for our collective liberation, *New Bones Abolition* honors the ancestors of centuries-long and present-day freedom movements and grounds their legacies as inheritances for the rebels and war resisters among us who are fighting for a future without police and state violence."

—**Charmaine Chua**, University of California, Santa Barbara, Global Studies

"It is impossible to read more than several pages of *New Bones Abolition* without confronting the long historical terror that saturates the present. This book is animated by the militancy of the Captive Maternal as a vessel of Black radical care and insurgent community, demystifying the liberal/nonprofit hijacking of 'abolition' while illuminating collective experiments in liberation that obliterate and make obsolete the anti-Black state—in and beyond the United States. Joy James identifies and dismantles the backdoor liberalism that endorses fraudulent 'radical' identities, organizations, and movements, offering a framework for collective study that builds liberationist analyses in the context of an increasingly multilayered, 'progressive' and reactionary counterinsurgency. I am grateful for this work."

—**Dylan Rodríguez**, author of *White Reconstruction: Domestic Warfare and the Logic of Racial Genocide*, University of California, Riverside, Department of Black Study and Department of Media and Cultural Studies

*

Praise for Joy James

"*Transcending the Talented Tenth* proposes original analyses of historical portrayals of the African American intelligentsia as a way of understanding the contested terrain on which contemporary black intellectuals work . . . . Joy James' work is a pioneering intervention."
—**Angela Y. Davis**, author of *Are Prisons Obsolete?*, University of California, Santa Cruz

"James reveals a radical tradition [in *Shadowboxing: Representations of Black Feminist Politics*] that could free us all."
—**Robin D. G. Kelley**, author of *Freedom Dreams: The Black Radical Imagination*

"In this extraordinary volume, James brings together the powerful voices of prison resistance, past and present, providing the intellectual foundations for a comparative approach to our understanding of criminal justice as a tool for political repression. *Imprisoned Intellectuals* creates a critical scholarly resource for interpreting criminal justice and its impact on race, gender, and class hierarchies of power."
—**Manning Marable**, author of *How Capitalism Underveloped Black America*

"Americans have a hard time thinking about race, gender, and class at the same time, especially when intellectuals are in question. But not Joy James. Her refreshing discussion of Black thought refuses to stop with men or the highly educated. This [*Transcending the Talented Tenth*] is what African-American Studies is about in the best sense of the phrase."
—**Nell Irvin Painter**, author of *Sojourner Truth: A Life, A Symbol*

"A superb collection, both instructive and inspiring. Joy James is to be complimented for *Imprisoned Intellectuals* and for her thoughtful introductory essay."
—**Dennis Brutus**, poet and former political prisoner of South African apartheid

"This Joy James reader [*Seeking the Beloved Community*] is at its core a portrait of 'the making of a dissident voice'. . . . What we most desperately need in a world that fears and silences opposition—or worse—are revolutionaries who speak truth to power and beckon us to stand with them in solidarity. *A luta continua*."
—**Beverly Guy-Sheftall**, author of *Alice Walker: Beauty in Truth*, Women's Research and Resource Center, Spelman College

"These broad-ranging essays in *Seeking the Beloved Community* circle around the topic of building community under siege. Communities can be 'thorny ties,' as Joy James notes, yet are vital for developing a critical consciousness of one's society. James also provides an astute analysis of the antirevolutionary trends in social theory today. Herein one will find the voice of a dissident humanist in full flower."
—**Linda Martín Alcoff**, coeditor of *Constructing the Nation: A Race and Nationalism Reader*

"*Imprisoned Intellectuals* is a unique and very significant contribution."
—**Bettina Aptheker**, author of *Communists in Closets: Queering the History 1930s–1990s*

NEW BONES ABOLITION:
CAPTIVE MATERNAL AGENCY AND
THE (AFTER)LIFE OF ERICA GARNER

NEW BONES ABOLITION:
CAPTIVE MATERNAL AGENCY AND THE (AFTER)LIFE OF ERICA GARNER

Joy James

Brooklyn, NY
Philadelphia, PA

ISBN: 978-1-94217-374-8 | eBook ISBN: 9781942173984
Library of Congress Number: 2023938203

10 9 8 7 6 5 4 3 2 1

Common Notions
c/o Interference Archive
314 7th St.
Brooklyn, NY 11215

Common Notions
c/o Making Worlds Bookstore
210 S. 45th St.
Philadelphia, PA 19104

www.commonnotions.org
info@commonnotions.org

Discounted bulk quantities of our books are available for organizing,
educational, or fundraising purposes. Please contact Common Notions at the
address above for more information.

Cover design by Josh MacPhee / Antumbra Design
Page Design and Typesetting by Suba Murugan

Printed by union labor in Canada on acid-free paper.

MIX
Paper from
responsible sources
FSC® C103567

CONTENTS

"NEW BONES"

we will wear
new bones again.
we will leave
these rainy days,
break out through
another mouth
into sun and honey time.
worlds buzz over us like bees,
we be splendid in new bones.
other people think they know
how long life is.
how strong life is.
we know.

—Lucille Clifton

ACKNOWLEDGMENTS

Suiyi Tang, Isaiah Blake, Ashley Shan, Nicole Yokum provided vital editorial and research support for *New Bones Abolition*. Tang located Erica Garner's tweets—which she describes as radical "songs"; software engineer Koh Wei Jie archived and preserved 11,000 tweets of Erica Garner messages for the New Bones Abolition's digital archives. Black Power Media (BPM), Black Anonymous, Prison Radio, and Columbia University law professors Bernard Harcourt and Jeff Fagan—all contributed to New Bones Abolition's digital appendix. Malav Kanuga, Erika Biddle, Stella Becerril, Lana Pochiro, and the team at Common Notions Press devoted significant resources and time to bring this text to the public.

My thanks to all contributors, especially the Agape-driven risk takers whose courage and clarity shook the streets and precincts to confront predatory state violence. May they continue to manifest strategies that safeguard our ethics, love, and lives.

CONTENT FROM PREVIOUSLY PUBLISHED WORK BY JOY JAMES APPEARS IN:

Joy James et al, The Abolition Collective/Black Internationalist Unions, *Abolition: A Journal and Community of Radical Theory & Practice*, https://abolitionjournal.org/bius/.

Joy James, "'New Bones' Abolitionism, Communism, and Captive Maternals," *Verso Blog*, June 4, 2021.

George Yancy, Joy James, et al., "A Tribute to bell hooks," *Los Angeles Review of Books*, January 15, 2022.

Ahmad Green-Haynes and Joy James, "Hacking the Codes of Black Power," *The Black Scholar*, vol. 47, no. 3, 2017.

Joy James, "Police Ethics through Presidential Politics and Abolitionist Struggle: Angela Y. Davis and Erica Garner," *The Ethics of Policing: New Perspectives on Law Enforcement*, edited by Ben Jones and Eduardo Mendieta. New York: NYU Press, 2021, pp. 179–202.

Joy James, "'Moving Targets,' #BlackLivesMatter: Anti-Black Racism, Police Violence, and Resistance," *Cultural Anthropology*, June 29, 2015.

Da'Shaun Harrison, Joy James, and Samaria Rice, "'Justifiable police homicide' and the ruse of American justice," *Scalawag*, March 8, 2022.

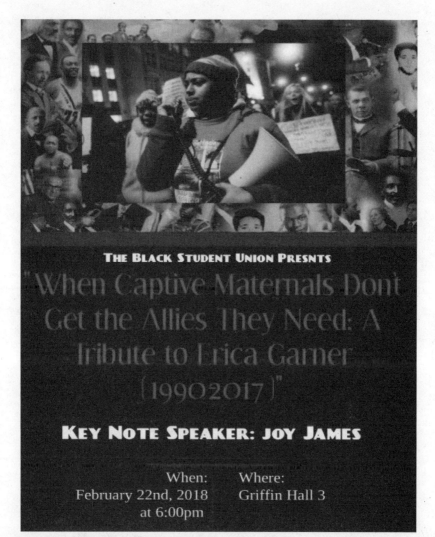

Figure 1: "When Captive Maternals Don't Get the Allies They Need: A Tribute to Erica Garner (1990–2017)," flyer, The Black Student Union, Williams College, February 22, 2018.

INTRODUCTION

On a December night in 2014, I found myself stuck in a cab traveling from Penn Station to upper Manhattan.[1] My African driver was frustrated, but also patient and sympathetic, as I became increasingly annoyed by the slow pace of traffic and the mounting cab fare. As we inched forward in traffic that had been rendered all but a standstill, the driver suggested that I simply walk back to Penn Station and navigate the subway. He then, without my asking, voided my $75 fare for the seven blocks that the cab had sat or crawled through.

The driver knew what I did not. His patience and generosity, I later realized, were inspired by an act of political and communal recognition. He understood that the traffic was snarled, not because of routine congestion in the metropolis, but because of street protests against predatory policing and anti-Black violence. I accepted what I first thought to be kindness and "charity" only to later recognize it as an expression of political solidarity and ethical community.

Exhausted by the Amtrak ride from my institutional work at the college, I made my way on foot through animated crowds back to then Pennsylvania Station (now Moynihan Hall-Penn Station) on West 34th Street. Energized by the shouts, chants, and bedlam, I gradually realized that this was not typical Gotham dysfunction, but a #NYCShutItDown mass protest over the NYPD murder of Eric Garner and the Staten Island Grand Jury's refus-

---

1. Nicholas St. Fleur, "They Shouted 'I Can't Breathe,'" *The Atlantic*, December 4, 2014, https://www.theatlantic.com/national/archive/2014/12/New-York-City-Eric-Garner-Protests/383415/.

al to indict Daniel Pantaleo police and other officers who killed Mr. Garner. Surprised and moved by the outpouring of *Agape*—love as political will—I began to see the shutdown of midtown NYC streets as an astute political strategy by organizers who wielded confrontation as a countermeasure to predatory policing and the dysfunctional bureaucracies that protected it.

During the following years, I occasionally participated in marches and watched from my apartment window as people flooded Harlem streets with chants and drums, songs and bellows—waves of color and determination. The protestors were boisterous, focused, undeterred by the wealthiest and most well-connected militarized police force in any US city, if not the Western world. I was impressed by the young organizers' strategies and their coordination of mass gatherings.

Along with millions of people within and beyond New York, I learned about the horrific death of Eric Garner on a street in Staten Island in July 2014 by watching the traumatic video of Garner's homicide by the NYPD. The footage captured on cell phone by Ramsey Orta—a friend of Mr. Garner's, who would later be imprisoned by the NYPD after releasing the footage to the Garner family and the public—was replayed endlessly by the media.

In a December 23, 2014 *New York Times* interview with philosopher George Yancy, I attempted to process my shock and rage:

George Yancy: Among my friends and colleagues of all races, the killings of Michael Brown, Akai Gurley, Tamir Rice, and Eric Garner and so many others like them have caused emotional pain—feelings of being sick and hurt, feelings of depression, angst, hopelessness. It's crazy.

Joy James: That's grief. And yes, it is crazy. Welcome to Black life under white supremacy.

Grief as a painful historical trajectory is one thing; to grieve intensely in the misery of the present moment is another. Ferguson, Staten Island, Brooklyn, and Cleveland (we can add Detroit for seven-year-old Aiyana Stanley-Jones, and Bastrop, Texas for Yvette Smith)—these disparate sites have forced diverse people around the country and internationally to huddle closer together as we scrutinize laws and policies that reward police violence with immunity.

Being denigrated and victimized by your designated protectors is shocking to the core, because their job is to protect and serve. We're stunned because our trust in law is violated; police departments tolerate hyper-aggressive officers by underreporting and under disciplining them. These officers are not "going rogue" in wealthy, white communities because those communities have the economic and political resources to discipline them.

Police are our employees whom we have to obey ostensibly for our own safety and that of the general good; but also, because they will hurt us often, with impunity, if we don't—and sometimes even when we do—obey.[2]

MEETING IMPACTED FAMILIES AND CAPTIVE MATERNAL WAR RESISTERS

Before and after Erica Garner died, I had met and worked with impacted mothers who had lost their children, siblings, or relatives to predatory police forces in North and South America. Chicago mothers, Shapearl Wells and Dorothy Holmes,[3] taught me a lot through their battles in Chicago against police involved in the killings of their sons. They also traveled out of the US to share and consult with other impacted families and mothers. Across generations and familial roles, the battle to maintain in public memory, state violence, and the necessary struggles for justice, altered their lives. There were contradictions given that victimization is not inherently a sign of valor and veracity. As I traveled outside of the US I was introduced to vulnerable people—some impacted by police violence, others impacted by the wounds of family violence and civilian violence. Their despair and desires did not always mirror the principled stances embodied in Shapearl Wells and Dorothy Holmes. I learned that it is not just bourgeois academics or journalists who bend reality to amplify their profiles—it is also those traumatized and lacking material stability and comforts.

---

2. George Yancy and Joy James, "Black Lives Between Grief and Action," The Opinionator, *New York Times*, December 23, 2014, https://archive.nytimes.com/opinionator.blogs.nytimes.com/author/joy-james/.

3. For student interactions with Shapearl Wells and Dorothy Holmes, see: https://sites.williams.edu/jjames/files/2019/06/Love-and-Justice-Transcription-1.pdf.

By coincidence or spiritual design, around this time, I met another gifted truth-teller, a young griot named Chaédria LaBouvier. The artist-activist wrote a compassionate and brilliant interview with Erica Garner, published in *Elle* magazine, discussed in Chapter 7, Captive (After)Lives. I first encountered the Afro-Cuban artist on a bus from the college town where I taught, to NYC. I recognized LaBouvier (class of '07) as gifted but did not realize that they were an abolitionist and a member of a family impacted by lethal police violence. LaBouvier's brother, Clinton Allen, was killed in 2013. During our long commute from the college to the city, the Afro-Cuban artist engaged me in conversation about their residency at their Ivy League alma mater. We spoke about artistic work and exchanged email addresses before we disembarked at the Port Authority Bus Terminal on West 42nd Street. When LaBouvier later asked to meet again, I suggested that we connect at a Harlem dojo for children on West 116th Street; it was a unique space created and led by Africans who taught Taekwondo to a multiracial community. Weeks later as we sat chatting in metal folding chairs off to the side of the dojo floor, we spoke quietly while watching young children train in self-discipline and self-defense. I became more focused on LaBouvier's narratives which began to detail police violence and abolitionist struggles. I gradually realized that I was sitting next to someone profoundly impacted by police terror and the dishonor of severed natality as police kill with (qualified) immunity and impunity.[4] Police predatory power is disproportionately wielded against Black people, especially Black males.

I learned later that LaBouvier had given the 2015 keynote address, "Mothers Against Police Brutality" at Williams College's annual "Claiming Williams."[5] College press described LaBouvier's discussion of her family tragedy in order to educate and galvanize people to resist lethal police violence. The contributor to *Elle*, *Medium*, and the *Bold Italic* had created The Allen Wells Project, a website named for her brother, who was killed by a Dallas police officer; she also recognized and honored antilynching crusader Ida B. Wells, author of *Southern*

---

4. For a discussion of "natality" and the loss of family kinship ties, see Orlando Patterson, *Slavery and Social Death* (Cambridge, MA: Harvard University Press, 1982).
5. Collette Flanagan and Chaédria LaBouvier, "Claiming Williams 2015 Keynote: Mothers Against Police Brutality," https://www.youtube.com/watch?v=CBzb9-3zZvE.

Horrors and The Red Record.[6] In the *Elle* article on Ferguson's police violence and family loss, LaBouvier describes police violence as a "feminist issue": "Women are so often on the front lines in the aftermath of these murders. They're the ones left behind to pick up the pieces, like my sister-in-law, who's now raising Clinton's twin boys without their father. We can't have this. Something has to change."[7] Police violence has a devastating impact on women caretakers, children as caretakers, and fathers and nonbinary and reproductive people who provide care.

Meeting and working with impacted families, I have seen firsthand that the work of familial care after predatory policing is predominately, *but not exclusively,* addressed by mothers. For some of those mothers who become activists—or who succumb to exhaustion and grief that can facilitate another family death—familial caretaking labor is passed onto their eldest female child. This was the passage that LaBouvier and Erica Garner had to navigate. They had mothers and elders, but the most radical work for accountability would be done by young Black women who were daughters or sisters of the slain.

Noting gender differences in the distributions of care labor, the Captive Maternal is about the *function* of care that becomes entangled with stages (and concentric circles) that include caretaking, protest, movement-making, marronage, and war resistance. The identity of the caretaker has no inherent value without an investment in care that becomes politicized through function. Hence, Agape as political will enables the longevity of self and community within a web of caretaking that is not inherently conventional or safe (in regards to predatory policing).[8]

At the Harlem dojo, LaBouvier briefly sketched strategies to bring honor to traumatized and dishonored families (including her own) who had lost members to predatory violence. I listened intently as I watched young children practice the arts to protect themselves from harm. I heard, above their Taekwondo and Korean language commands for maneuvers, shouts of self-affirmation and self-defense.

---

6. See Ida B. Wells, *The Red Record*, 1895 (e-book), https://www.gutenberg.org/files/14977/14977-h/14977-h.htm.

7. See Julia Munemo, "Challenging Police Brutality," Williams College, April 9, 2015, https://www.williams.edu/feature-stories/challenging-police-brutality/.

8. Flanagan and LaBouvier, "Claiming Williams 2015 Keynote: Mothers Against Police Brutality."

These underscored LaBouvier's voice as an "elder child," grown but grieving—one amid legions of impacted families bereft of loved ones lost to predatory policing or tortured by cops or prison guards.

During our few conversations, LaBouvier critiqued funders and nonprofits that offered compensation packets from the state in ways that normalized the monetization of Black death as political economy. She painfully addressed her personal need to maintain the memory of her brother, Clinton Allen, and the criminality of Dallas, Texas policing. This loss, noted in her interview of Erica Garner, allowed both to forge a spiritual and political connection with each other. Recalling my conversations with LaBouvier, I see the artist building abolitionist strategy upon a scaffold of broken bones. She spoke of writing a book that would trace and imprint upon memory and through text, the crime and the name of the white police officer who murdered her beloved Black brother. For future generations, this text would reveal the murder throughout his lineage—to children, grandchildren, and great-grands. We have to wrestle with bearing witness to murder in which white police, empowered and shielded by the state's inebriation with anti-Blackness, kill with impunity.

I was fortunate to have met LaBouvier. I did not have the opportunity to meet Erica Garner. Given her busy schedule I don't know if she would have had the time or interest to even meet with me. However, over several years of reflections following her death, I gradually recognized her contributions and strengths that offered clarity and political will to challenge predatory police powers. Both LaBouvier and Erica Garner shared insightful analyses of family members who lost loved ones to predatory policing. The traumas, distress, and rage alter the consciousness of those who were not impacted families. The loss of life at the hands of predatory police is a communal feeling of shock, rage and grief that can radiate across the globe. Hence the 2020 uprisings, amid the COVID-19 pandemic, were seismic. Before, during, and after George Floyd was suffocated in a slow death with a nonchalant killer employed by the state, civilians yelled, cried, and screamed, but could not interrupt the eight-minute affixation because they so feared the police. Civilians could tape video footage while traumatized, but could not raise hands for peaceful restraint as Manuel "Tortuguita" Terán did with both of their hands in the air. On January 18, 2023, Tortuguita was shot fifty-seven times by Georgia State Patrol while protesting "Cop City" in Atlanta's Weelaunee Forest. No one dared to place an open palm upon a uniformed shoulder in Minneapolis, Minnesota, and firmly instruct Derek Chauvin, who had both of his hands buried in his pant pockets and his knee pressed into Floyd's neck to "STOP." Despite our care, emotional intelligence, and political determination, without collective strategies, our caretaking freezes or falters. Becoming trained maroons capable of coordinating war resistance deflects or defies predatory violence. Analyzing our diverse roles as "caretakers" in revolutionary love, we explore how *Captive Maternal agency* encompasses the epicenter and the hypocenter of freedom struggles.[9]

BOOK STRUCTURE

New Bones Abolition: Captive Maternal Agency and the (After)Life of Erica Garner explores our capacity to care for and defend ourselves from state violence while also nurturing and being nurtured by individual selves and communities. *New Bones Abolition* notes the constant confusion and betrayals that mystify our radical impulses to address violators. *New Bones Abolition* is not a biography of Erica Garner. It does not attempt to paint a full portrait of a complex, fierce Black mother who became an antagonist of predatory and lethal policing from the July 2014 death of her father to her own death in December 2017. This book uses the Captive Maternal analytic to weave a narrative of a community, a collective informed by her tweets, "die-ins," organizing, and the ways we think as radicals, feminists, abolitionists, human rights advocates, impacted families, and communities. *New Bones Abolition* recognizes Garner as one of many leaders. As a working-class Black mother shaped by Agape—love as political will and communal care and protections—she shared her resistance against police violence with her family, community, and the world, and offered spiritual and material protections to deflect or defeat predatory

---

9. For additional discussion on the Captive Maternal, see Joy James, "The Womb of Western Theory: Trauma, Time Theft, and the Captive Maternal," *The Carceral Notebooks*, 2016, https://www.thecarceral.org/cn12/14_Womb_of_Western_Theory.pdf; Joy James, *In Pursuit of Revolutionary Love*; and the 2022 Captive Maternal Roundtable: https://www.youtube.com/watch?v=oi3IiKR6ZXQ

formations. With cadres, she battled local, state, and national governments, rejected corporate and nonprofit buyouts, and defied the intimidation of the NYPD.

Part I begins with Chapter 1, "Black Feminisms and Captive Maternal Agency," which reviews the contributions and contradictions of
agency by engaged caretakers and political actors. Chapter 2, "Old/
New Bones Abolition: Academic Conferences and Communal Gatherings," explores diverse communities in caretaking or protecting from
trauma, and violent death at the hands of police. "Movement Capture and Monetized Black Death," Chapter 3, discusses the hundreds
of millions of dollars funneled through nonprofits, private donors,
for-profit corporations, and state funding that sought to direct the trajectory of radical resistance to police forces into conventional reforms
and restoration of police budgets.

In Part II, "The Killing and Dishonor of Eric Garner," Chapter
4, reflects on trials, journalism, and NYC records to reconstruct Garner's death and the (lack of) ramifications for police killings. "Mother-
Daughter Doula," Chapter 5, discusses Garner's evolving agency as a
Captive Maternal who begins with liberal political statements and after betrayals by government and mainstream media moves into more
protests and movements that create a maroon community that refuses
to merge into duopoly politics and nonprofit largesse and management. Chapter 6, "Campaigning for Bernie and Against the DNC,"
reviews the stunning campaign ad that Erica Garner created for the
2016 presidential campaign of Vermont Independent Senator Bernie Sanders. In defiance of the Democratic National Committee and
President Barack Obama, Sanders ran as a "democratic socialist in
the framework of New Deal or FDR policies—and primaried the DNC
heir-apparent: Senator Hillary Clinton. Chapter 7, "Captive (After)
Lives," reflects upon the growth of political families and Black communities that emerge from trauma. It centers on Erica Garner's interview with Chaédria LaBouvier. Despite their different backgrounds,
shared grief, rage, and political thought connected both Black women.
This chapter concludes with Erica Garner's Harlem funeral, and re
flections by her mother, Esaw Snipes-Garner.

Part III opens with Chapter 8, "Police Violence and the Limits of
Legalism," which focuses on public attention to predatory policing and
the structural deficiencies of the legal system, as noted "The Limits

of Legalism," an article written by Da'Shaun Harrison, Samaria Rice, and me for *Scalawag*. Chapter 9, "International Alliances for Human Rights," examines human rights advocacy and alliances with international jurists and analyses who discuss the case of Eric Garner and anti-Black violence within policing practices in the United States. Chapter 10, "War Resistance: *We Charge Genocide* and *Return to the Source*" explores historical and contemporary political strategies to address contemporary crises.

The Conclusion, "Prioritizing Care and Ancestors," evokes the legacies of historical freedom, struggles from slavery abolition, civil rights, and Black revolutionary histories. Erica Garner's contributions register her as an ancestor. Despite the structural violations and predatory policing that sever natality and our connections with communities and ourselves, brokenness is mended through connections to the past, through the present, and into the future. The knowledge from those who watch over and care for us includes both the living and those who have transitioned. Hence, ancestors who fought to caretake, protest, march, create maroon camps, and engage in war resistance are never "dead" in spirit or in tutelage.

Figure 2: Jordan Engel, "500 years of Black Resistance." *The Decolonial Atlas*,
decolonialatlas.wordpress.com.

CHAPTER 1

BLACK FEMINISMS AND CAPTIVE MATERNAL AGENCY

BLACK FEMINISTS CAN BE CAPTIVE MATERNALS, BUT IT'S COMPLICATED

Feminism has no gender. To be a "feminist" is to advocate for equal rights and equity in resources for women and men (this would or should include trans wo/men and nonbinary people). If Black people lack equal rights and equity with (bourgeois) whites—and are not considered to actually be "human" and suffer disproportionate violence, severed natality, exploitation, and incarceration administered through the state and (vigilante) police forces—then this discussion is about more than gender. It is also about empire and colonialism, the ungendered and "queered" Black. The Captive Maternal as extension, companion, or alternative to Black feminisms is not inherently antagonistic to radical-centrist-liberal Black feminisms. Yet, unlike the majority of Black feminisms, the Captive Maternal is positioned as antagonist to the imperial state. Any forms of state feminisms that promoted Black feminisms—from Hillary Clinton to Gloria Steinem—would also have to be critiqued in order to gain greater clarity. The Captive Maternal journey is rooted in war resistance. Those promoting a militarized state would never become allies of the Captive Maternal—they would become allies of liberalism and compradors.

As noted in "The Womb of Western Theory: Trauma, Time Theft, and the Captive Maternal," US democracy was birthed in genocide, anti-Black animus, colonialism, capitalism, and imperialism. Black feminisms, in the plural, offer capacity for progress, but its diverse destinations are driven by centrism, liberalism, radical liberalism (the most popular form of abolition), radicalism, and revolution. Black feminisms in conflict with Captive Maternal constructs are incubators for state feminism. Black feminists could also be Captive Maternals. Given the varied forms of caretaking, Captive Maternals, even on the first stages of labor dedicated to home and social order, wield a function disciplined by strategy with interior emotional affects aligned with rebellion. Feminists are not inherently seeking rebellions against capitalism and colonialism. Captive Maternals acknowledge but do not always openly celebrate personal progress or gains under capitalism that largely accrue to (petite) bourgeoise sectors. Captive Maternals intuitively or consciously understand that the entire system is a predatory mechanism. Their "freedom dreams" are often laced with rebellions in which the old order collapses because someone enacted a move rarely conceived on a three-dimensional chess board. When David (and today's Davina) face Goliath and an entire army, persecuted people often become too terrified to fight. David, or Davina, thinking "outside the box" creates a war resistance strategy built on simple resources—a sling and a rock. Victories accrue from the war resisters to all—even those who fear the fight.

Captive Maternals resent and resist the theft or repurposing of their generative powers to stabilize state colonialism and police forces. Yet, every caretaker does not consciously reflect on their role in the social and political order. Captive Maternals intuit or scrutinize the inequality, dysfunction, and barbarity of power. To expand epistemology they must enter the fray and risk their (social) safety. To scrutinize the stratified (dis)order of things requires stepping beyond personal trauma and grievances to see and confront structures.

Even in the midst of labor hustles—not to be confused with brand or propaganda hustling—caretakers understand that the battles are not about an individual persona if battles of integrity are fought to secure and provide resources to self and others. To the extent that Black feminisms are aligned with state feminisms, care will not be subversive. Black feminisms aligned with state power boost one's individual or group ego to deflect from the fight to quell state predatory powers.

In the concentric circles of care, the dialectical spiral of struggle moves from caretaker, to protester, into movement maker, marronage, and war resister. Given that the majority of Americans, and US Blacks/

Africans, are *not* radical, the majority of Black feminists are not radical either (nor are the majority of trauma victims). As the Captive Maternal moves closer to marronage and war resistance, i.e., into the zones of direct confrontation with predatory police and state, most feminist, conventional abolitionists seek to reject, obscure or attack the militant Captive Maternal. My earlier work in *Shadowboxing: Representations of Black Feminist Politics* discusses "managerial" Black feminisms and (de)radicalizing Black feminisms—not to "cancel" Black feminism but to clarify that its diversity and hegemony do not seek or serve revolutionary anticolonial purposes.[1]

Most narratives placed into the public realm offer protagonists and punchlines. Hence, without a quest, discipline, or desire for duty, one has not a strategy but a form of entertainment. The story becomes the "political" contribution. The more drama the better; the storyteller as agent and victim and survivor becomes the major or minor celebrity, or political leader. However, the world of material struggle demands a communal ethics and security strategy. There is no security strategy without care. There is no care without Agape; love as political will or political will as love to vanquish all predators requires sacrifice and a confrontation with fear. Without disciplined collective agency, no movement goes beyond the performative.

For the Captive Maternal, function is central.[2] How we practice communal engagement with honor, and define "love" in a war zone, is pivotal for analyses and agency. The personal victimization narrative, although important, does not inherently render every story as virtuous or veracious. Capacity and agency discipline the ability to be truthful and the willingness to participate in communities with political structure and radical ethics. Prominent Black feminists bell hooks and Assata Shakur took their risks and made contributions as anti-imperialists and anticapitalists. hooks stayed on the epicenter of surface politics; Shakur was forced into the hypocenter of underground politics. Their analyses converge and diverge around the zones of marronage and war resistance that protect caretaking.

---

1. See Joy James, *Shadowboxing: Representations of Black Feminist Politics* (New York: Palgrave McMillan, 2000).

2. This is described in greater detail in "The Captive Maternal Is a Function, Not an Identity Marker," *Scalawag*, April 28, 2023, https://scalawagmagazine.org/2023/04/captive-maternal-joy-james/.

Caretaking becomes complicated with traumatized victims levitating narcissistic projections as a synonym for virtue or valor. Opportunistic behavior can be a zone of trauma and a zone of hustle and extortion. What would it mean to recognize that those marked by childhood poverty, parental dysfunction, or carceral entrapment will play you just as those privileged by wealth and comfort? Socialized or Agape-trained into caretaking for collectives and strangers, how should Captive Maternals prioritize their needs and those of others; or should they run a 24-hour service until they collapse or retreat from organizing and caretaking of others? To reject requests for self-discipline and self-regulation within shelters one did not build or stabilize is a refusal to acknowledge that structured homes, movements, and care require discpline. Entitlement based on personal narratives destabilizes security. Then who or what constitutes the vulnerable populations? It would seem to be deeply compassionate to open the door to varied addicts until one sees structure unraveling through an open door policy. Without structure, the care for the most vulnerable—the medically fragile, children, and elders—deteriorates. When discipline is attached to requests from unfamiliar adults—the proverbial stranger that some religions mandate one take in—financial support, medical intervention, listening therapy, middle-class family members living nearby, are insufficient to provide a safety network. The hubris of the Captive Maternal is to think that care can remedy all imbalances.[3]

Black freedom movements retain transformative agency but are constantly under siege. Their antagonists appear as more than state police forces seeking broken bones and nonprofits seeking ideological capture. Compradors, hustlers, and promoters clash with Captive Maternals. In a culture where narcissism is rampant and critical analyses scarce, hungry ghosts (not holy ghosts) have rapacious

---

3. Organizing to stop the 2022 execution of Kevin Johnson in Missouri, we spoke with Johnson on RSTV/*Black Power Media*, working with anti-death advocate Michelle Smith and found that our responsibility to care for and save Kevin's life faced the predicament of state violence disproportionately arraigned against poor and working-class Blacks. In the absence of a revolutionary struggle, the state executed Kevin Johnson in November 2022. See Kalonji Changa and Joy James, "Kevin Johnson Speaks from Death Row About His Impending Execution This Month," *Truthout*, November 16, 2022; and "The Philosophy of Care: Todd May in Conversation with Joan Tronto," *The Philosopher*, June 19, 2023. Political theorist Joan Tronto asserts that responsibility is inherent for caring as relational not obligatory. If "we are born into relationality" what does it mean for some to also be born simultaneously into anti-Black captivity?

appetites for name-recognition and nesting in zones in which they do not labor. To appear in the public or private arena means that one has arrived, as performances shape visibility, relevance, and ratings. The clarity of Black feminists generations ago is not easily discernible today. In *The Black Woman*, Toni Cade Bambara describes the disciplining of militancy:

> [W]e are just as jammed in the rigid confines of those basically oppressive socially contrived roles. For if a woman is tough, she's a rough mamma, a strident bitch, a ballbreaker, a castrator. And if a man is at all sensitive, tender, spiritual, he's a faggot. And there is a dangerous trend observable in some quarters of the Movement to program Sapphire out of her 'evil' ways into a cover-up, shut-up, lay-back-and-be-cool obedience role. She is being assigned an unreal role of mute servant that supposedly neutralizes the acidic tension that exists between Black men and Black women. She is being encouraged in the name of the revolution no less to cultivate 'virtues' that if listed would sound like the personality traits of slaves.[4]

Current disciplining goes beyond the discrimination levied at LGBTQIA+ and gender violence, the criminalizing of reproductive rights, and eugenics-based racial purity. Radical politics are reduced to self-presentations; without analytics or facts these become performances. What does it mean to exhibit the "personality traits of slaves" when different types of "slaves" exist? The Captive Maternals who remain closed mouth before attacks from unprincipled "low-status" and "high status" individuals/sectors that distort reality might themselves have a virtue problem—the need to prove their worth by stoically remaining on the cross to silently take abuse from the famous and anonymous attention-seekers who wish to be leaders; the house and field dichotomy is not just about class.

Malcolm X notes the "house" and "field" dichotomy in his March 26, 1964, "Message to the Grassroots." The house negro favors the "master" while the field negro hopes the plantation house burns down. Malcolm himself never worked for the state as a comprador but he was a hustler before being politicized and transforming into a rev-

---

4. Toni Cade, "On the Issue of Roles," in Toni Cade Bambara, ed., *The Black Woman: An Anthology* (New York: Washington Square Press, 2005), 106.

olutution in prison. It is easier to distinguish a Captive Maternal from a comprador who willingly enforces or promotes predatory policies. Today's hustlers are more sophisticated. Tech/media and white liberal benefactors allow them more exposure than they ever would have had during civil rights and Black liberation struggles. In the past movement era, to be noticed or noteworthy, one would have to take risks in order to participate in a movement disciplined by strategies, and risk their freedom and lives in SNCC- or Panther-like communalism. The staged performance projects both vulnerability and virtue; committment and risk for collective gains diminish if the political act to undo predatory structure is reduced to simulacra.

AVATAR BLACK FEMINIST BELL HOOKS

As was the case with Erica Garner, bell hooks was a maverick. However, Garner's productivity was tied to street protests, movement making, and care delivery from police homicide that severed an artery of natal belonging. hooks understood her privilege and her passion as a reader and author, when she returned to a small town in Kentucky, tracing the roots she planted in Berea College. Founded in 1855 by antislavery abolitionists, Berea became the first interracial and coeducational college in the South. Its epicenter was higher education of interracial students, and charity and advocacy for human rights. However, Berea hosted a hypocenter beneath its college buildings, it dug down to fashion an underground railroad to transport formerly trafficked people into "free states." By the time the Confederate troops fired upon and defeated Union forces at Fort Sumter in South Carolina, the official beginning of the Civil War in April 1861, Berea had been training in war resistance for six years. Kentucky-born hooks would call Berea "home," within the state where she grew up. Her marronage would include, Black, white, South Asian, Middle Eastern women, men, trans and nonbinary intellectuals.

Expressing her thoughts and analyses largely in text and lectures, hooks did not expand her epistemology to include organizing in the streets or prisons. Although she taught in prisons, teaching within a carceral site is not equivalent to radical organizing. Erica Garner and bell hooks were both shunned and disciplined by bourgeois morality:

hooks because of her manners, Garner because of the way her political militancy "talked back" to heads of city, state, and the nation. hooks became famous while taking risks as an ethicist, theorist, and feminist writer. It was hooks' critique of powerful Black feminists in celebrity culture that helped to sideline her among more respectable, academic feminists. hooks' ribald quip in the early 1990s about Oprah Winfrey servicing the male genitalia of white supremacist culture shares similarities with Garner's barb about Mayor Bill de Blasio's affinity for NYC's (second) Black First Lady, while lacking empathy for Black people and families grappling with a lethal NYPD.

Both Erica Garner and bell hooks were forced into self-invention respectively through familial loss—through police violence for Garner, and for hooks, childhood instability in the segregated Deep South. Both became transgressive satirists. Both were (self-)marginalized to varying degrees from "Black feminist respectability" because they rejected conventional boundaries. More precisely, hooks' rise focuses on the conflicted caretaker who does consciousness-raising through protest literature. hooks appears to have rarely, if ever, worked as an organizer within a political movement. Her refusal or failure to engage in the stages of protestor, street organizer, radical movement cadre, and war resister meant that she lacked the knowledge of organizers who could have informed her about specific, highly politicized police cases, such as the case of the Exonerated Central Park Five. The stages of collective actions that build epistemology that absorb the material conditions of war resistance are prerequisites for a fuller critique of capitalism, imperialism, and the militarized state.[5]

hooks' political conclusions carried blind spots. She did not organize with radical or under-resourced communities on the ground, and so she could not learn from informed communities. One key example of the impact of the failure to connect with grounded epistemology was hooks' pretrial writing about the "Exonerated 5"—previously known as

---

5. I critique hooks in *Transcending the Talented Tenth*, in a chapter that opens with a quote from Audre Lorde's *Sister Outsider*: "Survival is not an academic skill." Academic discourse and literary performance are not equivalent to communal material struggles against poverty and predatory policing. Developing an epistemology or paradigm that engages with material struggle is a form of competence that provides clarity about marronage and war resistance. See Joy James, "Captive Theorists and Community Caretakers: Women and Academic Intellectualism," *Transcending the Talented Tenth: Black Leaders and American Intellectuals* (New York: Routledge, 1997).

the "Central Park Five" that was ill-informed and presented the youths as guilty before their trial. In 1989, five Black and Brown teens were falsely accused and convicted of the viciously brutal rape and battery of white investment banker Trisha Meili in Central Park. hooks' writings about the rape and the teens, before and/or during their trials, asserted that they were guilty. In order to make points about sexual violence against women/girls perpetrated by men/boys, she apparently overlooked the facts (actually failed to do any substantive research or meet or speak with organizers for a fair trial). The contradictions and lies of the NYPD, welcomed by mass media, led her to print as facts, statements on the case shaped by coerced false confessions by the majority of the teens (but not Yusef Salaam—elected to the NYC Council in 2023—the only Muslim defendant and one of the few defendants with a highly visible and vocal mother, Sharonne Salaam, who maintained his innocence). An astute critic of pop culture, hooks mixed cop culture, predatory policing, and (white) media headlines to echo liberal white feminists and several prominent Black academics or authors to portray the youths as guilty.

Decades later, following the documentary *The Central Park Five* by Ken Burns, and legal exoneration after Matias Reyes, the actual rapist confessed, celebrity and entertainment Black feminists, Oprah Winfrey and Ava Duvernay would produce *When They See Us*. The film was emotionally-laden (a tearjerker) and depicted family stressors of the falsely accused, but incompetent portrayals of the political organizing and movements that fought against wrongful incarceration in the Central Park Five case.[6] Most academics relied on the framing of the *New York Times* for factual knowledge. *The New York Times* not only supported the false narratives and lies of the NYPD as it railroaded five Black and Brown teens into captivity, but also agreed to print Donald J. Trump's full-page advertisement calling citizens and governance to bring back the death penalty in order to have state murder of (innocent) children. hooks' *progressive* politics did not reflect the militancy and intellectual rigor of Captive Maternals who *organized* outside of academia.

---

6. See Joy James, "Searching for a Tradition: African American Women Writers, Activists, and Interracial Rape Cases," in *Black Women in America*, ed. Kim Marie Vaz, 131–155 (Thousand Oaks, CA: SAGE, 1995), https://sites.williams.edu/jjames/files/2019/05/Black-Women-in-America.pdf.

In a 2022 Philadelphia roundtable to honor her work, prominent Black feminists on stage asserted that hooks' critique of "heteropatriarchy" was her greatest contribution.[7] Yet, in a 2015 *New York Times* interview with philosopher George Yancy, when asked to explain her phrase "imperialist white supremacist capitalist patriarchy," hooks discussed a more complex form of "intersectionality" focused not on personal identity, but on predatory systems and structures: "We can't begin to understand the nature of domination if we don't understand how these systems connect with one another." According to hooks, the global arena is the "context of class, of empire, of capitalism, of racism and of patriarchy . . . an interlocking system."[8]

hooks does not highlight how liberal frameworks have shaped feminism and antiracism so that remedies to misogyny, gender oppression, transphobia, and white nationalism embed in liberal frameworks, or align with state feminism. (The most prominent state feminist ally of Black feminism would be Gloria Steinem, who worked for the Central Intelligence Agency [CIA] during the Cold War.[9]) hooks cruised through intellectualism structured by the white elite academy and its publishing houses. She wrote to safeguard the personal and therapeutic from disintegrating into fetish. She became a muse and mentor for feminists from varied class and ethnic-racial backgrounds. Yet, she did not provide protections against liberal capture. Although she wrote largely for liberal readers, hooks described how publishers courted her for potential books, only later to view her writing as "out of fashion." Never "fashionable" due to her lack of academic respectability, hooks remained popular through her accessible publications and talks which increasingly linked (Black) feminism to spirituality and hope with books such as *All About Love, The Will to Change, Feminism, Buddhism, and Liberation*, and *Salvation*. Spirituality became hooks' path for countering racism and patriarchy as state and social practices. Poverty and militarism grounded in the material struggles—such as

7. "Inaugural Bell Hooks Symposium," Uncle Bobbie's Coffee & Books, September 24, 2022, https://www.youtube.com/watch?v=1RZ1uesyfao.

8. George Yancy and bell hooks, "bell hooks: Buddhism, the Beats and Loving Blackness," *New York Times*, December 10, 2015, https://archive.nytimes.com/opinionator.blogs.nytimes.com/2015/12/10/bell-hooks-buddhism-the-beats-and-loving-blackness/.

9. See Joy James, *Contextualizing Angela Davis: The Agency and Identity of an Icon* (London: Bloomsbury, 2024).

work or prison strikes—would have been stages linked to spirituality but embodied in physical confrontations.

In *Teaching Community: A Pedagogy of Hope,* hooks reflects on Brazilian activist and educator Paulo Freire's statement: "It is imperative that we maintain hope even when the harshness of reality may suggest the opposite."[10] hooks followed this imperative for decades. ("Hope" is a complex and mixture of emotions, both the nonprivileged and privileged project emotional desires and fears about the past, present, and future; sometimes material conditions shape those projections.)

A Southern antiracist, anti-misogynist rebel, she traveled from Kentucky to Stanford in California, to Yale in Connecticut, and back home to Kentucky to teach and write. Seeing the entire world as a classroom, in *Teaching Community,* she writes of herself as a passionate teacher bringing "absolute grace to the art of teaching." She mentions the "union of theory and praxis" as "dynamic examples for teachers seeking practical wisdom." Still, little to nothing about organizing in communities or the streets appears on the page. Embodied in and embedded within the university/college and text, it is text and the classroom that connects her to struggle.

A professional teacher is not inherently a war resister. War resisters move upon the ground and from the epicenter to the hypocenter. hooks as an author and celebrated caretaker reveals the "life of the mind" and interior self "liberated" through text and meditation. The educator's task is to teach about and dissect the empire, patriarchy, classism, and racism. How to fight these structures—with more than one's mind—is not on the syllabus. The practice of the art of war resistance rarely unfolds, and should not unfold, in the classroom. This pedagogy of the people offers lengthy conversations and studies and practices.

Everyone has different skills. Thus, everyone has different roles to play—but not in isolation. hooks' goal is for "all passionate teachers to revel in a job well done to inspire students training to be teachers."[11] However, to link to the hypocenter likely requires spiritual and emotional intelligence that comprehends how the exterior surface interfac-

---

10. Paulo Freire cited in the front pages of bell hooks, *Teaching Community: A Pedagogy of Hope* (New York: Routledge, 2003).
11. hooks, *Teaching Community,* x.

es with the interior depth. hooks manifested gravity beyond conventional (Black) feminism as she grappled with spiritual teachings. She self-identified as a Buddhist Christian who was anti-imperialist and anticapitalist. Although her intellectual and political environments existed as stark contrasts to Erica Garner's revanchist battling of police in New York City. When hooks left elite academia to return to her birthplace, she moved to a rural, white town in Kentucky's Bible Belt. Her meditations reflected Martin Luther King, Jr.'s "beloved community." She invoked the works of Thich Nhat Hanh. hooks worked to contribute to the beloved community.[12] Daily, she entered her "laboratory" for intellectual work:

> Without all of those people engaged in civil rights struggles, I would not be here in this laboratory . . . how many black women have had the good fortune to write more than thirty books? . . . I try to read a [nonfiction] book a day . . . then I get to read total trash for the rest of the day. That's luxury, that's privilege of a high order —the privilege to think critically, and then the privilege to be able to act on what you know.[13]

For hooks, love is "the only way out of domination" and the only stable connector to other people and to "participating in every aspect of your life as a sacrament of love." Accordingly, teaching is connected to love. Referring to patriarchy and white supremacy as "a mental illness of disordered desire . . . [that] leads people to do completely and utterly insane things," hooks states that we must remember that we are in both "a spiritual crisis" and "political crisis" and should also recall that Martin Luther King, Jr. was "profoundly prescient" about "how the work of love would be necessary" for transformation.[14]

There is not much said in hooks' writings about love and spirituality connected to material struggles for food, housing, clean water, education, and protections from predatory policing. That is, revolutionary love shaped by *Agape* seems muted in her discussions and theory as does the existence of war resistance which manifests because of continued state and vigilante warfare against "out groups." The year

---

12. Yancy and hooks, "bell hooks: Buddhism, the Beats and Loving Blackness."
13. Yancy and hooks, "bell hooks: Buddhism, the Beats and Loving Blackness."
14. Yancy and hooks, "bell hooks: Buddhism, the Beats and Loving Blackness."

following the police killings of Eric Garner, Michael Brown, and Tray-von Martin, hooks sat for an interview in which she confided that she had become fearful of the police, referencing the 2015 death of Sandra Bland following a traffic stop in Texas. Bland was reported dead in her jail cell; coroner ruled the death as suicide. hooks reflected that she was experiencing a growing anxiety about the police.

hooks' *We Real Cool: Black Men and Masculinity* uses the story of Isis and Osiris to depict betrayal, war, death, and resurrection.[15] When, Isis, the stern mother-sister-lover, retrieves Osiris' dismembered and scattered body parts and sutures him together, she also battles his ene-mies. For hooks, this Egyptian myth which she sees as a "shared story," offers "soul-healing" for Black people living "in a culture that keeps black men and women further apart." Reflecting on this ancient myth, hooks quotes Malcolm X (el-Hajj Malik el-Shabazz) on facing suffering:

> Malcolm X said we have to 'see each other with new eyes' . . . that's where self-determination begins and how we are with one another. . . . So many black males and females have suffered men-tal abandonment . . . more than police brutality, that's the core for many of us of our trauma. Betrayal is always about abandonment. And many of us have been emotionally abandoned.[16]

For hooks, almost everything returns to the personal family, the pos-sibility of the *political family* as an essential organic entity to resist warfare is largely not addressed in her work. hooks correctly asserts that unattended wounds mean that children often lack models for "the opportunity to truly care for themselves in a way that's optimal for all."[17] Spirituality remains a key source for repair. But what kind of spirituality and what is its function in war resistance? hooks shares a self-assertion: "Feminism does not ground me . . . discipline that comes from spiritual practice . . . is the foundation of my life." Evolu-tionary struggles by the masses move or shape individuals. Agape is a collective experience and practice. In her spiritual transcendence, hooks assists but never merges with the masses. Abolitionist benev-olence for the incarcerated—who are to be helped or cared for and

---

15. See bell hooks, *We Real Cool: Black Men and Masculinity* (New York: Routledge, 2004).
16. Yancy and hooks, "bell hooks: Buddhism, the Beats and Loving Blackness."
17. Yancy and hooks, "bell hooks: Buddhism, the Beats and Loving Blackness."

"freed" by those with more social power, privilege, and leisure—turns movements into charity which aligns with the protocols of the state. What then is the possibility of cross-class solidarity and shared leadership? Are the poor to be assisted, fed, educated, and freed by their more professionalized and noncaptive caretakers, while the empire remains intact to continue to impoverish, starve, and violate the new crop of captives?

MAROON WAR RESISTER: REVOLUTIONARY ASSATA SHAKUR

Decades ago, the most remembered names among Black casualties were those whose risk-taking agency drove them to Agape and early deaths due to their organizing for liberation. Figures such as Fred Hampton, Mark Clark, Alprentice "Bunchy" Carter, and John Huggins joined revolutionary formations and disciplined themselves to the collective. They did not have the characteristics of the "slave." Social media marketing could not predict their contributions. Facts were relevant, and fact checkers essential. Police, FBI, compradors, and anti-revolutionaries created distortions formed while citizens were riding a media merry-go-round projecting willed blindness within war zones.

There has been much recent discussion of women in the Black Panther Party (BPP). The observation that at one time women were 60 percent or more of the BPP was a transformation that likely took place after the Party, led by Oakland's nondemocratic leadership, decided to forgo war resistance. The Party as a revolutionary formation peaked by 1971, although it continued as an organization into the mid-1980s. The concentric circles of care and self-defense delivered by the BPP 1966 formation originally named "The Black Panther Party for Self-Defense" motivated people across the globe and generations.

Black women were key in leadership and caretaking; they remain so today as the partners or daughters of Black Panthers. The daughter of Assata Shakur, K'Sisay Sadiki, notes in "Growing up Panther"[18] how the children of revolutionaries navigate the movement circles and care circles moving from the epicenter to the hypocenter. Often, trauma is

---

18. Susie Day, "Growing up Panther: An Interview with K'Sisay Sadiki," *San Francisco Bay View*, March 3, 2021, https://sfbayview.com/2021/03/growing-up-panther-an-interview-with-ksisay-sadiki/.

an endless cycle for Black Panther revolutionaries and political prisoners and their families. In her autobiography, Assata notes family trauma years ago:

> As we left the courtroom, [a friend] was standing in the hallway with K'Sisay, Kamau's two-year-old daughter. As Kamau walked near her, she held out her arms to him. Kamau took two steps toward her and the marshals jumped him and began beating him. . . . I will never forget the haunting scream of that child as she watched her father being brutally beaten.[19]

The contradictions, and betrayals, are profoundly felt. Black women partnered with Black Panthers, have called police to arrest their partners after reporting domestic infractions, aggression, or (alleged) abuse. Rather than seeking what abolitionists mandate—community intervention, healing circles, mediation—they allegedly called the cops not because of imminent physical danger but because of emotional pain. The arrests led the FBI to a high value political target hunted by the state. The US government wanted access to Assata Shakur, and so arrested the father of Shakur's daughter who would not agree to entrap Shakur. Kamau Sadiki was convicted of a cold case crime and sentenced to life inside a Georgia prison, according to the Jericho Movement.

For some it is difficult to fathom why not to call the police, but consider the police shootings and killings of people in their homes, including Atatiana Jefferson in Fort Worth, Texas in October 2019.[20] Communal need for security has to address verified and unverified claims of physical harm. The 911 call—"He's got a gun!"—led to the arrest and conviction of Assata Shakur's co-defendant Kamau Sadiki.[21] (Ironically and tragically, that is the same call that cops make before they open fire on an unarmed civilian.) Arrested and charged with "crimes" of past deeds tied to the Black lib-

---

19. Quoted from Day, "Growing up Panther."
20. "Say Their Names," Green Library Exhibit supporting the Black Lives Matter movement, Stanford University, https://exhibits.stanford.edu/saytheirnames/feature/atatiana-jefferson.
21. See "Assata Shakur.org," http://www.assatashakur.org/kamau.htm; and Freddie Hilton (Kamau Sadiki), National Jericho Movement, https://thejerichomovement.com/profile/hilton-freddie-kamau-sadiki.

eration struggle, war resisters were given life-death sentences by the state. Triggered by trauma in domestic disputes, familial pain enters the public record.

Since the state largely neglects or punishes Black families, its punitive powers are trained to intimidate and dishonor the general Black mass. It reserves its surplus power to decimate Black radical discipline for political acts which are strategic. The most valued function is to complete assigned tasks with sufficient discipline; as such, revolutionaries and war resisters are rare. Not only do they take immense risks, they understand that their individual autonomy can become a liability in struggle if no one commits to following plans. Few seek liberation from capitalism and imperialism (those desires or ambitions are not present in the definition of feminism). Becoming "equal" to patriarchs or men does not defeat colonialism. Queen Elizabeth transcended patriarchy while unleashing a genocide in Africa.[22] In the United States, the first Black woman president seeks to become its second Black imperial president.

There are insufficient analyses on how (Black) feminisms align with imperial state feminism; consider relationships structured by position and proximity, as well as time, in terms of generations linked to but alienated from each other. The epicenter is the location on the surface of the earth positioned directly above an underground point, the hypocenter, or "focus" of a fault line. The earthquake can have little impact on those at a great distance from the underground or those standing on the surface of politics. The hypocenter below the earth's surface is where the earthquake starts. In war terminology, it is the center of the bomb explosion or "ground zero." Most Black feminisms, ranging from centrist to radical liberalism, interact at the epicenter. They share or compete for space and the meaning of struggle on the surface of politics within zones stabilized by state power, but rarely engage with the burden of material struggles shouldered by their icons waging war against colonialism and anti-Black terror.

The move to adjacency to the radical past and surviving Panthers is a catalyst for the revolutionary imagination which present gener-

---

22. See "Queen Elizabeth's Policies Resulted in Kenyan Freedom Fighters Living in Concentration Camps," *Global Black History*, April 14, 2022; and Caroline Kimeu, "'A brutal legacy': Queen's death met with anger as well as grief in Kenya, September 12, 2022.

ations relate to as virtue and valor. Yet, the majority of the present generation are like the past generations: they are not revolutionary, and some are antirevolutionary because of careerism and corporate funding, and recruitment to join the state. Venerated Black Panther and Black Liberation Army veteran Assata Shakur—known by most only through her memoir, *Assata: An Autobiography*—exists at the hypocenter with a $2 million bounty after surviving illegal, lethal Federal Bureau of Investigation (FBI) COINTELPRO tactics and NJ troopers.[23] To publicly (re)claim oneself as the "daughter" or "student" of Assata is a preference that projects a familial attachment that logically promises protection.

Mixing a parental role model with Black Power imagery within the walls of academic/nonprofit/corporate environments is tricky unless you are moving towards the hypocenter and willing to engage in war resistance. Academia and nonprofit organizers brought Shakur to the epicenter through visual culture and oration. Faculty have been teaching *Assata: An Autobiography* for over twenty years before Barack Obama was elected as the first Black president of the United States of America in 2008. Nearing the close of Obama's second term as a liberal comprador, in May 2015, Marquette University revealed its animus against a Black (feminist) revolutionary—who was shot, captured, incarcerated, and escaped from prison to find haven in an island nation that won and stabilized the only revolutionary war waged against capitalism and imperialism in the Americas—when Black Alpha Kappa Alpha Sorority sisters painted a mural of Assata Shakur on the wall of the University's feminist center.

The Marquette student government largely backed the university administration's puniative response to the mural and its statement. Some students attempted to protect employment for Susannah Bartlow, then director of the Gender and Sexuality Resource Center. International communications chairman of Alpha Kappa Alpha Sorority Inc., Leona Dotson, issued a statement on the mural, noting that the university approved it before it was painted on a wall in the Gender and Sexuality Resource Center: "The chapter, along with other university staff and students, painted a mural that featured an image and quote by Assata Shakur to promote student thinking about their ed-

---

23. Assata Shakur, *Assata: An Autobiography* (Chicago: Lawrence Hill Books, 1987).

ucations and history. Unfortunately, Ms. Shakur's entire history and background was not fully researched. If that process had occurred, she would not have been featured in the mural."[24] A Black sorority supported the administration whitewashing a mural of Assata and firing the white woman who headed women and gender studies. The Black sorority apparently censured the students who feigned innocence about Black liberation movements hunted and "neutralized" by lethal and illegal (hence the monetary settlements to families and survivors) FBI, CIA, and local police forces. Academics have taught Shakur's memoir for decades, but email requests for them to petition against this censorship were ignored. Betrayals of radical freedom struggles align with the agency of the comprador class.

BLACK FEMINIST COMPRADORS

The Captive Maternal relies upon function within a world structured by anti-Black violence, queer and transphobia, patriarchy, capitalism, colonialism, and imperialism. Resisting violence is not just a personal affair, it is a political obligation. Self-defense is not violence. What one does to resist violence is more important than what one says to denounce it.

Black feminisms have made important contributions to discourse and practices. However, Black feminism often aligns itself with state feminism (for the last fifty years, founded and funded by Steinem). Gender identity expanding with intersectional personal or communal identities—race, neurodiversity, sexuality, class—cannot substitute for structural analyses of systems such as (neo)colonialism, capitalism, and imperialism. Empires roll with extreme violence as a maintenance program and to ensure their longevity. If personal or communal identity does not have interlocking or concentric circles of protections as strategy against state warfare, then one must abide by state predatory formations.

---

24. See "Gender and Sexuality Resource Center director is gone after Assata Shakur mural removal, Marquette community responds," *Marquette Wire*, May 19, 2015, https://marquette-wire.org/3929295/tribune/gender-and-sexuality-resource-center-director-gone-after-assata-shakur-mural-removal-marquette-community-responds/.

Intersectional identities do not enhance political acumen even if those identities magnify vulnerabilities to policing and predatory behavior from vigilantes and civilians. Compradors embody the same identities as the virtuous and the opportunistic, from those providing healthy caretaking to those hustling to be cared for. Black feminism is not a panacea against policing. Through the state, it has become an emerging signifier of the police apparatus. For example, Vice President Kamala Harris was a district attorney who sought to discipline and fine poor and working-class parents who could or would not force their children to attend schools—that functioned as carceral centers—on a regular basis. Consider the political archetypes of powerful Black women, informed by Black feminism, which offer no clear differentiation between centrist, liberal or radical Black feminisms (in the plural).

In the realm of police power, former Chicago mayor Lori Lightfoot was the first Black lesbian to win a mayoral election in Chicago. Her unwavering support for the Chicago Police Department (CPD) often downplayed its notorious violence. In 2014, CPD white officer Jason Van Dyke shot seventeen-year-old Laquan McDonald, who is Black, sixteen times for slashing car tires. Van Dyke was sentenced to seven years in prison for the murder, and released in 2022, after serving three years. The CPD is known for police brutality and torture to garner false confessions from hundreds of Black victims who decades later sought, and continue to seek, financial compensation.[25] CPD murders before and after the December 4, 1969, assassinations of Black Panthers Fred Hampton and Mark Clark (orchestrated by the FBI) have lingering malevolence. Crime is real, so too is police criminality. Consider another large city with Black feminist leadership—Atlanta. Mayor Keisha Lance-Bottoms pushed for the funding of the militarized destruction of a city forest in a Black neighborhood in order to pave the way for "Cop City" (mentioned earlier concerning Tortuguita's murder by troopers).[26] Funded by the Atlanta Police Foundation,

---

25. See Jon Burge, *The Marshall Project*, https://www.themarshallproject.org/records/331 jon burge.

26. Also see Rev. Matthew V. Johnson, Jr. and Joy James, "A Letter of Concern to Black Clergy Regarding "Cop City," *Logos: A Journal of Modern Society and Culture* 22, no. 2 (Spring 2023), https://logosjournal.com/2023/a-letter-of-concern-to-black-clergy-regarding-cop-city/.

JP Morgan,[27] Delta Airlines, Home Depot, and other large corporations, "Cop City" was to promote police morale after the protests following the murders of George Floyd and Rayshard Brooks in Atlanta, while expanding the militarization and colonization of urban centers through removal and violent policing of Black people, the poor, and working classes.[28]

After her mayoral term ended, Lance-Bottoms left Atlanta to work in the Biden administration. Her credentials as a "Black feminist" were never revoked but her function as a captive maternal was overridden by comprador status. Through her loyalty to state feminism and predatory policing, Lance-Bottoms sold or coerced Atlanta, despite citizen protests, into spending $30 million (now ballooned to $67 million) to build "Cop City" as a militarized zone that will displace Black working-class communities that coexist with the forests and promote anti-Black gentrification.

A more recent portrait of how Black feminisms have morphed into state feminism would be NYC's Keechant Sewell, the first Black woman NYPD commissioner. March 2022 data reports ethnic/racial breakdown of the NYPD as: 44.5 percent white; 30.2 percent Hispanic; 15.5 percent Black; 9.9 percent Asian; 0.10 percent Native American).[29] Sewell resigned in June 2023 after eighteen months serving as the NYPD chief commander. She was made subordinate to a special NYPD manager situated within City Hall.[30] Mayor Eric Adams, also Black, overrode her mild disciplining of top brass NYPD. (It is speculative about whether Sewell would have ever attempted to censure a white NYPD brass.) This conflict—not antagonism—between Black female and male NYPD leadership could be explained in part through Black feminism; however, conventional Black feminism does not appear to offer polyvariant or context-sensitive analyses in which

27. Funders of Jeffrey Epstein, JP Morgan will provide a multimillion-dollar settlement to the survivors of human trafficking.

28. See Joy James and Kalonji Changa, "The Rubik's Cube of Cop City," *Inquest*, July 18, 2023; and "Urban Warfare and Corporate-Funded Armies,"*nquest*, July 20, 2023.

29. See Annie McDonough, "NYPD reveals training details and demographics of neighborhood safety teams," *City & State*, March 30, 2022, https://www.cityandstateny.com/politics/2022/03/nypd-reveals-training-details-and-demographics-neighborhood-safety-teams/363849/

30. Yoav Gonen and Katie Honan, "Police Commissioner Keechant Sewell Resigns," *The City*, June 12, 2023, https://www.thecity.nyc/2023/6/12/23758688/police-commissioner-keechant-sewell-resigns.

patriarchy is situated within colonialism and imperialism. To anchor a predatory democracy, some forms of Black feminism as state leadership seem to offer "correctives" to state violence while working to stabilize its policing structures. The imaging of (Black) maternal care is projected onto society in order to legitimize overpolicing and soften the negative impact of predatory state powers.[31]

Press reported City Hall "micromanaging" the NYPD commissioner throughout her eighteen-month tenure. The final straw appeared to be when she attempted to discipline Chief Jeffrey Maddrey who has close ties to Mayor Adams. Following Civilian Complaint Review Board (CCRB) recommendations, Sewell had sought to discipline NYPD Chief of Department Jeffrey Maddrey by removing 6–10 vacation days after he abused his authority by voiding the arrest of retired NYPD officer Kruythoff Forrester. Forrester was arrested on Thanksgiving eve, November 2021, by Brooklyn police in the 73rd Precinct, Brownsville, which is predominantly Black, for chasing and pointing a gun at three twelve-to-fourteen year-old boys whose basketball hit Forrester's storefront security camera. When arrested, Forrester was in possession of the firearm described by the boys. Maddrey, previously Forrester's commanding officer in the 73rd Precinct, visited the precinct and demanded Forrester's release. Maddrey challenged the loss of paid vacation in an administrative trial, while Mayor Adams—former NYPD—publicly stated that he acted appropriately despite Yoav Gonen's video montage for the March 9, 2023 *The City* exposé.

Sewell's public statement offered no criticism of the nepotism and police violence: "I have made the decision to step down from my position. I will never step away from my advocacy and support for the NYPD, and I will always be a champion for the people of New York City." Some might focus on the patriarchal move of men dominating the NYPD and NYC government and social politics. However, that would elide the crises of predatory policing and Sewell's contributions to it. African-American Clergy & Elected Officials supported Maddrey

---

31. For perspectives on the Captive Maternal and policing and repression, see Joy James, "The Womb of Western Theory: Trauma, Time Theft, and the Captive Maternal," in *Challenging the Punitive Society*, Carceral Notebooks, Volume 12, 2016, ed. Perry Zurn and Andrew Dilts, https://www.thecarceral.org/journal-vol12.html; Joy James, *In Pursuit of Revolutionary Love: Precarity, Power, Communities* (Brussels and London: Divided, 2023); and Joy James, "Maternal (In)Coherence: When Feminism Meets Fascism," *Parapraxis*, November 21, 2022, https://www.parapraxismagazine.com/articles/maternal-incoherence.

and Forrester who are both Black. Threatening with a gun in hand and chasing Black male children whose basketball hit a camera while they were playing on the street is a form of violence and child abuse.[32] Organizing in war resistance to resist predatory policing is a political not a performative act. Most avoid the Captive Maternal stage of war resistance which follows marronage.

MARRONAGE: FULCRUM FOR FREEDOM

Despite the betrayals and the compradors, the morphing of Black feminisms into state feminisms, the avenues for circumventing carceral networks and predatory policing remain intact. All stages of organizing are not "equal." Captive Maternal stages within political struggles require caretaking, protests, movements. These are essential in community building, but marronage is what offers sanctuary.

Marronage is a zone where the concentric circles of care mindful of security apparatuses move closer to the epicenter—the surface of political struggle, positioned directly above the hypocenter (the underground zone of explosion—where US and CIA coups and assassinations operate against liberation movements). The hypocenter "ground zero" is the underground terrain where the intensity of the fight for freedom is. Gaslighting by the state—and by individuals who distract themselves (and others) from war resistance—makes it difficult for us to (publicly) face our fears of protofascist violence. Marronage opens the cognitive and material corridor to war resistance; it is the stage in which revolutionaries manifest.

Of the multiple stages of the Captive Maternal—caretaking, protest, movement, marronage, war resistance—marronage is the zone for radical communities who devote substantial time and resources to stay with and protect each other, in order to thrive under predatory policing and capture. Afropessimism asserts that globally Blacks have grappled with apocalyptic reincarnations for half a millennium, or a millennium and a half if one includes Arab enslavement of Africans. Spaniards and Portuguese defeated the Arabs and Africans and Islam,

---

32. See Yoav Gonen, "WATCH: Videos Show NYPD Chiefs Intervened Before Voiding of Ex-Cop's Gun Arrest," *The City*, March 9, 2023, https://www.thecity.nyc/2023/3/9/23632499/nypd-police-jeffrey-maddrey-video.

that colonized and civilized parts of Europe. After the expulsion of "the Moors" in 1492, Western Europe began to traffic humans as commodities through chattel slavery, waging war on the African continent, on the Atlantic waters, and on the American continent.

Historical examples of marronage throughout the Americas are plentiful.[33] Captive Maternals stole themselves from enslavement through resistance, life, and death. Cinque on La Amistad commandeered the Spanish slaving vessel with other Africans in 1839. Arrested by the US he took his case to the Supreme Court (former president John Quincy Adams was his attorney) and gained his release, along with other surviving Africans to return to Africa. Although land wars had decimated his village and disappeared his people, Cinque had fought and won a war on water and a legal battle on land. Other rebels, such as Nat Turner and Harriet Tubman, ran from plantations or burnt them down and fought in liberation wars. Insurrections were linked to freedom movements. In US democracy, captivity is normative within not only prisons, jails, and ICE detention centers, but also in work camps, factories, domestic servitude, military camps, and human/sex trafficking. Captives steal themselves and their time back from "masters," bosses, employers, guards, cops, judges, rapists, and pimps. They constantly build marronage sites.

Captive Maternals are not marked by personal gender identities, or class/social status, but by their *functions* in service—from caretaking to war resistance—are the most significant thing about their personas. From the initial stages of the compromised caretaker or protester and movement-maker and marronage comes the rebel stage before war resistance to anti-Black violence, poverty, colonialism, and imperialism.[34] The earlier stages of caretaking stay within conventional political and social norms. People discipline themselves to accept compromises and compliance in order to obtain job security, secure housing, health care, food, and education, sometimes to save a life, including their own. The maroon community allows for some auton-

---

33. UNESCO, "Maroon Communities in the Americas," https://slaveryandremembrance. org/articles/article/?id=A0060#:~:text=The%20institution%20of%20slavery%20 was,in%20the%20Caribbean%20and%20Brazil.
34. See Orlando Patterson, *Slavery and Social Death: A Comparative Study, With a New Preface* (Cambridge: Harvard University Press, 2018).

omy and protections from carceral sites such as prisons, parole, welfare, and foster care.

Captive Maternals as maroons for centuries transpose exhaustion, exploitation, and resentments into rebellions and fugitivity. Lynching, state violence, and police murder push Captive Maternals into movements. Movements create freedom schools, underground societies, mutual aid associations, a range of co-ops. Physical, sexual, cerebral, emotional selves, collective and individual, manifest outside the carceral gates in fields, swamps, mountains, beyond the gaze of prison guard, social worker, police.

Vulnerable Captive Maternals often lack material stability afforded to the Black bourgeoisie and wealthy whites.[35] They are often shackled to the state's carceral zones: social work, foster care, detention centers, jails, prisons, psych wards. Agency and marronage exist even in hell.[36] Marronage is essential for an evolutionary trek that confronts or departs from predatory violence. To attain that zone, one must first traverse the stages and contradictions of the Captive Maternal. Captive Maternals can provide care because they are bullied or shamed into doing so. Others willingly provide care with reluctance and exhaustion to personal, familial, communal, and political formations. Agape-fueled care is love disciplined by political will. It transcends the personal and the familial. This is the level in which the self—that can only manifest within communal—expands its awareness. Self-love encompasses the collective. For a people trafficked for centuries—whose color registers them as "slave" in the psyches of others and their own communities—the process of care would involve stealing oneself back. Marronage seeks to claim the self without victimization by violence, dishonor, and death—emotional, psychological, intellectual, spiritual, biological.[37]

Marronage and war resistance are woven into emotional, spiritual, intellectual, and physical training. In a democracy structured for predatory acts, people grow bent without healthy culture. The journey

---

35. See Cheryl Harris, Whiteness as Property, *Harvard Law Review*, June 10, 1993, https://harvardlawreview.org/print/no-volume/whiteness-as-property/.

36. Dante Alighieri's *The Divine Comedy* offers nine circles of Hell, the last circle which focuses on treachery. Within the framework of the Captive Maternal, this would be the zone of the comprador. It is a "frozen wasteland." See Matt Staggs, "A Visitor's Guide to Dante's Nine Circles of Hell," https://www.penguinrandomhouse.com/articles/a-visitors-guide-to-dantes-nine-circles-of-hell/.

37. James, "The Womb of Western Theory."

back to ourselves requires new frames. Our battles to contain harm and dishonor are painful if not brutal. They suture over the ruptures of natality through political, personal, familial, communal care. Care is politicized in order to address mechanistic state capture and murder through the histories of human trafficking and enslavement, antebellum/postbellum mass rape and torture, convict prison lease system, Black Codes, Jim Crow, Cointelpro, and CIA assassinations. Atrocities produce mutations of grief, loss, and rage. Rather than succumb to acquiescence, some become rebels. Whether pacifist or militarist, war resisters engage in the most intense level of struggle for the Captive Maternal because they are willing to confront violence. Captive Maternal labor was repurposed to stabilize the state and corporate culture that counters or cannibalizes Black freedom. Even when violated, Captive Maternals still mutate across stages of agency. Compromised caretakers often fear to demand justice due to the loss of livelihoods, protections, or positions within the social order schooled into us. Protesters call out injustices. Frustrated by the lack of structural change, they evolve into movement builders who build maroon sites and sanctuaries.

Captive Maternals sacrifice in order to stabilize families, political economies, communities, and cultures, and offer protections from police forces, state trafficking into prisons and ICE camps, and foster care. Captive Maternals use pain to reconstruct opposition to predation and thus (re)build potential for proto-revolutionary formations. The barriers to opposition include fear, depression, indoctrination, and betrayal by the ill-informed opportunist, parasitic operative, and comprador. Inevitably, the most active of Captive Maternals will ask, Who and what protects me?, a query this text cannot fully address.

Engineering marronage, communities form firewalls against poverty and police violence. What is personal/familial/communal health, security, peace, and pleasure within a state and society apprehensive about Black autonomy and independence? Some maroons become war resisters when they fight police terror, lynching, and incarceration. Agender or ungendered Black caretakers, as Captive Maternals with diverse political interests and intentions, have resisted democracy's predatory practices—such as the Three-Fifth Clause, and Thirteenth, Fourteenth, and Fifteenth Amendments—for centuries.

In 2020, a Black male pastor in Rochester, New York, gave an interview on WBAI, a NYC-based public radio station. In that interview, following the murder of George Floyd, the reverend tersely declared to the state and corporations (which fund police unions and foundations such as the Atlanta Police Foundation, the architect for "Cop City"): "*If you kill us, we will kill your economy.*" Movements progress when activists can levy or deliver a penalty for murder (since the state refuses to discipline its militarized police forces). An impact upon antagonists might be a deterrent, interrupting the flow of funds would also be useful to steer corporations to stop funding the sectors and politicians that they decry for sowing anti-trans and anti-LGBTQIA+ violence, and violence against undocumented people, violence against the working class and laboring poor, the racialized, Indigenous, and African-descended. The stage of marronage separates organizers from corporate funders and conventional society. Maroons who retreat from conventional politics are more likely to be survcilled and targeted by police.

CONCLUSION

Organizers understand the necessity of redefining citizenry as an activism that can contain state predation, and contingents form marronage to hold community together in war resistance. Transformed by trauma, most Black people—LGBTQIA+, impoverished, working class, (petite) bourgeoisie—are not inherently radical. Some are intensely hostile to radicalism, others seek respectability and responsibility and employment through liberalism. Few manifest as radicals and revolutionaries given that hypervisibility brings hyper*vulnerability*. Blacks remain dehumanized across many registers. (For example, Donald Trump's "sh**-hole" countries reference to African asylum seekers and undocumented people at the southern borders and in ICE camps is not a US aberration.)

Erica Garner and cadres committed to struggles that surpassed their specific traumas. They used personal pain but did not make a political campaign out of family trauma; they opened a corridor to move from the epicenter closer to the hypocenter. Erica Garner's expressed radicalism through rhetoric and Twitter went beyond the performative and personal grievances; she used her loss and trauma to make calls for radical action. Without virtue signaling the autobiographical (Taibbi notes in his book on the Garner family her candor about contradictions and familial flaws), Garner chose militancy that also showed grace.[38]

38. Harlem Renaissance Church Pastor Jordan distinguishes between a *moralism* that mandates the right thing as opposed to *relativism* which mandates individually doing whatever one wants. Although restorative justice or connections "keep the door open," at times one wants to slam it shut and lock it to bar out intruders and hungry ghosts. Grace means that we are entitled to what we did *not* earn. Still there is intentional labor required; the ideal goal is not correct behavior but right relationships. Past childhoods stalk the present. Childhood repetitive conflicts allow adult and childhood-parental blame, attacks, and lies to become the recycled norm. Healthy conflict would retain the relational if true relation—rather than a hustle—had existed. There can be no relations when narratives are embedded in outright lies or lies by omission. "Connection before correction" is what Renaissance advocates. See Renaissance Church, "Galatians: Conflict in the Family of God (Full Service – Sunday, June 25, 2023)," https://www.youtube.com/watch?v=SWHyQi5sWkQ.

CHAPTER 2

OLD/NEW BONES ABOLITION: ACADEMIC CONFERENCES AND COMMUNAL GATHERINGS

SPOTLIGHT ON ACADEMIC SKELETONS

Contradictions embedded within abolition are amplified by academia. The University of Pennsylvania and Princeton University claimed and profited off the bones of MOVE children murdered by Philadelphia police in the 1985 bombing of Osage Avenue.[1] Medical and anthropological centers and departments routinely capture and use as teaching tools or exhibits, the bones of those defeated in colonial wars and their aftermaths. The bones of Indigenous families/communities, and the bones of Black families/communities over centuries have been stolen by state and corporate entities. The Black men who joined John Brown in the 1859 raid on Harper's Ferry to push the US forward toward abolishing slavery were either executed in the streets or at the gallows. Their bodies were dismembered by white mobs; intact bodies were donated to medical schools for dissection. However, John Brown's body was given a ceremonial burial in the north by his family and abolition community. Police forces routinely disappear people into jails and prisons. Some die while others are directly killed in their encounters with police forces and prison guards. How does academia grapple with this historical and contemporary violence?

---

1. Elaine Ayers, "The Grim Open Secret of College Bone Collections," *Slate*, April, 30, 2021, https://slate.com/news-and-politics/2021/04/move-bombing-victims-princeton-penn-museum-history-anthropology.html.

The disposability of the impoverished and the racialized is a key feature of policing. Police are known in their administrative paperwork to designate murdered people who were drug-addicted or exploited sex workers—and *Blacks in general*— as "NHI" or "No Humans Involved." Institutional contempt and disposability coexist with other forms of dishonor from elite academia and its purchases. There are ways in which Black life and death, as well as Black revolutionary struggles, are captured by the state and corporation.

Prestigious academic institutions collect the papers of revolutionary political prisoners hunted, tortured, and held captive by the state: Brown University has the papers of Mumia Abu-Jamal.[2] Yet, Brown discusses "mass incarceration" with little to nothing said about political prisoners. Elite universities appear to have not waged an active public campaign to petition for Abu-Jamal's right to an evidentiary hearing and to uphold ethics in order to stabilize democracy. Princeton University purchased the papers of another Panther veteran, Dhoruba bin Wahad, who went underground into the Black Liberation Army. He was framed and incarcerated for nineteen years and eventually awarded a financial settlement from the state.

NJ TROOPERS "STORM" PRINCETON'S ABOLITION CONFERENCE

In 2011, Princeton University invited me to speak on a panel at an abolition conference sponsored by African American Studies. Their request was for me to speak in New Jersey about Black Panther and BLA veteran, Assata Shakur, who was shot by New Jersey troopers, acquitted in multiple trials led by her attorney, her aunt Evelyn Williams (author of *Inadmissible Evidence*), only to be convicted in a last trial (with attorney William Kunstler) of the shooting death of New Jersey State Trooper Werner Foerster. Shakur was shot and wounded by the troopers in a car check stop. She had no powder residue on her hands indicating that she had held or shot a gun when Troopers injured her and killed her Panther/BLA companion Zayd Shakur. I was committed to speaking on a panel to increase political education

---

2. News from Brown, "To advance research on incarceration, Brown acquires personal papers of prisoner Mumia Abu-Jamal," August 24, 2022, https://www.brown.edu/news/2022-08-24/incarceration.

about political prisoners by using the prestige of Princeton. My research, writing, and travels led me to become deeply impressed with Panther and Black Liberation Army veteran Assata Shakur. My writing on Shakur, e.g., "Framing the Panther,"[3] was shaped by Harlem Panthers who had worked with her to deliver care to Black communities in NYC. For me, even though I did not use the language at the time, Assata Shakur was/is a Captive Maternal whose stages of development went from caretaking to protesting, movement making, marronage, and war resistance.

For Princeton, in New Jersey, I had some concerns about how I would discuss Shakur in a state where NJ Troopers and police tried to kill her by shooting and torturing her when she was hospitalized; and later, by sentencing her to death in prison, before she was liberated by comrades (as noted, Silvia Baraldini and Sekou Odinga were imprisoned for decades for assisting in a nonviolent prison escape of a political prisoner). Shakur's $1 million bounty would grow to $2 million under the Obama administration. Her memoir is popular on progressive campuses. It never occurred to me that perhaps I was invited to speak on Shakur as a victim of police violence and carceral repression because no other academic in New Jersey would take on that task. My colleagues on the panel were all white, which appeared to be true of most panels. I was the second or third speaker, and as I settled in my seat to give my talk, I noticed the double doors to my upper left open. I glanced up to the entry for the walk down to the stage. White New Jersey State Troopers cued their entrance into the auditorium when I began to speak. This would be replayed by white Brazilian attorneys in São Paulo when I began my keynote on Erica Garner in 2018. Several years earlier, white NYPD officers entered a lecture hall at The New School in New York City when our panel of Black activists began talking about police violence.

During my 2011 Princeton talk, I quietly, periodically glanced at the door to my left where the troopers had gathered, but they were of course not that quiet. I asserted from Princeton's stage that Assata Shakur was innocent of the death of New Jersey Trooper Werner

3. Joy James, "Framing the Panther: Assata Shakur and Black Female Agency," in *Want to Start a Revolution: Radical Women in the Black Freedom Struggle*, ed. Dayo Gore, Jeanne Theoharis, and Komozi Woodard (New York and London: New York University Press, 2009), 138–160.

Foerster. Some maintain that when NJ Troopers shot Assata Shakur and killed her companion, Zayd Shakur, they might have hit Foerster in "friendly fire" (as was the case when Georgia State Patrol shot unarmed forest protector "Tortuguita," Manuel Pacz Terán).[4] My conference talk referenced *Assata: An Autobiography* which recounts how NJ troopers/police tortured Shakur while she was shackled to a hospital bed. Shakur credits a white German female nurse, who ushered the white troopers out of her room, for saving her life. As an academic, I sought to contribute an analysis appropriate for the academic environment in which I would be speaking. In actuality, as a Captive Maternal invested in war resistance, my function was to be clear about the distinction between state predators and Black communal liberators.

NJ Troopers and police rarely attend Princeton University conferences. Campus security though tend to have close ties to local police, as both constitute some aspect of police forces. In the car with Vermont license plates and Black occupants randomly stopped on the New Jersey turnpike was Sundiata Acoli who escaped, was captured, convicted, and incarcerated as a political prisoner for over fifty years. Eleven years after the Princeton conference, he was released in 2022, at the age of eighty-five.

Despite the troopers' visibility, the lack of response among the attendees was notable. Dissonance for the gathering appeared not to stem from police, but from a young Black woman who questioned the function and purpose, the very relevance, of the conference.

A young Black woman seated in the center front row of the auditorium calmly posed a question to our panel. She identified herself as teaching at a working-class vocational college with low-income and impoverished Black and Brown students living under conditions of scarcity, violence, police aggression, and imprisonment—all struggles that multiracial academics had discussed in their papers throughout the day. The young professor noted that every academic presenting papers that day came from elite private institutions where students were shielded from the vulnerabilities and violence stalking her own students. Immediately, a prominent Black professor chastised her for

---

4. See Tracey Tully, "Sundiata Acoli, Black Nationalist Who Killed NJ Trooper in '73, Wins Parole," *New York Times*, May 10, 2022, https://www.nytimes.com/2022/05/10/nyregion/sundiata-acoli-black-liberation-army-parole.html. Tully asserts that Acoli killed Foerster.

lacking appreciation of the gathering and pointed to a young Black male Princeton student who was graduating that year, as the brain-child of the event. Although verbally attacked, she kept her composure and remained seated. From the stage, I interrupted to affirm her critique by noting that abolitionist conferences at elite institutions had become the national norm—not the exception—as the most popularized forms of abolition. No one else—all the panelists appeared to be ivy league or elite academics—spoke. My lone voice of support proved less powerful than that of Princeton academics, students, and representatives of nonprofits who were reticent to speak on her behalf, or panelists and audience members who agreed with the dismissal of a class analysis.

I witnessed the protest of one anonymous Captive Maternal bravely determined to organize and instruct, despite censorship from the Black bourgeoisie, as a stage of Captive Maternal agency. Her protest impressed upon me the need to analyze and publicly discuss the roles of elites in abolition. Those who daily show up for working-class and underfunded students—those most likely to be harassed and violated by police forces—are the Captive Maternals who confront poverty, homelessness, police violence, and incarceration, not just within the intellectual realm of reading, speaking, conferencing and teaching, but also within the material realm of struggle and scarcity. These very realms are distanced from or present as abstractions to elite universities and colleges.

2015 APSA IN SAN FRANCISCO, POLITICAL SCIENTISTS PROTECT OBAMA

Four years later I had another wake-up call at an academic conference. In San Francisco, the American Political Science Association (APSA) was hosting its 2015 annual conference. I accepted the invitation to be a respondent to the papers presented by the white male assistant professor who invited me, and chaired the panel with his colleagues who were also assistant professors: a Black woman, a Black man, and an Indigenous woman. After the discussion, I was invited to join them for lunch. (The Black woman had another engagement.) At lunch, an academic linked to the HBCU casually commented that academics were using their training in critical theory to stealth-edit President Barack Obama's public statements on lethal and predatory police forces, in order to make POTUS appear more committed to and ethically aligned with those outraged at anti-Black police violence. This conference was held in the fall, months after Freddie Gray's death by severed spine at the hands of Baltimore police in April 2015. As a reflex action, in reference to the news about POTUS, I unthinkingly blurted out at the lunch table, "Mother-f*****!"

The mood immediately shifted from the congratulations for a well-presented panel to a cool reception. The young Black male wore a confident smirk at my perceived *faux pas*. The white male academic's face dropped in disappointment. The Indigenous woman who had made the statement in a casual way had little expression, but it seemed as if she felt sorry for me given my lack of decorum. Diminished in stature, I apologized to the younger profs who quietly and quickly departed. I sat for a while reflecting, then realized that my shreds of remorse were eclipsed by my rage. If the information were accurate, my colleagues had spent years as academics or professional abolitionists attending White House invitations to meetings and task forces, to make the President and his administration—Obama visited federal prisons in his second term—seem relevant and engaged in addressing prisons and police abuses. Colleagues were "airbrushing" the administration, in similar ways that CNN commentator and founder of the Ella Baker Center, Van Jones, would airbrush the Trump administration by stealth-editing Jared Kushner's portfolio on prison reforms. US foreign policy which also furthered captivity and death through drone strikes and United States Africa Command (AFRICOM) was rarely discussed in academic abolition circles. Academics who were stealth-editing for the state logically were working for lobbyists and state-aligned corporations.

My guttural responses and swearing at injustices no longer embarrass me. This Captive Maternal shifts stages as she ages. I see betrayals in all administrations and in the most well-funded start-up movement organizations. I wonder now why I was embarrassed in 2015 to curse in front of promising young professors. Captive Maternals are not role models for careerists. Advancement is for the oppressed communal formations that cannot be liberated by "Black Excellence" unless it is deployed in war resistance. My curse about and around the POTUS included his academic informers. It was an expression of agency and agony. Collectively, the communities were exhausted about reading, studying, and viewing photographs or video screens or texts that recounted the police murders of Eric Garner, Michael Brown, Tamir Rice, and in 2015, Freddie Gray. Identifying as a Captive Maternal, I realize that today—with the exception of a pro forma courtesy apology for vulgarity, I don't mind blurting out a sincerity that reflects both frustration at government and fear for vulnerable communities. I would rather curse than curtsy around corrupt state power and corporate funders that perform care without delivering it to oppressed communities. The state remains predatory even when forced to make concessions after protests and movements. It steals our generative powers as caretakers. Given the betrayals augmented by academia, punditry and decorous dialogue, I needed to access Captive Maternal agency that could be rude, abrasive, and even weird. Eventually, gradually, I began to leave the enclosure of academic convention and likeability.

CAMPUS BSU SPARKS MEDITATION AND ANALYSES OF ERICA GARNER

On December 30, 2017, media reported that Erica Garner, at the age of twenty-seven, had died after suffering a massive heart attack causing extensive brain damage, on Christmas eve. I had no idea at the time that she was ill, and that community and advocates (such as myself) had failed to sufficiently rally for better care and medical support. The most militant, committed to revolutionary love, are easily ignored or dismissed by those comfortable with Black suffering and police oppression. Mourning her death, I decided to recognize her passing in my classrooms and in my public talks. I determined that for one year, beginning in 2018, wherever I was invited to lecture or keynote as an academic—whether Toronto, São Paulo, or my college—I would only speak of Erica Garner (1990–2017). That "one-year" tribute acknowledging her contributions grew to several years, and finally was invested into *New Bones Abolition*.

Erica Garner had passed when students were on winter break from campus. After winter study, the spring semester began in early

February. At the start of the semester, a former student of mine and a leader within the Black Student Union (BSU) emailed to ask if I would fill in for a Black History Month speaker who canceled their February campus talk. I said "yes" and stated that I would talk about the organizer-revolutionary lover Erica Garner. The BSU was attempting to break down the political isolation and anti-Black animus that encircled the frozen aspects of the white and wealthy elite college formed in the eighteenth century through genocidal land and labor extraction. The BSU students created a montage of historical images of Black intellectuals and political actors that merged time and space within resistance movements. Their visual poster-flyer imprinted a color photograph of Garner, with bullhorn in hand, leading a protest through NYC streets over a collage of old black-and-white photographs of Black movement leaders, or what is now commonly referred to as the "Black radical tradition." The students blended the past with the present moment (of loss). The photo was spot on: Erica Garner had joined the ancestors, and the visual underscored the transition and the connections that cross time and space. I expected a modest gathering for the talk, but the cavernous Griffin Hall was pretty full on the ground floor (a few people were even in the balcony). The BSU's February 2018 Black History Month keynote, sponsored by Williams, was my first opportunity to speak in public about Erica Garner.

Some seats were occupied by students because a professor appeared to have made attendance to the event an assignment for his class. Largely white males, likely political science majors, those students took notes and conferred among themselves occasionally during the talk and Q&A. Black and other BIPOC students seemed more relaxed and better able to comprehend the concept of the Captive Maternal in relationship to Erica Garner than the white male students who never attended any of my talks/lectures. One student would assert when called upon in Q&A that my presentation was "poetic" but lacked political analysis about the young Black mother. It took me a moment to realize that although Garner had developed one of the most powerful political ads in the twenty-first century for the "maverick" presidential candidate Senator Bernie Sanders (I-VT), she was still stereotyped as a nonintellectual; her political intellect overlooked because she was viewed as a poor or working-class Black mom who could not have conceived, pitched, and directed the "It's Not Over" campaign ad. Without a college (elite) degree or position in formal politics or nonprofits, few radicals manifest to elites as not only their peers but also potential teachers. Later, several female BIPOC students told me students, who were not in our seminar where we had discussed Black radicalism, seemed unable to grasp political leadership emanating from Black working-class militants terrorized by police, funded by taxpayers, who could kill with impunity, especially if the target was Black and working class or low-income.

Following the BSU Black History Month, I began to study more deeply the contributions and sacrifices made by organizers such as Erica Garner and her cohort of radical activists. Elite students seemed to know little of Black history or contemporary resistance struggles to state violence. That ninety-minute encounter during the shortest month of the year became a "teachable" moment for me. I listened to conflict in queries seeking answers and antagonism in declaratives dressed as queries that sought to uphold the police as essential to law and order. The majority of the gathering was not Black. It did not need to be. Marronage, a historical and contemporary flight and fight against captivity, at times reflects the "rainbow" vision (which culminates in "all power to the people, none to the police") of Fred Hampton, the Black Panther leader murdered by the Chicago police and FBI.

Throughout 2018 and beyond, I dedicated my spare time to meditations, political analyses, and tributes to Erica Garner. I routinely screened her 2016 political campaign ad for Senator Bernie Sanders (discussed in Chapter 6, "Campaigning for Bernie and Against the DNC") when I was giving public talks and when I was home alone. Whereas some replayed the video of her father's execution, I watched as she created out of pain and loss a presidential campaign advertisement seeking justice and safety for vulnerable communities. As my planned one-year homage grew into several years, I would screen the election video in North and South America. Eventually, talks developed into several articles: "The Captive Maternal and Abolitionism" and "Abolitionist and Ancestor: The Legacy of Erica Garner."[5] The aca-

---

5. See Joy James, "The Captive Maternal and Abolitionism," *TOPIA: Canadian Journal of Cultural Studies* 43 (Summer 2021), 9–23; Joy James, "Abolitionist and Ancestor: The Legacy of Erica Garner," *American Literary History*, April 1, 2021, https://doi.org/10.1093/alh/ajab006.

demic reflecting and writing on the contributions of Erica Garner did not deter antagonists and white nationalists at home or abroad.

ANTAGONISTS VERSUS COMRADES

In July 2018, I traveled to São Paulo, Brazil to give a keynote on crime and punishment for a conference of international jurists—*Instituto Brasileiro de Ciências Criminais* (IBCCRIM). The conference was held at an upscale hotel that seemed unaccustomed to having to accommodate Black guests (the janitorial staff were all Black, the folks at the front desk were all white). In São Paulo, white and Black attorneys and scholars greeted me. Two Black feminist Brazilian scholars hugged and welcomed me and then sat beside me on the dais as respondents to my keynote. I settled and reviewed my notes. The lecture hall had filled to capacity. From an elevated sound/video booth in the upper tier on my right, a female Brazilian translator repeated in Portuguese or English the introduction provided by the Black women academics who read my bio and welcomed me to the international conference with speakers from Europe, the US, and Latin America. They patiently waited to field queries after my keynote but it became a thirty-minute stressor—for some—as white male reactionary attorneys burst through the doors of the upscale hotel in São Paulo and attempted to turn my keynote into their personal Colosseum, within which they would pose as gladiators for international white nationalism. Black women professors, at the first level of the Captive Maternal, sat stoically and silently on the dais beside me as I spoke about Erica Garner and against white supremacy and predatory policing, while reactionary white male attorneys created a ruckus at the entry doors of the hall, laughing as I spoke about Black murder at the hands of white police.

There were two antagonistic narratives: theirs in loud jeers and mine in a quiet voice before a microphone amplified my words for the Brazilian woman translator in the upper tier booth. I was not disillusioned or traumatized by the battle to dominate the public-private arena through voice. From the dais, I looked down to the main audience in the center of the hall, while periodically glancing to my left at the suited, well-heeled white male attorneys punctuating my talk with their boisterous jeers and prancing at the entrance doors. Their performance was meant to derail my presentation. But in their opposition, they only deepened the analyses of Black death—and the loss of Eric Garner, Erica Garner, named and unnamed casualties, and a fight for democracy despite state violence. The verbal attacks pushed me mentally and emotionally toward the crossroads where *Esu/Elegua* (*Elegbara* among Afro-Brazilians) waited. I returned the contempt of the antagonists. Orisha and ancestors (discussed in the Conclusion) led me not to stumble. Shrugging off white nationalist derision, I offered no verbal or facial response or change in my cadence or speaking style, as I continued to discuss the contributions of Erica Garner. Intellectual warfare was one of Erica Garner's gifts. How the intellect is wielded in battle is at times shaped by individual temperament; we had/have different styles, but I had studied her courage.

The majority-white Brazilian audience began to shift in their seats, embarrassed by their counterparts. The tribute to Erica Garner was never paused or fractured. My contempt for racist antagonists centered me. Minutes after the heckling started, white Brazilian women defense attorneys, appearing mortified, rose from their seats and walked back to the doors where their white male colleagues heckled and herded them out of the hall. At the end of Q&A, I took photos with Black Brazilian academics and attorneys in the hall. They appreciated the tribute and the analysis, and perhaps most of all my quiet contempt for their homegrown white supremacists. I had stated to Black Brazilians and to the larger audience that perhaps, given that, globally, the US had the largest imprisoned population per capita, and Brazil the most murderous police forces, we could align our abolition movements. There was little interest in discussing that alliance.

Throughout my stay in São Paulo, my thoughts were embedded in the words and images of the screening of Erica Garner's 2016 presidential campaign video ad for Senator Bernie Sanders (I-VT)—in which Sanders declares that any police officer who kills a (Black) civilian without legitimate self-defense should be imprisoned. To my recollection, no major figure in the Democratic Party had publicly asserted that position. The opposition's mockery of the desire to quell and reign in anti-Black violence in predatory policing and white nationalism would not be translated by the white woman in the media booth who channeled my English into Portuguese. Garner's English-language political ad screened with Portuguese subtitles. Some understood intellectually, politically, and/or emotionally, my statement as I closed the screening: "We fought. . . and we lost."

After six years of reflecting on the gifts of Erica Garner and other caretaking militants, I have begun to realize that we did *not* "lose." We were never defeated despite the exhaustion, forced retreats, "collateral casualties," and political imprisonments, police torture, and terror. My remembrance and study of Erica Garner helped me to develop steely composure from which to observe and counter white supremacists-in-play. Erica Garner remains a present reminder of our collective capacity. She and her cadres challenged the NYPD, the New York City Mayor, the New York Governor, and the President of the United States. We can transition from conflicted caretaker, protester, movement builder, maroon space holder, and await the calls for the war resistance. There were, and are, allies.

After the keynote, several print and media news outlets asked for interviews. I was able to speak then more about rising white nationalist terrorism, and vigilante and predatory police violence in the United States. Progressive Brazilian journalists, jurists, attorneys, and academics wanted to be in dialogue. Later, I accepted an invitation to travel to the offices of human rights attorneys and sit for an extensive video interview about racism and US policing. The attorneys and videographer and I hugged as they wished me well on my return to the US, which I had described as a predatory zone and a deeply flawed democracy.[6] Leaving Brazil, I recognized that my US passport and visa made it easier for me to protest white nationalist antagonists. The other Black women on the dais wielded their own agency, silently. I appreciated that I belonged to a Black internationalist alliance of war resistance and war resisters cracking their bones while embedded in the imperial US.

---

6. US presidential elections are determined by the electoral college which overrules the general public's choice. Millions of voters chose Al Gore over George W. Bush and later Hillary Clinton over Donald J. Trump (after they chose Clinton over Sanders in the Democratic primary). The elections of (dis)avowed and (un)repentant white nationalists celebrating and upholding predatory policing stems from a legacy of anti-Black enslavement and exploitation through the Three-Fifths Clause; that clause structured the electoral college to disproportionately favor Southern enslavers as presidents because they could count captives on their plantations as "representation," without the consent of the captives. Despite the historical trajectory, corruption and violence, severed natality of terror baked into the apparatus of democracy, Captive Maternals continue to resist.

After I returned to the US, I continuously met radical Black activists who had organized with Erica Garner in NYC, and later resisted police violence after the police murder of George Floyd. Their battle scars from the NYPD included being assaulted in Manhattan protests for not standing on a sidewalk. After an upper-level administrator did performative kneeling in Central Park with largely affluent, white protesters distraught with police violence that they rarely had to endure, the same NYPD officer oversaw peaceful protesters, Green Caps [legal observers], journalists, and human rights observers being kettled (with metal gates) and beaten in the South Bronx. NYPD corralled activists and detained them from returning home to make curfew imposed by the city. Minutes after the curfew went into effect, around 8:00 p.m., police set upon civilians, swinging batons into their heads for "violating" curfew that civilians could not obey because they were being forcibly and illegally detained outdoors on June 4, 2020.[7] Six years after the police executions of Eric Garner, Michael Brown, Jr., and Tamir Rice, two years after the death of Erica Garner, who had been organizing from 2014 until December 2017, organizers had been on the battlefield for over six years. Some of the organizers became contributing authors to the *Black Anonymous Timeline and Analysis* (accessible via the digital link in the Further Resources section at the back of the book) which traces political lineage in war resistance from civil rights through the Black Power into the BLM movements. Different views of political struggles continue. In order to clarify contradictions and identify productive communities and destructive compradors, those views must engage with radical actors such as Erica Garner.

FRACTURES MENDED WITH POETRY

In April 2021, I received an unexpected gift from a dear friend from seminary, Sally McNichol, who sent me Lucille Clifton's poem "New Bones" in an email gift just as I was finalizing my talk for UC Davis' Humanities Center, "Mellon Sawyer Seminar on Contemporary Struggle: abolition x communism." I read the brief poem and decided

---

7. "Kettling Protesters in the Bronx: Systematic Police Brutality and Its Cost in the US," *Human Rights Watch*, September 30, 2020, https://www.hrw.org/report/2020/09/30/kettling-protesters-bronx/systemic-police-brutality-and-its-costs-united-states.

I would share it with the conference. I renamed my talk "'New Bones' Abolition, Communism, and the Captive Maternal." The Mellon Sawyer Seminar on Contemporary Political Struggle summarized key points from the panel for their blog, noting that opening my talk with Lucille Clifton's poem was an attempt at "seeking new bones and new structures in our revolutionary struggles," as I encouraged the audience to be aware of the ways in which academia is not amenable to revolutionary struggles and the growth of new bones.[8] My presentation on "New Bones" asserted that academia often fails "to recognize the intellectualism and abolitionary praxis of the working class," and how academic abolitionism is often "hampered by its desire to speak for people rather than with them, and by its ties to capital." As I stated in my talk, if capital is financing our freedom movements, then they are not freedom movements. Who controls the terms of discourse about "revolutionary" struggles shapes strategies? I contended that we can only get new bones if we return to the power and intellectualism of 'the people who die first and die poor.'

After hearing the April 2021 talk, Verso's editors emailed to ask me to submit the paper as a blog article.[9] When I submitted the essay, an editor deleted the section on the Captive Maternal, and the addition of "Black feminism" was suggested as a replacement for "Captive Maternal." Black feminism and Captive Maternal are not synonyms, I explained. The function, specificity, and complexity of ungendered Black caretaking, protest, movement forging, marronage, and war resistance are the markers that identify the functions of the Captive Maternal. They are not intersectionality or Black feminist identity markers. Within the context of anti-Black violence and denigration through enslavement, colonialism, capitalism and imperialism, incarceration, and rape, I had sought new formulations. I maintained to the editor that although the concept of the Captive Maternal is unfamiliar to most, if the article were to be published by them it would have to include the analytic of the Captive Maternal. The stages of the Captive

---

8. See "Growing New Bones as the Crossroads of Abolition and Communism," UC Davis Humanities Institute, May 17, 2021, https://dhi.ucdavis.edu/featured-stories/growing-new-bones-crossroads-abolition-and-communism. Speakers included Silvia Federici, Charisse Burden-Stelly, Kathi Weeks, and moderator Charmaine Chua.

9. Joy James, "'New Bones' Abolitionism, Communism, and Captive Maternals," *Verso* (blog), June 4, 2021, https://www.versobooks.com/en-ca/blogs/news/5095-new-bones-abolitionism-communism-and-captive-maternals.

Maternal encapsulated agency. Any reflection on epistemology would have to include experience with the material world. Hence, Captive Maternal agency is—to channel Bernard Lonergan's *Insight*—the unspoken step after experience, reflection, and judgment. Action is essential to the Captive Maternal. It is not so much *cogito, ergo sum* but rather an Agape-driven *facio, ergo sum*. Caretaker, protester, movement-maker, maroon creator, war resister—the loving act to quell violence means that for the Captive Maternal it is not about the profile, persona, or performance, it is all about the action.

When the blog article was finally published, I thought that I and Black US rebels were being trolled. Above the article was a photograph of heavy-set, dark-skinned Black people jumping up and down on police cars. It appeared to be some "King Kong" choreography reconfigured for the contemporary moment. I contacted a senior editor and suggested the image be replaced immediately with a "Decolonial Atlas" (printed in this book) of half a millennium of Black rebellions against capture and police/state terror, which came from an anonymous donor tied to the academy. Fortunately, the editor became an ally who complied and included the map of war resistance leveraged by Black captives over the centuries.[19]

Clifton's poem reflects Captive Maternal agency and epistemology. It offers a meditation upon the knowledge that we retain despite structural violence, denials, gaslighting, and the narratives of what "other people" say constitutes our reality. Those who share the lineage of anti-Black human trafficking, enslavement, and mass rape as foundational experiences with Western democracy recognize or veil material, and psychic worlds with unique proximities to dishonor social death, imprisonment, and murder. We define and resist the structures and traditions that confine us. *New Bones Abolition* reflects our knowledge and our desires concerning how to obtain peace and "honey time" when structured violence is arrayed against us and our communities. Our material struggles and epistemologies are shaped by our functions that range from conflicted or celebratory caretakers to war resisters. Our capacity to love through political will shaped by

10. I am grateful for that ally, though it appears he left the press. He nonetheless assisted me so that "'New Bones' Abolitionism, Communism, and Captive Maternals," could become a printable pamphlet.

Agape, politicizes caretaking if we have strategies for self-care. Whether or not one acknowledges the "Divine Mother" and "Divine Father" or any gender formation, it is the function or actions of Captive Maternals that resist predation. Clifton's gift of poetry, shared by a beloved friend, was soothing as it helped me to stabilize and think more critically of the possibilities for community and individual/communal protections.

CONCLUSION

Elite abolitionist conferences instructed me in hierarchy, professionalism, and commodification within academic settings.[11] One is more likely to grow new abolition bones after witnessing *and experiencing* the contradictions of popularized and monetized abolition while those most vulnerable to broken bones, police violence, and imprisonment remain preyed upon. The concepts of "New Bones" and "Captive Maternals" are entwined, yet maintain their distinct functions. New Bones serves as a metaphor. Captive Maternal serves as an analytic. Both concepts gesture toward radicalizing politics with the capacity for growth, and the mandate to mutate through stages of concentric or broken care. The metaphor of "New Bones," as a visual, projects the images of our brokenness and our healing processes through development of defenses against breakage and betrayal. We absorb and inflict wreckage, yet we mend, mutate, and move toward Agape, communal marronage, and war resistance. Revolutionary love is a catalyst for caretaking that cannot be appropriated by the state and capitalism. The generative powers to stabilize ourselves, kin, community and resistance should not be stolen from Captive Maternals in order to stabilize the state and corporation. Captive Maternals, evolving upon varied stages, reveal an analytic. Their function is not only to offer care but to create a fulcrum that can leverage predatory policing despite a corrupt or imperial democracy out of our communities. In the language of burn units, forward-thinking Captive Maternals transition from zones

---

11. See Chapter 3, "Seven Lessons in One Abolitionist Notebook: On Airbrushing Revolution," *In Pursuit of Revolutionary Love* (Brussels and London: Divided Press, 2023).

of coagulation to zones of stasis, and from there they build protective marronage to limit further and future harm.

Chapter 3

MOVEMENT CAPTURE AND MONETIZED BLACK DEATH

Traumatized families impacted by police violence and murder experience overwhelming grief, depression, and political intimidation and fear—along with rage—following police homicides and state violence that kill loved ones. Tens of thousands had mobilized after Trayvon Martin's death in 2012 and the 2013 acquittal of his murderer. As a Black child growing up, Erica Garner would have heard narratives about police and vigilante violence and white impunity for aggressions. Police killings are legalized by the courts as "justifiable" through police procedures or as self-defense. They were never labeled as "murders" by the state or majority of mainstream media. Erica Garner and her allies, as well as sizable segments of the public, never identified these deaths as justifiable or as acts of self-defense. These chapters interchange "murder" with "homicide" when describing police who are dealing with unarmed individuals facing white supremacy, classism, anti-radicalism, as well as predatory state violence and police forces.[1]

Impacted by NYPD violence, organizers function as a collective and skilled doula, helping to instill guerrilla intellectualism within justice movements increasingly financed by liberal, statist and corporate sectors and funders. Principled confrontations with predatory police forces and state bureaucracies would not be replicated among

---

1. For a discussion of anti-Blackness and violence, see Selamawit Terrefe, Frank Wilderson III, and Joy James, "An Ontology of Betrayal" presentation, *Captivity, Betrayal, Community*, 2022–2023 Williams College Just Futures Roundtable Series, online, November 15, 2022, https://www.williams.edu/justfutures/past-events/.

celebrity sectors that had access to hundreds of thousands or multi-million-dollar stipends of support. Before and after the homicide of her father, Eric Garner, the activist allowed police homicides or murders of Black civilians to radicalize her in ways that made her ill-suited for distributions built upon the monetization of Black death.

INSURANCE POLICIES AND PAYOUTS STABILIZE STATE CRIMINALITY

Before mega nonprofits and corporate donors could distribute hundreds of millions of dollars to social justice organizations, spectacle(s) of public lynching, as with the historic and barbaric postcards of anti-Black lynching in the twentieth century, are captured in images collected through cell phone photos or footage. The graphic and disturbing images circulate through an (inter)national viewer market. Some view for entertainment, others for education and/or ethical concerns. The (global) citizen responds with protests and demands for less violence and predatory policing or unfettered vigilantism. The massive protests worldwide in 2020 saw millions of people take to the streets in protest of predatory policing. In 2023, news media reported that police forces had killed more civilians that year than in any year since 2013, when police began tracking the number of its killings of civilians.[2]

The monetization for/of Blacks murdered by police is not a form of caretaking or reparations. It is an insurance policy paid for by Black Americans and other taxpayers. Those funds—as compensation for the state taking life it cannot resurrect—are garnered from taxes paid by Blacks, the working class, and others penalized and disproportionately hunted (think of "stop-and-frisk" discussed in Part III). Conventional caretaking, protest and movements rarely move to the upper register or stages of marronage and war resistance, against predatory policing and contemporary lynching. Disenfranchised communities mourn and grieve under the shadow-play of the carrot-and-stick. This false binary or dichotomy deflects from the fact that corporate funders

---

2. See Sam Levin, "'It never stops': killings by US police reach record high in 2022," *Guardian*, January 2, 2023, https://www.theguardian.com/us-news/2023/jan/06/us-police-killings-record-number-2022.

that help protest and educate about lethal policing also fund predatory police and maintain elite hierarchies in state bureaucracy. As stated in *In Pursuit of Revolutionary Love*: "Finance capital does not fund freedom movements." Those latter two stages disrupt the hegemony and authority of the state and its bankers who disproportionately direct the state through secret campaign donations (enabled by the Supreme Court's 2010 *Citizens United* ruling[3]). In the carrot-stick analogy, the state wields two clubs to "correct" protesters as ethical citizens. Bankers and (non)profit corporations provide the soft clubbing of "carrots" to ensure that funded abolitionists stay within the garden of civil and human rights advocacy that protests, but eventually aligns with the interests of the state as a colonial project.

The brutal clubbing by the state of street protests and criminal pursuits of whistleblowers—from the late Daniel Ellsberg through Edward Snowden and Chelsea Manning—who leaked documents to the public to expose the duplicity and war crimes of the state—coincides with invitations to White House think-tank sessions to curb predatory policing.[4] In the first decades of the twenty-first century, during the two-term (2009–2016) administration of the first Black president of an imperial democracy, the era of "Black Lives Matter" emerged. The catalyst was not just the police murders of civilians, but the massive street protests that followed. Those unruly spectacles of love and rage had to be managed. Hence, the managerial elite carrying the visage of the Black feminist as imago functioned as some form of "magical negress" in leadership without sustained public scrutiny over the influence of funding or ties to the DNC.

I critiqued the emergence of managerial politics shaping the trajectory of Black feminism into varied forms of liberalism in 1999.[5] The apocalypse that (the artist formerly known as) Prince sang about

3. "How Does the Citizens United Decision Still Affect Us in 2022," *Campaign Legal Center*, January 21, 2022, https://campaignlegal.org/update/how-does-citizens-united-decision-still-affect-us-2022?gclid=CjoKCQjwnMWkBhDLARIsAHBOftoiXmk-hhHPjt-3LAOZMSM72J5Ff1-q_AHM_in-t9pE-d-W-jZ4mnGUaAqiMEALw_wcB.

4. "Whistleblower Daniel Ellsberg: Civil Disobedience Against Vietnam War Led Me to Leak Pentagon Papers," *Truthout*, May 18, 2018, https://truthout.org/video/whistleblower-daniel-ellsberg-civil-disobedience-against-vietnam-war-lcd-me-to-leak-pentagon-papers/?gclid=CjoKCQjwnMWkBhDLARIsAHBOftob-Z8xPCjDwC8NziO78SKUMqMHelUI-Tef-GhoZ_WpS3ZGZodamDzQaArzFEALw_wcB.

5. Joy James, *Shadowboxing: Representations of Black Feminist Politics* (New York: Palgrave McMillan, 1999/2000).

was not actually the end of the world but the expansion of state and corporate hyper-sophistication of steering activism into capture. The continuous state killings of Blacks in the public square have a significant impact on our collective and individual psyches. Traumatized, we seek stability, structure, and financial support. It's a bit Hansel and Gretel, but it might not be safe to accept all offers for shelter if you don't control the terrain and the "open-door policy and funding" requires that we enter into a house that our community did not build and does not control.

CHRONOLOGY AND CATALOG—BLACK DEATHS AT THE HANDS OF POLICE

For the last decade, US society and the globe have witnessed spectacles of killings predominantly of Blacks. It's true the gun violence and shootings at churches, mosques, synagogues, schools, festivals, and malls is stunning. Somehow those tragedies are wrapped into a human collective of random, psychotic violence inflicted by civilians who are deranged or "demonic," or carry a death wish that they cannot execute without a large audience forced to scream and cry at the performance. Black death at the hands of the police is different. It feels more personal, an intimate form of violence for the Black psyche as the rational mind balances the imbalance of millions of dollars after the murders. In a March 9, 2022 article, "The hidden billion-dollar cost of repeated police misconduct," *The Washington Post* asserts that more than $1.5 billion was spent to settle claims of police misconduct. And, usually the police who are litigated against are repeat offenders.[6] The following catalog fashions a form of "roll call." On February 26, 2012, Black seventeen-year-old Trayvon Martin was murdered by vigilante George Zimmerman in Florida. Through the Florida court's "stand your ground" defense, in 2013 Zimmerman was acquitted in the second-degree homicide of Martin.[7] According to the

---

6. "The hidden billion-dollar cost of repeated police misconduct," *Washington Post*, March 9, 2022, https://www.washingtonpost.com/investigations/interactive/2022/police-misconduct-repeated-settlements/.
7. In 2005, Florida had extended its "castle doctrine" law to state: "a person who is not engaged in an unlawful activity and who is attacked in any other place where he or she has

Black Anonymous Timeline, UCLA Professor Marcus Anthony Hunter coined or created the phrase "Black Lives Matter" in 2012, before it was popularized by BLM founders. In 2014 police homicides—state murders—of Black people became sensationalized in media. As noted earlier, two years after Trayvon was murdered, the demise of other Black casualties were made international in 2014. On July 17, 2014, Daniel Pantaleo and other members of the NYPD killed Eric Garner through chokeholds and chest compression on a Staten Island street, for refusing to comply with their orders. The video of Eric Garner's slow and painful death—or more accurately, his murder by cops—while pleading and panting eleven times "I can't breathe," shocked and enraged many. It stoked the memories and narratives of lynching spectacles inflicted over centuries, from antebellum slavery, through the postbellum convict prison lease system, into Jim Crow and mass incarceration, ICE camps and "womb collectors"—all eras in which war resisters were punished through assassinations or caged for decades as political prisoners. Garner's 2014 death would be replicated in some ways in Derek Chauvin's 2020 killing of George Floyd (as a police officer Chauvin would have read about or screened the "I Can't Breathe" cell phone video of Garner's death at the hands of the NYPD). On August 9, 2014, Ferguson, MO police officer Darren Wilson shot and killed eighteen-year-old Michael Brown. Ferguson police left his body in the street for four hours while blocking family and friends from approaching him. On October 20, 2014, Chicago police officer Jason Van Dyke shot teen Laquan McDonald sixteen times. In the aftermath of protests, the police commissioner was fired, and the state attorney general was voted out of office.[8] On November 22, 2014, Cleveland police officer Timothy Loehmann shot and killed twelve-year-old Tamir Rice, who had been playing with a plastic toy gun in a park near a youth recreation facility. Tamir was sitting quietly by himself when the police car raced onto the pavilion, and, within

---

a right to be has no duty to retreat and has the right to stand his or her ground and meet force with force, including deadly force, if he or she reasonably believes it is necessary to do so to prevent death or great bodily harm to himself or herself or another or to prevent the commission of a forcible felony." See "Self-Defense and 'Stand Your Ground,'" National Conference of State Legislatures, last modified March 1, 2023, https://www.ncsl.org/civil-and-criminal-justice/self-defense-and-stand-your-ground.

8. See "16 Shots: The Police Shooting of Laquan McDonald," WBEZ Chicago (podcast), https://www.npr.org/podcasts/643309816/16-shots-the-police-shooting-of-laquan-mc-donald.

seconds, Loehmann began shooting without warning or commands. As Tamir's fifteen-year-old sister ran to assist him, police tackled her, shackled her, and left her cuffed in a squad car as Tamir bled to death. The police offered no assistance to the dying child.

Other deaths by police or vigilantes would follow. Most, but not all, would be based on gun violence: Breonna Taylor,[9] Alton Sterling,[10] Sandra Bland, Ahmaud Arbery,[11] Atatiana Jefferson,[12] Rayshard Brooks,[13] Tyre Nichols,[14] and more. US gun culture, an extension of its predatory police culture, marks a number of deaths of unarmed Black people.

Police are not the only sectors valorized and defended by white nationalism that can take Black life with near impunity. In NYC, in May 2023, Jordan Neely was murdered by a white retired Marine Sergeant, Daniel Penny, who put him in a chokehold on a subway car floor.[15] Daniel Penny was not a formal member of the NYPD. But his lethal act was reminiscent of NYPD function and its own killing in 2014 of Eric Garner. Jordan Neely had been yelling in the subway that he was hungry and unhoused and that he did not care if he was imprisoned if he killed someone. Frightening words for some, but he had no weapon and he approached no one. He needed care. At age fourteen, Neely had discovered his mother's body hacked to pieces in a trunk. He subsequently became emotionally and mentally dysregulated after

9. Current and Former Louisville, Kentucky Police Officers Charged with Federal Crimes Related to Death of Breonna Taylor, US Department of Justice, August 4, 2022, https://www.justice.gov/opa/pr/current-and-former-louisville-kentucky-police-officers-charged-federal-crimes-related-death.

10. "Alton Sterling," PBS Newshour, https://www.pbs.org/newshour/tag/alton-sterling.

11. Jennifer Rae Taylor and Kayla Vinson, "Ahmaud Arbery and the Local Legacy of Lynching," The Marshall Project, May 21, 2020, https://www.themarshallproject.org/2020/05/21/ahmaud-arbery-and-the-local-legacy-of-lynching?gclid=CjoKCQjwnMWkBhDLARIsAH-BOftrOLOiQWuvLV7Dx7D8wLr-OWr3MV4r6XZXFAQHx7QQ6nkurFahRNfIaAmF-yEALw_wcB.

12. William Melhado, "Former Fort Worth police officer found guilty of manslaughter of Atatiana Jefferson," Texas Tribune, December 15, 2022, https://www.texastribune.org/2022/12/15/fort-worth-police-officer-atatiana-jefferson.

13. Becky Sullivan, "Atlanta to pay $1million to the family of Rayshard Brooks, killed by police in 2020," NPR, November 22, 2022, https://www.npr.org/2022/11/22/1138650659/rayshard-brooks-shooting-police-atlanta-family

14. "Tyre Nichols," Guardian, June 2023, https://www.theguardian.com/us-news/tyre-nichols.

15. Samantha Max, "Daniel Penny arraigned in chokehold death of Jordan Neely," All Things Considered (podcast), May 12, 2023, https://www.npr.org/2023/05/12/1175915027/daniel-penny-arraigned-in-chokehold-death-of-jordan-neely.

discovering the gruesome murder. That trauma was likely played out in the subway car, when Neely, who was Black, and had only expressed frustration in words, was put in a nearly three-minute chokehold by ex-Marine Daniel Penny, who is white. There were several men, one Black and one white, who assisted Penny so that Neely could not escape from slow suffocation. That replayed the murder of Eric Garner, this time by self-deputized "citizens" or "vigilantes" who refused to ignore Neely or slip him a five- or ten-dollar bill for food. It was not the responsibility of the volunteer cops or vigilantes to feed Jordan Neely. And it was also not their responsibility to kill him.

Juan Alberto Vazquez, who witnessed the extrajudicial killing, told *NBC New York* that Neely had entered the train and began "aggressive speech, saying he was hungry, he was thirsty, that he didn't care about anything, he didn't care about going to jail, he didn't care that he gets a big life sentence." According to Vazquez, Neely never touched Penny, or likely any other person in that subway car. Yet Penny initiated and engaged in a fifteen-minute physical confrontation with Neely, and imprisonment of Neely's body, likely as he was trained to do as a marine sergeant.[16] The NYPD spoke with Penny and then released him to go home.

Sectors of society considered him a "hero" or promoted that image because they understood selling an image of unlicensed Black violators and "peacekeeper white vigilantes" and the financial profits from public executions of Blacks. Within weeks, $1.8 million dollars was raised for Penny's defense by organizations associated with Christian nationalism and white nationalism. Kyle Rittenhouse, the white teen who shot three white men, killing two, at a BLM protest, was heralded as a hero by President Trump and white nationalists. Even if white nationalist organizations that raise massive funds for white killers do not also finance Black police or vigilantes who execute Black civilians in the public square, there are avenues to pay compradors to inflict harm on Black communities.[17] Penny and his funders—who

16. Marlene Lenthang, "What we know about the chokehold death of Jordan Neely on a NYC subway," *NBC News*, May 5, 2023, https://www.nbcnews.com/news/us-news/jordan-neely-chokehold-death-what-we-know-so-far-rcna83102.

17. White billionaire Harlan Crow's two decades of secret funding for Justice Clarence Thomas to promote reactionary legislation appears aligned with the state's violence against working class, poor, imprisoned, and Black communities; the lethality of the violence is not as performative as police forces and vigilantes.

likely kept the lion's share of the financial catch—knew how to monetize Black death while claiming that the killing had nothing to do with Blackness. Reportedly Penny received $500,000. It's as if this were a bounty or bonus from funders who desire a public statement, a performative act caught on public cameras and disseminated through media, its pornographic violence appears.

Is it a stretch of the imagination to consider that if a tall young white woman with conventional personal "beauty" screamed that she was hungry and homeless and didn't mind dying or going to jail if she could not get food and shelter—but she never touched anyone—that Penny would grab her from behind, wrestle her to the dirty floor and strangle her, that it would not be seen as snuff porn? Consider again that another white man aided by a Black man, held Jordan Neely down as he tried to escape from Penny choking him. Just as three years earlier—yet without volunteers to participate in the harm that would lead to murder—onlookers screamed and took cell footage standing on a Minneapolis sidewalk as George Floyd was murdered. Different types of murder porn, similar viewers. Without training or strategy, Captive Maternals often lack a plan for intervention in which the communal can salvage life at risk from vigilantes and police forces. However, spontaneous care remains powerful. The August 5, 2023 collective battle, for instance, to protect Black co-captain Dameion Pickett in Montgomery, Alabama from a brutal beating by irate whites told to move their boat so that a riverboat could dock, became a celebrated moment of Black resistance.

"BLM" DOES NOT MEAN "BLACK LIBERATION MOVEMENT"

After the public police or vigilante murders of working class and poor Blacks, pundits and academics rose to become celebrities and paid organizers as corporate donors funded and flooded movements sparked by working class, low-income, and militant communities. Black Anonymous notes, in its "Timeline and Analysis," how during the civil rights movement era corporate funders, liberalism, and movement careerism deradicalized militancy and steered people into the Democratic Party.[18] Contemporary police and prison abolitionists are shaped by the diverse politics of activists and academics who are not always aligned. When street activism and elite academia do overlap, it is often because the latter builds on the backs of the former. Examine the fissures between those who engage in risk-taking political struggles (such as political prisoners) and those who are compensated for seeking reforms. The fault lines might at times appear to be thin or imperceptible given that political prisoners tortured for years and decades need "deals" to get out of hell, precisely because movements have not effectively forced the state to stand down in its predatory policing and imprisonment schemes.

Despite the purchase of the loyalties of movement sectors, Captive Maternals can align with state actors who play myriad roles. In the past, taking donor capital came with the mandate to ignore or just pay lip service to rebels and political prisoners. Today, political prisoners are incorporated into donor largess. There is little rebel speech, but much promise about new growth as if the radical movements of decades past could be re-engineered under the conditions of star recognition. The war resistors confront not just police forces, presidents and politicians, but cultural figures, entertainers, celebrity academics, advocates, and abolitionists.

After the 2014 deaths of Eric Garner, Michael Brown, Laquan McDonald, and Tamir Rice—millions took to the streets. Then hundreds of millions of donor dollars poured into organizations and monetized political struggles. Predatory policing increases Black suffering. Violence and protests become morbid spectacles—similar to nineteenth and twentieth-century lynching—that become entertainment, news, and traumatic cautionary tales. Riding the wave of street protests, wealthy donors invested in "Black Lives Matter" and "movement millionaires" manifested. Radicalism became amplified by collections of phrases, chants, and signs.[19] At first glance, the invocation of in-

---

18. See "Black Anonymous Timeline and Analysis" (for the June 12, 2021 Summit for Accountability in Social Justice Movements and Juneteenth Archives), https://abolitionjournal.org/wp-content/uploads/2021/06/Black-Anonymous.-_Timeline_-6.12.2021-Summit-for-Accountability-in-Social-Justice-Movements.docx.pdf?189db0&189db0.

19. By 2020, nonprofit and for-profit corporations, such as Amazon, would flood hundreds of millions of dollars into BLM. This funding created "movement millionaires," real estate acquisitions, celebrity activists, and pundits who became professional speakers about under-resourced and over-policed neighborhoods.

surrection against white nationalism, colonial capitalism, and imperialism seems evident. Yet the rhetoric does not reflect the funding nor the actions outside of training pedagogy that stays within duopoly democracy and deference to police forces by not highlighting their lethal strategies as structural not accidental. There is a disconnect from the surface of radical struggle, usually articulated in academia by radical liberals, and the depth or underground of struggle, articulated by those who directly, not by adjacency or rhetoric, participated in the hypocenter, the underground, where police forces—local, federal, international—routinely violate civil and human rights.

Black Panther Party/Black Liberation Army (BPP/BLA) veteran Dhoruba bin Wahad asserts that if "BLM" had been designed as "Black Liberation Movement," its twenty-first century strategies would have been focused on radical goals, not alignment with funders and teaching abolition in elite or middle-class universities and colleges. "Black Lives Matter" is implemented if one has a strategy to stop the predator and the structural reduction of undervalued communities as prey. Civilian violence has to be addressed as well. This brings one back to security. Therapeutic interventions are not always sufficient for stopping physical harm in the moment. Civilian violence through domestic and child abuse, rape, theft, predatory drug sales, sex and human trafficking, gun violence, labor exploitation—all must be quelled. The state—including foster care, a carceral and policing extension of the state—does not provide adequate protective care. Its punitive measures are haphazard and brutally inflicted upon nonelite civilians. In its violations of UN and civil rights protections, the state flaunts its own criminality and closes cases with funds taken from taxpayers (which disproportionately are not billionaires who hide assets offshore). To make Black life matter requires strategies for security and safety that deflect or negate predatory violence. Since the state will wear us down by lighting incendiary projects against socialist and communal-focused politics, the feasible path forward on the journey of a Captive Maternal would be to neutralize predatory capitalism, imperialism, and mercenary warfare. Obviously, the zone of the war resister is an arena of hyper-vulnerability to state and vigilante violence.

The funded BLM highlights Panther lineage, and its Ten Point program for survival programs in service of the people: free breakfast/ food security programs to sickle cell anemia testing, housing security, release from mass incarceration, and protections from white nationalists such as the Hells Angels and racist police forces.[20] However, why do nonprofits think the police would burn the breakfast programs (literally destroy cereal for hungry families) at the height of marronage and war resistance, but not burn real resistance marronage today? The state funds the services it destroyed the Panthers for providing. This may seem like a twister but actually has a logic: the state and predatory police forces want communities to depend upon their formations for survival. Hence, the survival programs of communities attempting to liberate themselves from dependency upon a stratified and indifferent state are, as marronage, largely prohibited. BLM as a Black Liberation Movement—not a lobbying effort to the public/state/banks for Black humanity to be recognized by state formations structured by capitalism, colonialism, and imperialism—would literally combat fascism to establish and defend a transformative culture.[21] A transformative culture—care, protest, movements, marronage, war resistance—would undo the state as we know it. The state, as imperial project or predatory policing—has consistently mandated that such transformative cultures will be punished or purchased.

Black and resister communities have faced a barrage of state violence—from local police to FBI, CIA, and the Drug Enforcement Administration (DEA). The end results of gunshot wounds, asphyxiation, the literal and figurative broken bones and necks of vulnerable civilians avoiding (and militants confronting) state violence have led to political prisoners among mass incarceration or general poverty through loss of jobs for low-profile radicals. Captive Maternals attempt to keep their jobs or academic placements until out of disgust they walk off the plantation. The most vulnerable activists for justice and liberation though are mobilized in streets and among under-resourced communities. They tend to have low visibility and limited funds. Routinely surveilled, indexed, harassed, and arrested, they are most likely to be

20. "(1966) The Black Panther Party Ten Point Program," BlackPast.org, https://www.blackpast.org/african-american-history/primary-documents-african-american-history/black-panther-party-ten-point-program-1966/.
21. Rebel Diaz's *Which Side Are You On?* remix with male Captive Maternals Dead Prez and Rakaa Iriscience is one example of cultural resistance, see https://www.youtube.com/watch?v=jSZWslqjfPE. Suiyi Tang, who contributed significantly to Part II of this book, hears Erica Garner's tweets in defense of a movement for Black lives as "songs" created for social justice organizing.

injured, incarcerated, or killed by police forces or white supremacist vigilantes. Meanwhile, a stratum of the movement comprised by elites (both those already in existence and those in the making) benefit as personal identities blur with progressive or leftist ideologies and form radical liberalism.

ACCOUNTABILITY IN SOCIAL JUSTICE MOVEMENTS

If BLM formed in 2014 without unionizing its members and workers to ensure collective decision making, then job security, fair labor compensation, and workers' political leadership to set agendas would be heavily compromised. According to the collective authors Black Anonymous, who published a "Timeline and Analysis" for the Summit for Accountability in Social Justice Movements,[22] billionaires such as Warren Buffett provided funding bridges to BLM through philanthropic platforms such as Thousand Currents, NoVo, ActBlue, and the Tides Network.[23] BLM titular leaders, as well as Black political celebrities, visited Ferguson during the rebellion following the police killing of Michael Brown.

On July 24, 2015, "Movement for Black Lives" (M4BL) emerged from a gathering of about fifty organizations and several thousand activists in Cleveland, OH, who sought to form a new network: Movement for Black Lives (M4BL). The Black Led Movement Fund also emerged and would direct millions of dollars into the network. In 2016, Ferguson activist Darren Seals publicly critiqued Black Lives Matter, asserting that academics and affluent Blacks leveraged white philanthropy to control a spontaneous movement and curtail its grassroots and militant agency. Seals posited that these newly funded organizations were not providing adequate support for communities to resist police violence and obtain resources for daily living. Seals denounced BLM founders receiving millions of dollars while impoverished St. Louis was struggling. Seals later alleged that local police had pulled him and his fourteen-year-old brother over and warned them

---

22. This section summarizes the "Black Anonymous Timeline and Analysis."
23. Sean Cooper, "Is Warren Buffett the Wallet Behind Black Lives Matter?," *Tablet Magazine,* October 26, 2020, https://www.tabletmag.com/sections/news/articles/warren-buffett-black-lives-matter.

to "choose your enemies wisely." Local leaders, like Ferguson activist Darren Seals, detailed how community response reignited Black rebellions for freedom and security. The FBI would gather a 900-page file on Seals, just as the Bureau functioned in past Black freedom rebellions. Of those 900 pages, all but forty-five pages were redacted (the forty-five pages had massive strike outs). The FBI had asked local police to harass Seals and engage in traffic stops of Seals. The FBI described Seals to police forces as a "dangerous revolutionary."[24] Shot six times, Seals' body would later be found dead in a burning car.[25]

In 2016, the Ford Foundation (which was created in 1936 and during the Cold War was funded by the CIA to combat communism and freedom movements) committed $100 million to the Movement for Black Lives. That year, BLM gave Thousand Currents (formerly the International Development Exchange, founded in 1985 for the "Global South") control over BLM finances. By 2017, in addition to Darren Seals, other Ferguson activists were killed or incarcerated or lost family members. They included Edward Crawford,[26] Deandre Joshua,[27] and the son of Ferguson organizer Melissa McKinnies, Danye Jones, who was found hung in a tree in the yard of their house.

In July 2020, Thousand Currents transferred financial control and management of BLM to the more massive Tides Foundation, which had more connections to financial elites and global capitalism. Hundreds of millions of dollars were donated or pledged in 2020 by the Ford Foundation, the MacArthur Foundation, and the Doris Duke Charitable Foundation. Incorporating in Delaware, in 2020, BLM formed a political action committee (PAC) that allowed the organization to receive and disburse (but not always be transparent about) large donations to fund electoral candidates. On November 8, 2020,

---

24. Ryan Krull, "Ferguson Activist Darren Seals Was Surveilled by FBI, File Shows," *Riverfront Times*, September 16, 2022, https://www.riverfronttimes.com/news/ferguson-activist-darren-seals-was-watched-by-the-fbi-file-shows-38501846.

25. Elliott C. McLaughlin, "Top Ferguson activist found shot in burning car, police say," CNN.com, September 7, 2016, https://www.cnn.com/2016/09/07/us/darren-seals-ferguson-activist-found-dead-shot-burning-car/index.html.

26. Christina Coleman, "Edward Crawford, Ferguson Activist in Iconic Protest Photo, Found Dead," *Essence*, October 26, 2020, https://www.essence.com/news/edward-crawford-ferguson-tear-gas-photo-dead/.

27. Hilary Hanson, "Deandre Joshua Identified as Man Fatally Shot During Ferguson Protests," *HuffPost*, November 26, 2014, https://www.huffpost.com/entry/deandre-joshua-shot-killed-protests_n_6225380.

Joe Biden was elected the forty-sixth President of the United States (POTUS). Kamala Harris became the first (Afro-Asian) female vice president. BLM campaigned for Biden-Harris, but their request to meet with the Biden administration after the election was declined. In April 2021, BLM, a recipient of millions of dollars of donations from Facebook, Google, and Amazon, was being critiqued, and according to Black Anonymous, Facebook began preventing people from sharing articles critical of BLM. Jeff Bezos' Amazon—which fights labor unions seeking decent wages and safe working conditions—gave limited funding to BLM and $100 million to CNN commentator and abolitionist Van Jones. Amazon, along with other corporations, heavily donates to police foundations and uses its products to develop police departments.

Also in 2021, financial statements revealed BLM had raised $90 million after the March 25, 2020 murder of George Floyd. According to Black Anonymous, during the 2020 fundraising year/cycle, the vast majority of Black people killed by police were Black men, who were 239 of the 241 Blacks killed by police. Responding to public scrutiny over the funds raised after George Floyd's murder, BLM created a fund to distribute $20 million to thirty groups in 2021. Of those thirty, twenty-three were LGBTQ organizations.

Black Anonymous' "Timeline and Analysis" poses queries to the community: "Given the alliance between the CIA and philanthropic organizations, why would self-described socialists and communists accept hundreds of millions of dollars from "Amazon, Pepsi and other corporations that fund police departments . . . [and] destroy the lives of working class and poor Black people?" Black Anonymous points out that Seals and other Ferguson activists had warned about the emergence of a "Black movement" dependent upon white corporations (with Black-facing leadership). Yet, the majority of the activists or leftists ignored the warnings and dismissed those who raised such warnings. They pointedly ask if "this movement" has "a place for people like Darren Seals?" And if so, "how would someone like Seals be integrated into a heavily financed nonprofit professing Black freedom?" From the view of a Captive Maternal, I would say that Seals would have needed a marronage community that could protect him from the FBI, police forces, and opportunistic freelancers. As he became more visible as a war resistor, Seals or any working-class Black militants in the zones of marronage and war resistance would be highly vulnerable.

The tracking of (missing) funds became a distraction as funding flooded into Black liberation formations administered by Blacks but controlled by whites; apparently none of that funding was used to form a community security apparatus to protect militant protestors targeted by police and the FBI. President Obama told James Comey, his FBI director, that its "Black extremity index" to track "Black terrorists" within civil and human rights movements was not a "real thing." Obama never fired Comey who continued to peddle lies about a "Ferguson Effect" among BLM activists in the streets (not the boardrooms) who were labeled "terrorists" by police forces and the FBI as both recycled murderous fantasies enacted by the anticommunist, white supremacist J. Edgar Hoover.[28]

POPULARIZING BLACK LIVES OR BLACK LIBERATION?

Elevating "movement leaders," liberal publications such as the *Washington Post*, *New York Times*, and *New York Review of Books* assured the rise of political celebrities and thereby built a firewall against calls for accountability to those who had access to social and financial capital without any structural obligation or responsibility to grassroots or marginalized communities whose vulnerabilities sell papers and media clicks.[29]

Organizers at the base, or on the ground, became increasingly vocal in their demands that direct-democratic social movements be accountable to the masses. When those demands were not met, they began to disassociate or distance from a centralized BLM. The NYC chapter of the Black Lives Matter Global Network Foundation was one of the first to openly separate from the national organization headed by Patrisse Cullors, Alicia Garza, and Ayọ Tometi. In their January 5, 2018 communique to the public, the local organization noted its three years

---

28. Clara McCarthy and Sabrina Siddiqui, "FBI Director Concedes He Has Little Evidence to Support 'Ferguson Effect,'" *Guardian*, October 26, 2015, https://www.theguardian.com/us-news/2015/oct/26/fbi-director-ferguson-effect-crime-policing-james-comey.
29. See Glen Ford, "Black Lives Matter Founder Launches Huge Project to Shrink Black Lives, 2019," *Black Agenda Report*, April 13, 2022..

of organizing with Black New Yorkers and activists across the city, and around the country and globe. Formed as a "decentralized network," Black Lives Matter NYC proved instrumental "in building the Global Network in various capacities that ranged from website and digital media development, artistic production, national chapter capacity-building, substantial financial support, major campaign formulation."[30]

A founding chapter of the BLM Global Network, the NYC Black Lives Matter chapter emerged from the Fall 2014 Black Lives Matters Ride to Ferguson, following the police killing of Michael Brown. "The uprising of the greater St. Louis community served as a catalyst for a national, Black-led movement to form," according to their statement, which refers to the "instrumental contributions of Black trans women, and hundreds of Black people gathering and organizing [who] formed the basis for what would become the BLM Global Network."[31] They also noted their contributions in supporting families of victims of state-sanctioned violence as an important aspect of their political work.

By 2018, BLM NYC would assert autonomy from the BLM Global Network in order to figure out and further the goals of Black liberation struggles:

> We see this as a continuation of the radical Black liberation and the Black power struggle that has spanned centuries around the world. We believe in the right to self-govern and our need to become ungovernable to institutions that do not serve our interest of freedom, autonomy, and liberation. We view the struggle for Black liberation as a human rights struggle. Black liberation is necessary and imperative for global liberation. . . . Though we will no longer identify as Black Lives Matter NYC or have any direct affiliation with the Global BLM Network, we will continue to do our work as Black liberation fighters. . . . We want to build the worlds we seek now.[32]

Incarcerated intellectuals noted the contradictions within leadership on the outside. Stevie Wilson spoke about the Imprisoned Black Radical Tradition, as opposed to the Black Radical Tradition often raised by

---

30. "A Statement from Black Lives Matter NYC," Black Lives Matter NYC, January 5, 2018, https://web.archive.org/web/20180109085658/http://blacklivesmatternyc.com/.
31. Black Lives Matter NYC, "A Statement from Black Lives Matter NYC."
32. Black Lives Matter NYC, "A Statement from Black Lives Matter NYC."

academic abolitionists. For Wilson, there was a lack of peerage among abolitionists not just shaped by class differences but also shaped by legal status: "free" or incarcerated.[33] The same contradictions shaped by vulnerabilities to prison and police violence and access to platforms of political leadership also appeared around the protests and arrests surrounding "Cop City."[34]

For-profit and nonprofit businesses coexist with federal System for Award Management (SAM) tracking of official federal grant monies. Investment capital's incursions into protest cultures poured the foundation for movement millionaires to overshadow the necessity of war resistance, as political influencers became prosperity preachers, and movements began to look like reality shows performing abolition (e.g., the author recalls years ago seeing one episode of their reality show, where the Kardashian sisters argue and sling insults such as "faux abolitionist 'ho'"). With a massive audience, academic and political celebrities shape an (inter)national narrative that protests and creates "movements" in line with the funders' guidelines, but do not address marronage as an organized formation to *resist* predatory and paramilitary police violence used against *peaceful* protesters.[35]

The Black Lives Matter Global Network Foundation attempted to address impacted families. Yet, some mothers, such as Samaria Rice, alleged that the foundation and other nonprofit movement entities profited off the vigilante/police murders of their children. That is, the nonprofits swim in the revenue streams monetizing state/vigilante killings of Black people. Rice's critiques, which reflect family protections and personal trauma, are also structural critiques of US capitalism and predatory policing. Monetized Black death is structured in fundraising *and* civil rights advocacy. Former organizers who worked with Erica Garner and the movements that she championed contributed to the "Black Anonymous Timeline and Analysis," to highlight the

---

33. See, for example: Steve Wilson's work at *Rust Belt Radio*, https://rustbeltradio.org/2019/11/20/ep33/; Abolish Slavery National Network, https://abolishslavery.us/; August Nimtz, "Marxism and the Black Struggle: The 'Class v. Race' Debate Revisited," *Journal of African Studies* 7 (1985); and National Alliance Against Racist and Political Repression (NAARPR) Executive Director Frank Chapman's recent book, *Marxist-Leninist Perspectives on Black Liberation and Socialism* (Minneapolis: Freedom Road Socialist Organization, 2021).
34. See Joy James, "The Rubik's Cube of 'Cop City,'" *Inquest*, forthcoming.
35. "New York Police Planned Assault on Bronx Protestors," *Human Rights Watch*, September 30, 2020, https://www.hrw.org/news/2020/09/30/us-new-york-police-planned-assault-bronx-protesters.

contradictions and funding that follows spectacle lynching. The above engagement with their research and assertions provides context for the complications and contradictions shaping the movements within which Erica Garner made her contributions. However, Black Anonymous did not foresee the emergence of "Freedom Scholars" whose *scholarship* on, not physical *engagement* with, nonacademic working-class and impoverished sectors being awarded $250,000 each to further the goals of academic abolition.

Their primary funder was/is the Marguerite Casey Foundation, which derived part of its massive portfolio through the capture or demise of Black families, the target of foster removal based on poverty and Blackness and not harm to their children. Scholar Dorothy Roberts has written extensively about the dangers of foster care as a carceral system with racist biases. Anticarceral academics and authors receive funds from a massive agency that monetizes Black families and facilitates their dismemberment which becomes a form of death for Black, Indigenous, and largely impoverished or under-resourced families. The "Freedom Scholars"[36] awards went to diverse academics, progressives, and radical feminists. Individual $250,000 distributions went to BIPOC academics from the Casey Foundation, a foster care nonprofit critiqued by legal scholar Dorothy Roberts. The new training grounds and instruction (e.g., digital platforms at elite universities or foundations) offer abolitionist training to dismantle the repressive carceral state while being funded by the carceral state's liberal wing, including Casey and the DNC advocate Pritzker Foundations.

What would it mean for each poor family to receive a $250,000 voucher for development, education, and therapeutic support for their "at risk" children? The academy is already monetized of course. Yet, this appears to be a much more thoughtful intervention, begun in 2020, the year in which funder largesse into movements and rebellions significantly rose. The Freedom Scholar site states that the Marguerite Casey Foundation provides "unrestricted support to leaders in academia whose research provides critical insight from and to social justice leaders whose ideas encourage us to imagine how we can radically improve our democracy, economy and society." The foundation's

---

36. Marguerite Casey Foundation, "Freedom Scholars," https://www.caseygrants.org/freedom-scholars.

verb is *"imagine"*—the verbs "organize" and "resist" do not appear in this political framework.

The Casey Foundation states the metric for becoming a Freedom Scholar includes evidence of "a commitment to scholarship benefitting movements led by Black and Indigenous people, migrants and queer people, poor people, and people of color." The awards are also incentives to shape movements,[37] as Freedom Scholars are funded to promote the award recipient's role "in cultivating and nurturing movements for justice and freedom." For a quarter of a century, since the 1998 launch of Critical Resistance with funding from large corporations, academia has developed the central hubs for the development of the progressive idea of "freedom." Philosophers have explored the meanings of enslaved captives seeking underground railroads and maroon societies, for centuries. Academics' worldview is largely structured by discourse, reading, and observation. Scholars without PhDs are hosted in the academy as nonacademics, viewed as "community intellectuals," where "awardees are proven movement leaders who entered academia and academics with a demonstrated commitment to supporting social movements." If on top of one's standard annual salary there is a $250,000 incentive to formulate "freedom" in the absence of working class, impoverished, or incarcerated peers, freedom has been monetized. That form of freedom shapes intellectual autonomy and productivity linked to an epicenter bound to elite academia and think tanks, as the hypocenter recedes from focus.

In *Torn Apart*, scholar and foster care abolitionist Dorothy Roberts states that "children exited foster care with more developmental problems than they had when they entered—and worse problems than the children who were left at home."[38] The impact of predatory policing on

---

37. The *Hammer and Hope* digital publication to inspire and train abolitionists at Columbia University is funded by the Casey Foundation and the Pfizer family.

38. See Dorothy Roberts, *Torn Apart: How the Child Welfare System Destroys Black Families—And How Abolition Can Build a Safer World* (New York: Basic Books, 2022), 240. Roberts also cites the work of Joseph Doyle, who specializes in the economics of government policy, summarizing his research findings: "Doyle found that the children placed in foster care fared worse than those who remained at home at home on every outcome." See Roberts, *Torn Apart*, 241. "Disproportionality" shaped by racial bias, specifically anti-Blackness, revealed that Black children are removed at higher rates although their families are not significantly marked by child neglect or abuse. Today's patterns still reflect this: "Black children made up 76 percent of the sample in Chicago's child welfare system, although they were only 26 percent of school-age children in Cook County." See Roberts, *Torn Apart*, 241.

(Black) families is significant. If police do the reporting, the child(ren) are most likely to be taken whether or not the reporting is accurate, given police authority over the lives of families. Likewise, social workers have disproportionate power in the removal of children.

In a roundtable on "Family, Freedom & Security," Joyce McMillan of JMacForFamilies notes that the majority of reasoning for removing children is the poverty of the family, not discernible or physical harm against the child(ren). Amanda Wallace, a former social worker and founder of "Operation Stop CPS," resigned from her state job to become a movement organizer calling for resistance to foster care and Child Protective Services (CPS). She asserts that some states balance their budgets through the economies of "child trafficking" children into foster care and obtaining federal dollars for private foster care systems (likened by some to having a similar role to private carceral sites such as prisons).[39]

Dawn Wooten, the whistle blower on ICE (US Immigrations and Customs Enforcement) camps and coerced hysterectomies, noted at the roundtable that ICE prison guards would threaten mothers with the loss of their children if they did not agree to hysterectomies, ICE's eugenics program.

According to Human Rights Watch's 2022 report "If I Wasn't Poor, I wouldn't Be Unfit": The Family Separation Crisis in the US Child Welfare System,"[40] one in three children in the US will be interviewed or interrogated by a child welfare investigator and Black children are twice as likely than white children to be removed from their homes, although Black homes are just poorer than white homes. Poverty is punished with child removal, but capitalism does not have a "fix" for poverty. If child removal is a carceral system that monetizes the "death" or dismemberment of Black families, then how could it become the (financial) source for abolitionist care?

39. See Joyce McMillan, Samaria Rice, Amanda Wallace, Dawn Wooten, moderated by Joy James, "Family, Freedom & Security," roundtable discussion, Williams College, February 28, 2023, https://www.youtube.com/watch?v=tBjo6TxiZic.
40. See "If I Wasn't Poor, I Wouldn't Be Unfit": The Family Separation Crisis in the US Child Welfare System," *Human Rights Watch*, November 17, 2022, https://www.hrw.org/report/2022/11/17/if-i-wasnt-poor-i-wouldnt-be-unfit/family-separation-crisis-us-child-welfare.

CONCLUSION

Protesters align with liberalism but identify as radical more often if they are well-funded and have access to liberal promotional platforms. Liberalism does not advocate "marronage." Maroon comes from the term "Seminole," the Indigenous and Africans who refused enslavement or the missions' carceral systems. Historically, maroon camps were not strictly determined by race/ethnicity. Base camps—constructed as rebel camps—included the Indigenous, Afro-Indigenous, African, and European—all who fled chattel slavery and servitude. Any in-depth discussion of abolition, "community" and "love" needs to outline its relationship to, and strategic moves against predatory policing. Presidential or state task forces, richly funded nonprofits appear pragmatic, strategic, and sensible. Yet, if these endeavors are mergers of state management and corporate largess, then think tanks, White House conferences, and city cops speaking at community centers continue to control the stage as royalty deigns to be in the presence of proletariat and peasants. We are not going to be able to abolish funders and nonprofits steerage of abolition. But this is the complicated and contradictory milieu within which Erica Garner and her collectives "fought the good fight."

Corporate culture is the enemy of war resistance. Massive funders are the "soft" power behind the militarized state. Foundations have emerged as the CEOs of police culture. The Atlanta Police Foundation is the brawn and brains behind organizing Atlanta's city government to protect and construct its deadly "Cop City." That project seeks to bulldoze a forest and gardens, vivisect, and gentrify a Black working-class community and terrorize when not killing organizers seeking land trust preservations and nonmilitarized lethal police forces.[41] There are distinctions between the Marguerite Casey Foundation and the Atlanta Police Foundation (APF), backed by Delta Airlines, Bank of America, and JP Morgan. Both maintain their coffers through the "care economy" of the state—foster care and militarized policing —sectors which disproportionately harm Black working-class and under-resourced communities.

---

41. James, "The Rubik's Cube of Cop City."

Transitioning through Captive Maternal stages to strategize how to fortify concentric circles of care that materially—not just rhetorically—confront colonialism and imperialism is a punishable offense for the Casey Foundation and APF. Employment, reputations, and lives attacked due to nonconformity can train some into becoming a "responsible" abolitionist who is more likely to be compensated for their labor. Critics of multimillionaire/billionaire donors are unlikely to become recipients of donations. Likewise, meeting with state officials might be infiltrated by state surveillance of resisters, as paid officials appear in churches, mosques, and synagogues to share a performance of care for "the community."

Erica Garner and organizations such as FTP (Free the People/Feed the People/F*** the Police) realized over several years that countering predatory policing is a domestic form of warfare. The imago of Henry Kissinger seems relevant to some of these funders that harm the poor and working class[42]—a war criminal whose "kills" in the US wars in Southeast Asia and elsewhere in the "Global South" encompass millions of lives—remains beloved and accepted by human rights liberals and both duopoly parties. Kissinger's genocidal war in Vietnam was defeated, but Henry's House of realpolitik is deeply rooted in political mayhem that publicly performs as civility.[43] Today, abolitionists continue living under conditions of surveillance, poverty, precarity wages, and asymmetrical warfare with states and corporations. Part II discusses how the catalyst of painful loss for the Garner family sparks and radicalizes abolition.

42. Jonathan Guyer, "I Crashed Henry Kissinger's 100th-Birthday Party," *New York Magazine*, June 8, 2023, https://nymag.com/intelligencer/2023/06/the-elite-dont-want-to-talk-about-henry-kissingers-party.html.
43. See "Return with Honor: Ho Chi Minh," *American Experience/PBS*, https://www.pbs.org/wgbh/americanexperience/features/honor-ho-chi-minh/.

Part II

Figure 3: Erica Garner, image still, "It's Not Over" video, February 11, 2016.

CHAPTER 4

THE KILLING AND DISHONOR
OF ERIC GARNER

CONTEXT

Matt Taibbi's *I Can't Breathe: A Killing on Bay Street* is essential reading for understanding the violence arrayed against Eric Garner and
racially fashioned and dishonored communities surveilled and targeted by predatory policing.[1] In his acknowledgments, Taibbi writes
that this book—a difficult and pain-filled process—was only possible
because of the candor and generosity of Erica Garner and her friends
and family:

> First and foremost, I want to thank Erica Garner, daughter of Eric,
> who insisted upon telling all sides of her father's story, including
> those that were painful and uncomfortable. Erica's courage in telling
> both her story and the story of her family's ordeal was a continuing
> inspiration. Moreover, the fact that she and many family members
> and friends continued to go out on the streets and protest, often
> when there was no media around and there were only small crowds
> of supporters, spoke to a determination to find justice that sadly was
> matched only by the relentless ignorance and insensitivity of the city
> bureaucracy.[2]

This chapter uses the work of legal scholars and journalists to reflect
on Garner's death at the hands of the NYPD. As discussed earlier, law

---

1. Matt Taibbi, *I Can't Breathe: A Killing on Bay Street* (New York: Spiegel & Grau, 2018).
2. Taibbi, *I Can't Breathe*, 308.

enforcement targets specific neighborhoods: low-income, racialized ones, with hyper-violence focused on Black targets. Legal investigations on stop-and-frisk procedures indicate that whites disproportionately are not stopped even as they have a higher rate of carrying illegal drugs. Elite college campuses remain havens for illicit drugs where working-class and middle-class cops are unlikely to violate the rights of affluent white students. The state has a criminality problem: its own.

The violence of police forces against unarmed civilians includes the use of the lethal chokehold. Legal scholar Shaun Ossei-Owusu describes a "sordid, deadly history" and police "potential defenses" for the use of an "undeniable, four-century chokehold that *racism* has had on non-whites."[3] According to Ossei-Owusu, the LAPD killed sixteen people from 1975–1983 with chokeholds. Twelve of the victims were Black, although Blacks were roughly 12 percent of the population during that time. He describes a press conference where LAPD police chief Daryl Gates defined Blacks not as victims, but bodily deficient: "It seems to me that we may be finding that in some blacks when it [the chokehold] is applied, the veins or the arteries do not open as fast as they do on normal people."[4] Ossei-Owusu cites the 1983 case *City of Los Angeles v. Lyons* (461 U.S. 95), in which the Supreme Court decision held that plaintiff Adolph Lyons lacked standing to challenge the LAPD's use of chokeholds as official policy. Lyons had sought a Supreme Court injunction on the LAPD's use of the chokehold after police placed him in a chokehold during a traffic violation, although he had offered no resistance. Police held him face down, choking for air, "spitting up blood and dirt" and "urinating and defecating"[5] on himself. After torturing him, LAPD officers gave Lyons a traffic citation and released him. The Court ruled against Lyons because he could not show that he would be subject to the chokehold again. Ossei-Owusu asserts that "race" or anti-Black rulings were typical during the "Rehnquist-led SCOTUS" which regularly denied relief to plaintiffs to stop LAPD chokeholds.[6]

---

3. Shaun Ossei-Owusu, "'I can't breathe!': Police overreach, Eric Garner and the chokehold of racism," *Salon*, July 22, 2014, https://www.salon.com/2014/07/22/i_cant_breathe_police_overreach_eric_garner_and_the_chokehold_of_racism/. Emphasis added.
4. Darryl Gates, quoted in Ossei-Owusu, "I can't breathe!"
5. Ossei-Owusu, "I can't breathe!"
6. Ossei-Owusu, "I can't breathe!"

News outlets sought video or images of police and/or whites killing Blacks because it created revenue or monetized Black death. An anonymous Black news editor allegedly asserted that the "Black Person Abused by Police" story was a constant-in-demand news item. If "the phenomenon of unarmed Black dudes getting shot by the cops" missed a publishing deadline, it would still be useful for print in a few weeks with slight editing for details "when the next Black kid gets killed."[7]

Black victims are often demonized or animalized not just by police forces but also by pundits and the press. On *ABC News'* video report of Garner's death on Friday, July 17, 2014, the following caption editorialized the tragedy: "Caught on Camera—NYPD Chokehold Investigation—400 Pound Suspect: I Can't Breathe." Emphasizing Garner's size references racist stereotypes of the threatening "big black buck." Darren Wilson, the white police officer who shot and killed eighteen-year-old Michael Brown in Ferguson, Missouri, used the same trope to win his exoneration. Journalist Lucy Steigerwald echoes Ossei-Owusu's concerns, further noting that although the four emergency medical service (EMS) workers who failed to assist Eric Garner while he was unconscious on the sidewalk were restricted to desk duty and banned from responding to 911 calls, no NYPD officers at the scene of Garner's death were placed under investigation.

Steigerwald draws attention to another video showing nearly four minutes of NYPD officers "gently shaking" Garner's still body, noting that police search his pockets but seem unconcerned "that their suspect hasn't moved in minutes." Although NYPD officers are trained to provide CPR, they are rarely punished for withholding it. Cell-phone footage captures a bystander asking, as Garner is placed onto a stretcher, "Why does nobody do CPR?" To which a NYPD officer replies, "Because he's breathing." There are multiple attempts to exonerate the NYPD for Garner's death. Ossei-Owusu notes that "Causality arguments will equate Garner's weight with imminent threat, or as cause of death" as arguments maintained that "his preexisting health conditions (asthma, diabetes, sleep apnea) coupled with his resistance, and not the chokehold, caused Garner's death."[8]

---

7. Ossei-Owusu, "I can't breathe!"
8. Ossei-Owusu, "I can't breathe!"

For Steigerwald, the penalty for Black males who assert their civil rights could be death. Noting that "I can't breathe" were Garner's last words, the journalist finds Garner's "penultimate words" equally, if not more disturbing "because they consisted of a man committing the fatal error of standing up for himself. . . . It's too dangerous to stand up to the police, particularly for a black male in a place like New York City." The journalist does not believe that the NYPD "who brought him down" planned to kill Garner. They would though, for their own exoneration and self-protection, highlight Garner's obesity and asthma as the reasons he died. As Steigerwald notes, the police claim "he didn't survive his interactions with those protecting and serving him. Qualified immunity . . . is not so much that police did wrong, as that it's bad to resist them." The journalist, who is not a Black male, processes in her mind a protective policing to shield Garner from claiming his civil rights: "When you see Garner yell, 'I was just minding my own business. Every time you see me you want to mess with me. I'm tired of it. It stops today!' You want to tell him: no, no, no, just give in! Obey police orders, because your life is forfeit if you don't."[9]

THE SECRET GRAND JURY

On September 29, 2014, Staten Island District Attorney Dan Donovan convened a secret grand jury which listened to evidence and testimony (including from Officer Pantaleo) for over two months. The District Attorney's office announced that the grand jury would not indict Pantaleo on December 3, 2014, just nine days after a Ferguson, MO grand jury stated that it would not indict Darren Wilson, the white police officer who shot and killed Michael Brown (whose body was left in the streets for four hours as the community gathered and became more distraught).

Following the grand jury's verdicts exonerating Eric Garner's killer,[10] protesters hit the streets. The NYPD, along with 170 other cities' police forces, were impacted by protests. Thousands protested

---

9. Lucy Steigerwald, "NYPD and EMS Workers Failed to Help Eric Garner After Cop Choked Him," *Vice*, July 21, 2014, https://www.vice.com/en/topic/bad-cop-blotter.

10. See Jeffrey Fagan and Bernard E. Harcourt, "Professors Fagan and Harcourt Provide Facts on Grand Jury Practice After Staten Island Decision," Columbia Law School, https://www.

and disrupted in NYC streets, where 300 protesters were arrested.[11] As Garner's death had been caught on video, the continuous newsfeed and visual "trauma porn" shocked and numbed varied sectors of the public. These visuals reflected a long history of spectatorship of racial violence, from trafficking to enslaving to lynching to mass incarceration. A white NYPD officer, assisted by other white officers, choked a Black man to death on a public street while the man gasped or cried out eleven times "I can't breathe."

After the Staten Island grand jury failed to indict Pantaleo, US Attorney General Eric Holder, Jr. announced a federal investigation, which he said would be "independent, thorough, fair, and expeditious." Holder called Garner's death "a tragedy" and "one of several recent incidents across our great country that tested our sense of trust" in law enforcement. When Holder retired in 2015, his replacement, Attorney General Loretta Lynch, who had also served as a prosecutor in NYC, assigned the Garner case to the Justice Department's civil rights division in Washington, DC.[12]

On July 13, 2015—one day short of the first-year anniversary of Eric Garner's murder—New York City Comptroller Scott Stringer suddenly settled with the Garner family for $5.9 million, which effectively ended further public litigation. The Comptroller's statement noted that the settlement "acknowledges the tragic nature of Mr. Garner's death" and that NYC "has not admitted liability." (At the time of Erica Garner's death on December 30, 2017, no funds had been released to the family.)

In July 2016, as the presidential election heated up, the NYPD completed its internal investigation into Pantaleo, but released no information. While NYPD Commissioner William Bratton informed the public that the case would proceed after the US Attorney decided if there was a civil rights violation,[13] *CityLaw* Fellow Jonathon Sizemore argued for a public trial so that communities could scrutinize

law.columbia.edu/news/archive/professors-fagan-and-harcourt-provide-facts-grand-jury-practice-after-staten-island-decision.

11. Jonathon Sizemore, "Eric Garner's Death: No Justice, No Peace," *City Land: New York City Land Use News and Legal Research*, March 16, 2017, https://www.citylandnyc.org/eric-garner-death-no-justice-no-peace/.

12. "Eric Holder's Complex Legacy," *Democracy Now!*, September 26, 2014, https://www.democracynow.org/2014/9/26/eric_holders_complex_legacy_voting_rights.

13. Sizemore, "Eric Garner's Death: No Justice, No Peace."

the charges, facts, and legal remedies and retain some faith in the legal system:

> When a police officer is videotaped killing an unarmed man with a chokehold, and the police officer's innocence is determined under a grand jury's shroud of secrecy, that confidence is severely under-mined. As Chief Justice Warren Burger wrote, "the open processes of justice serve an important prophylactic purpose, providing an out-let for community concern, hostility, and emotion."[14]

Garner's family had also called for the arrests of the other NYPD of-ficers involved in the killing: Justin D'Amico, who admitted to filing arrest paperwork that exaggerated the charges against Garner shortly after Garner's death, and Lieutenant Christopher Bannon, after being told that Garner was in cardiac arrest texted another officer that things "were not a big deal."[15] None were disciplined in any serous fashion. The only officer indicted was a Black woman, NYPD Sergeant Kizzy Adonis, charged with failing to supervise other officers at the police crime scene. Adonis' 2019 departmental disciplinary trial was can-celed when she pled guilty. On August 21, 2019, the NYPD announced her punishment: the loss of twenty vacation days.[16]

On August 29, 2019, Daniel Pantaleo was fired for using a depart-ment-prohibited chokehold resulting in Eric Garner's death. NYPD Commissioner James O'Neill made the announcement that Pantaleo lost his badge because of a "reckless" chokehold on Garner: "No one believes that Officer Pantaleo got out of bed on July 17, 2014 thinking he would make choices and take actions during an otherwise routine arrest that led to another person's death. But officers' choices and ac-tions even made under extreme pressure matter."[17] Pantaleo had been on desk duty since killing Garner. With his firing, although Pantaleo

14. Sizemore, "Eric Garner's Death: No Justice, No Peace."

15. P.R. Lockhart, "The officer who used a chokehold on Eric Garner was fired. But the case is far from settled." *Vox*, Aug 27, 2019, https://www.vox.com/identities/2019/8/27/20833639/daniel-pantaleo-eric-garner-nypd-protests-activists-de-blasio.

16. Lockhart, "The officer who used a chokehold on Eric Garner was fired. But the case is far from settled."

17. Lockhart, "The officer who used a chokehold on Eric Garner was fired. But the case is far from settled."

would no longer receive a pension, he was allowed to keep money he had paid into it.[18]

As was the case with Mumia Abu-Jamal seeking a new evidentiary hearing in 2023, while some Black wo/men served the state as compradors, others battled state forces and bureaucracies.[19] Eric Garner's mother Gwen Carr demanded justice. Rejecting restorative connections, she charged the city with criminal collusion: "By refusing to schedule a disciplinary trial for Adonis, de Blasio and the NYPD are actively participating in an ongoing cover-up." The family called for the House of Representatives to hold committee hearings, and advocated state legislation to make police use of chokeholds a criminal offense. The chokehold was already prohibited but police retained discretionary use of it.[20]

The Garner family and local activists filed a petition with the state court and a letter of inquiry with the NYPD and the city's Civilian Complaint Review Board (CCRB), in an effort to get more information about the aftermath of Eric Garner's death. NYPD officers argued that the decision to hold Pantaleo accountable for Garner's death was unsupportive to them and made their jobs more difficult.[21] Police unions held press conferences stating that officers were unfairly punished. Pantaleo's GoFundMe page, created in August 2014, garnered contributions. By December 2022, 3,500 donors had given a total of $178,703 to support Pantaleo, although the campaign did not meet its $250,000 goal.[22]

Ultimately, no one would face prosecution, criminal liability, or disciplinary actions in the immediate aftermath of Garner's death. There would be no accountability to the public that witnessed and felt the grave injustice. The grand jury ruling represented the norm found in the Luis Baez case when the 1979 grand jury also refused to indict the NYPD officer who killed Baez. Thirty-six years later, the Garner

18. Lockhart, "The officer who used a chokehold on Eric Garner was fired. But the case is far from settled."

19. Noelle Hanrahan, "Mumia's Response to the Judge's Decision," *Prison Radio*, April 4, 2023, https://www.prisonradio.org/news-update/mumias-response-to-the-judges-decision/.

20. Lockhart, "The officer who used a chokehold on Eric Garner was fired. But the case is far from settled."

21. Lockhart, "The officer who used a chokehold on Eric Garner was fired. But the case is far from settled."

22. "Officer Daniel Pantaleo's family help fund," GoFundMe, https://www.gofundme.com/f/officer-daniel-pantaleos-family-legal-fund.

grand jury indicated that the convention of police immunity would remain the norm. That Garner was not emotionally dysregulated and spoke the same language as the NYPD that killed him gives pause, distinguishing the case from that of Elizabeth Mangum and Luis Baez. For Baez, Brooklyn District Attorney Eugene Gold reported that the grand jury had issued no statement but had simply "voted no true bill." A Grand Jury vote of "no true bill" indicates "no criminal liability" against those charged. Involving the federal government was an option, but the US Attorney of the Eastern District conducted a federal investigation of Baez's homicide that also exonerated the NYPD.[23]

SHIELDING POLICE CRIMES

Although the NYPD had banned chokeholds in November 1993, police had continued to use chokeholds with "tacit acceptance—and sometimes, explicit approval—of department leaders."[24] *ProPublica* journalist Topher Sanders notes the exception clause(s):

> The patrol guide provides no allowances for using the maneuver, defined as 'any pressure to the throat or windpipe which may prevent or hinder breathing or reduce intake of air,' but other department guidelines note that chokeholds will be reviewed on a case-by-case basis 'to determine whether, under the circumstance, the actions were reasonable and justified.'[25]

The New York City Civilian Complaint Review Board (CCRB), which investigates police misconduct, has documented forty instances of officers using prohibited chokeholds since Garner's death to June 30, 2020. The report states that there were 880 complaints of NYPD chokeholds from July 2014 to June 30, 2020. Journalists at *ProPublica* and *The City* analyzed CCRB's chokehold reports in two databases, concluding that light punishments that did arise stemmed from

---

23. Joseph P. Fried, "Police Ruled Not Liable in Killing," *New York Times*, November 21, 1979, https://www.nytimes.com/1979/11/21/archives/police-ruled-not-liable-in-killing.html
24. Topher Sanders and Yoav Goan, "Still Can't Breathe: How NYPD Officers Continue to Use Chokeholds on Civilians," *The City*, January 21, 2021, https://www.thecity.nyc/2021/1/21/22241444/nypd-officers-chokeholds-still-cant-breathe.
25. Sanders and Goan, "Still Can't Breathe."

NYPD leadership's contempt for the CCRB. As NYPD Chief Joe Esposito (2000–2013) remarked at the time: "People who don't do this for a living are trying to make rules for people that do it every day."[26]

Meanwhile, lawsuits against the CCRB revealed it to be more of a NYPD surrogate than a hapless "our hands-are-tied" civilian advocacy group. CCRB Executive Director Jonathan Darche stated that recommending severe punishment for police violence "could hurt the board's ability to influence disciplinary outcomes."[27] The CCRB is dependent upon the police for evidence against and for punishment of criminal cops, so essentially, the NYPD controls the CCRB.

The Legal Aid Society filed a Freedom of Information (FOI) request in December 2014, seeking CCRB's summary of the number of substantiated complaints brought against Officer Daniel Pantaleo before Pantaleo and other NYPD officers killed Garner. According to Legal Aid, it needed the information to engage the NYPD in "a discussion on improving police investigative and disciplinary systems." The CCRB declined, which led to the Legal Aid Society filing an Article 78 petition in New York County Supreme Court arguing the information was necessary "to inform a public discussion about policing accountability."[28]

Defending itself by stating that releasing the summary could subject Pantaleo to "harassment or public humiliation," CCRB also argued that the disciplinary records could not be disclosed to the public due to New York Civil Rights Law Section 50-a, which bans access to police personnel performance records without the prior consent of the officer or a court order.[29] Through advocacy, 50-a would be repealed under the Cuomo administration several years after Erica Garner's death. If she had lived, Erica Garner would have likely boycotted the signing of the Eric Garner Anti-Chokehold Act as a symbolic and ineffectual act. In July 2020, New York Attorney General (AG) Letitia James held public hearings on NYPD violence against peaceful protests in the wake of George Floyd's homicide. The AG's report contributed to litigation against the NYPD and NYC Mayor Bill de Bla-

---

26. Sanders and Goan, "Still Can't Breathe."
27. Sanders and Goan, "Still Can't Breathe."
28. Sizemore, "Eric Garner's Death: No Justice, No Peace."
29. Sizemore, "Eric Garner's Death: No Justice, No Peace."

sio for civil rights violations.[30] During the hearings, I watched NYPD Commissioner Dermot Shea assert that among the current legislative changes inspired by BLM only the repeal of the 50-a shield law had a real impact on the police department.[31] The NYPD subsequently filed a lawsuit to challenge the repeal that released to the public records of police violations.[32]

Manhattan Supreme Court Justice Alice Schlesinger ruled that the CCRB was a city agency, independent of the NYPD, so the requested CCRB's summary would not be "personnel records" under Section 50-a. Even if the court considered as Pantaleo's personnel record, the judge maintained that "disclosure was warranted because the CCRB could not prove that the summary could abuse Pantaleo. Mayor Bill de Blasio participated in suppressing Pantaleo's records that detailed his history and habit of harming civilians without cause. When New York City appealed Judge Schlesinger's decision, Pantaleo's files remained sealed.[33]

The repeal of New York's 50-a law, which shields police violence by banning civilians from knowing about NYPD misconduct, was supposed to foster change in controlling police predatory violence. In the Garner case, New York City's CCRB recorded seventeen complaints filed against Pantaleo, from 2009 to 2014, the year he killed Eric Garner. CCRB opened eight cases and substantiated several cases of abuse. In a 2011 case, CCRB substantiated abuse of power during a vehicle stop and search, in which Pantaleo's punishment was to receive "instructions." In a similar case in 2012, the departmental disciplinary trial found Pantaleo guilty and he was punished by having to forfeit two vacation days.[34] Despite its dismal record of holding police ac-

---

30. Jake Offenhartz, "Federal Judge Promises "Rocket Docket" for NYPD Protest Lawsuits," *Gothamist*, February 3, 2021, https://gothamist.com/news/federal-judge-promises-rocket-docket-nypd-protest-lawsuits.

31. Joy James, "'Amnesty for All': Anti-Racist Activism to Control the Police Violence and Protect Protestors," *Abolition Journal*, August 18, 2020, https://abolitionjournal.org/amnesty-all/.

32. Caitlyn Jordan, "After Section 50-a repeal, New York police unions are fighting in court to keep misconduct records secret. So far, they're losing," Reporters Committee for Freedom of the Press (RCFP), November 5, 2020, https://www.rcfp.org/50-a-repeal-police-misconduct/.

33. See *Luongo v. Civilian Complaint Review Board*, 15 N.Y.S.3d 636 Sup. Ct., NY City Supreme Court, 2015.

34. Sonia Moghe, "Disciplinary record of ex-officer who held Eric Garner in chokehold is finally released," CNN, June 23, 2020, https://www.cnn.com/2020/06/23/us/eric-garner-officer-misconduct-complaints/index.html.

countable for predatory violence, CCRB chair Fred Davie's statement to CNN praised grassroots organizations for fighting to change laws to make police abuse records public, "The repeal of 50-a is a major step toward bolstering public confidence in the disciplinary system, allowing for more comprehensive reporting about police misconduct, and ultimately, changing the dynamic between police and civilians for the better."[35]

Pantaleo's disciplinary records were leaked to the progressive news website *Think Progress* in 2017. For five years, Carr petitioned for the Obama Department of Justice (DOJ)—led by a Black woman, Attorney General Loretta Lynch—to decide if the DOJ would charge Pantaleo. But Lynch let the case sit, with no action or engagement on the issue of the violation of Garner's civil rights. This play reflects the comprador more than the conflicted caretaker. In January 2017, weeks before Donald Trump took office, Lynch designated the file on NYPD policing to Trump's incoming conservative Attorney General, and former Alabama senator, Jeff Beauregard Sessions III, who was sworn in on February 9, 2017. Trump fired Sessions in November, accusing him of being "disloyal." Subsequently, Trump appointed Attorney General William Barr. AG Barr announced in July 2019 that there would be no federal investigation into Pantaleo's killing of Garner and civil rights violations. On July 16, 2019, almost five years to the date of Eric Garner's murder, US Attorney for the Eastern District of New York Richard Donoghue announced the Department of Justice (DOJ)'s conclusion to the investigation of NYPD officers violating Garner's civil rights:

> We are here to announce that, after an exhaustive investigation, the Department of Justice has reached the conclusion that insufficient evidence exists to prove beyond a reasonable doubt that the police officers who arrested Eric Garner in Staten Island on July 17, 2014 acted in violation of the federal criminal civil rights statute. Consequently, the investigation into this incident has been closed.[36]

---

35. Fred Davie quoted in Moghe, "Disciplinary record of ex-officer who held Eric Garner in chokehold is finally released."
36. Richard P. Donoghue, "Statement by United States Attorney Richard P. Donoghue," press release, July 16, 2019, United States Attorney's Office: Eastern District of New York, https://www.justice.gov/usao-edny/pr/statement-united-states-attorney-richard-p-dono-ghue.

The ruling did not surprise the family and communities seeking justice and reforms. In a press conference, Garner's mother, Gwen Carr, delivered the family's statement in response to the DOJ announcement: "We're here with heavy hearts because the DOJ has failed us, although we looked for better from them. Five years ago, my son said, 'I can't breathe' eleven times, and today, we can't breathe because they have let us down."[37] Erica Garner told the public that despite Pantaleo's removal from the NYPD, her fight would continue: "Justice for New York City means Pantaleo is fired and there's no murdering cop on the police force." She championed the Eric Garner Law, legislation that would ban police chokeholds and revoke legal protections that amounted to immunity for police involved in violence or killings.

CONCLUSION

Rarely is there closure for the public — let alone the family—for victims of police violence and murder. Yet, a ritualized panacea for predatory policing exists: legislation. Politicians keep blocking or passing bills, and police forces continue to brutalize and murder civilians. After years of litigation, and protests to the media and in the public square, families and civil and human rights organizations petition for new laws. Such legislation at times functions as a marker, even a tombstone registering the name and identity of the slain. Police lynching spectacles are not just funereal in terms of tragic deaths; they also create a container around the state murders by triggering legislation that promises protections that rarely manifest in actual court cases or in the curbing of predatory policing.

After the 2020 summer protests in the wake of the Minneapolis police murder of George Floyd, the New York State Assembly repealed the 50-a law and passed the Eric Garner Anti-Chokehold Act.[38] Gwen

37. Gwen Carr, quoted in Kevin Johnson and William Cummings, "'Today we can't breathe,' DOJ will not bring civil rights charge against NYPD officer in death of Eric Garner," *USA Today*, July 17, 2019, https://www.usatoday.com/story/news/politics/2019/07/16/justice-department-not-bring-charges-death-eric-garner/1741169001/.
38. Assembly Speaker Carl E. Heastie, "Assembly Passes Eric Garner Anti-Chokehold Act," news release, June 8, 2002, https://nyassembly.gov/Press/files/20200608a.php.

Carr appeared with Governor Cuomo at the 2020 signing of the Act.[39] Other impacted families refused to appear at the signing event with Governor Cuomo (see Further Resources), considering the performative signing of the act to be window dressing. Two weeks after the governor signed the new law,[40] a NYPD officer was captured on video placing a man in a chokehold.[41] It is unclear if that officer was fired from their job.

High-profile police brutality and murder allegations against the NYPD continue. The absence of reliable criminal convictions for police officers raping, injuring, or killing civilians remains the norm. New York State Attorney General Letitia James held investigative public hearings on NYPD brutality against peaceful protestors following the police murder of George Floyd in Minneapolis.[42] After denying police routinely brutalized or violated civilians, the NYPD Police Commissioner asserted that the Eric Garner Anti-Chokehold Act, now law, was inconsequential because the NYPD had already banned it, and the NYPD was protected if they used a chokehold. The Orwellian statement is accurate. After five years of pay raises and promotions for Daniel Pantaleo, NYPD Commissioner James O'Neil fired him in August 2019. No police officers among the five who applied chokehold or chest compression that led to Eric Garner's death were prosecuted for murder. Social media attributed a succinct impact statement made by Erica Garner—allegedly after Baltimore police killed Freddie Gray in 2015—several years before Pantaleo was fired: "I would do everything in my power not to see another Eric Garner."[43]

39. Alexa Lardieri, "Gov. Andrew Cuomo Signs 10-Bill Police Reform Package into Law," *U.S. News & World Report*, June 12, 2020, https://www.usnews.com/news/politics/articles/2020-06-12/new-york-gov-andrew-cuomo-signs-10-bill-police-reform-package-into-law.

40. Sonia Moghe, "New York City Council passes sweeping police reform bills," CNN, June 18, 2020, https:///www.cnn.com/2020/06/18/us/new-york-city-passes-police-reform-bills/index.html.

41. Amir Veram, Mark Morales, Sonia Moghe, and Ganesh Setty, "NYPD officer in 'disturbing apparent chokehold incident' had previous civilian complaint cases on his record," CNN, June 22, 2020, https://www.cnn.com/2020/06/22/us/nypd-officer-record-chokehold/index.html.

42. New York State Office of the Attorney General, "Preliminary report on the New York City Police Department's Response to Demonstrations Following the Death of George Floyd," July 2020, https://ag.ny.gov/sites/default/files/2020-nypd-report.pdf.

43. Eric Levenson, "What's next for Eric Garner's family now that the NYPD officer has been fired," CNN, August 20, 2019, https://www.cnn.com/2019/08/20/us/eric-garner-family-next/index.html#:~:text="I%20will%20do%20everything%20in,it%27s%20not%20supposed%20to%20happen.

CHAPTER 5

MOTHER-DAUGHTER DOULA

THE VULNERABILITIES OF BLACK MOTHERS

Erica Garner, as a Captive Maternal, stems from her merger of family care and political risk-taking for freedoms against predatory policing. An impacted family member of a victim of lethal policing, Erica Garner displayed intellectual and political agency that shaped liberation strategies and struggles. She increasingly played the "wild card" against state bureaucracy and conventional or performative politics that claimed transformative radicalism. She was unpredictable in deferring to conventional and party/boss politics except her increasing radical opposition to such politics. A Black mother caretaker with meager material resources, Erica Garner mutated into an avatar and an ancestor.

The Captive Maternal is ungendered in terms of its function. However, gender retains a material, psychological and emotional impact on our lives. Erica Garner's role as a Black mother was both private and political (she placed her seven-year-old daughter as a central interlocutor in the *It's Not Over* presidential campaign ad for Bernie Sanders). Motherhood and birthing made her more susceptible to fragile health and maternal mortality. In particular, maternal and child mortality rates are devastating for Black women who bear the brunt of medical crises driven by poverty, indifference and neglect, and the impact of anti-Blackness on psyches and bodies.

Erica Garner's first heart attack occurred during the birth of her son, Eric. Four months later, on December 30th, 2017, she died from a second heart attack which followed an asthma attack. Her enlarged heart grappled with stress that *Womanly* author Kandace Fuller traces to *trauma* from NYPD killing her father, *stress* from organizing against predatory policing, and a *maternal mortality crisis* in which US Black women face extreme vulnerability."[44]

Fuller notes that according to the National Institute of Health, women are at greater risk than men for psychological risks of depression, post-traumatic stress disorders that contribute to heart disease, and this negatively impacts their ability to recover. The high precarity for young women such as Erica Garner, who was in her late twenties when she died, having the combination of a parent murdered and becoming a movement actor or leader who is continuously ignored or rebuffed by state powers would be debilitating.

Focusing on her vulnerabilities and victimization at the hand of the state and medical establishment is important. The unstated or understated factors of stressors spiking after one publicly embraces radicalism—punished within and beyond Black formations and communities—is rarely addressed.[45] In low-income communities, Black families face "food deserts" that exacerbate childbirth complications stemming from obesity, heart disease, and diabetes. Fuller notes that for Black women and women of color "fighting social and political oppression has a direct impact on the mental and physical health of women as they struggle "on the front lines of every battle in the war against inequality," allies offer a succinct message: "protect your hearts."[46]

DAUGHTER-AS-ACTIVIST

Born in New York on May 29, 1990, in Brooklyn's Woodhull Hospital, Erica Garner died on December 30, 2017 in Woodhull Hospital. Three years prior, the young mother was transformed when, in July 2014,

---

44. In *Womanly*, Fuller notes that NYC Black mothers are twelve times "more likely to die from prenatal and childbirth complications than white mothers" while US Black mothers are 243 percent more likely to die than white mothers. Racist biases lead doctors to dismiss or downplay the health needs of Black mothers and due to lack of financial resources Black women disproportionately have access to under-equipped/staffed hospitals but not quality care afforded affluent white patients in "upper-class hospitals." Kandace Fuller, "The Heart of Erica Garner," *Womanly Magazine*, no. 2: Matters of the Heart, https://www.womanlymag.com/matters-of-the-hearts/articles/the-heart-of-erica-garner.
45. Fuller, "The Heart of Erica Garner."
46. Fuller, "The Heart of Erica Garner."

several members of the NYPD applied a chokehold and chest compression that asphyxiated her father, Eric Garner, on a Staten Island street. Following the police murder of her father, Erica Garner struggled through the stages of grief and through activism. She would also have to contend with the exposure and manipulations of mass media while she painfully grew into political consciousness that understood the entanglement of community care and confrontation with police and state. The traumatized working-class Black daughter-mother evolved into a political leader who could not be "bought or bossed."[47]

Initially, Garner engaged in protests and petitions, then she waited for justice. With no accountability offered, betrayed, she broke from liberal politics embraced by officials and liberal democracy and mainstream abolitionists who spanned from centrist through progressive to radical liberals. She eventually rejected the deferential or polite petitioner role prescribed for impacted families who are told not to annoy the state or society with their grief, and to never show rage at the government or police. The apologia of "we do not mean to offend" is often seen as a prerequisite for monetary compensations following the murder of kin by police forces and a "seat at the table" with politicians and power brokers for the state and civil society.

Erica Garner did not align with administrators and mainstream politicians, nor did she swim in corporate revenue streams. Garner was neither a comprador nor a sideline hustler. She did not portray herself as a victim although she consistently publicly spoke about the police killing of her father, Eric Garner. She verbally castigated police and politicians—in impassioned and emotive ways—but even when she spoke about her pain she focused on the strategies and goals to stop predatory policing. Without positioning her personal victimization as virtue or valor, Garner engaged in material political struggle. Her loss was tragic, but it was her function not her identity as an impacted family member that recognized but did not focus on victimization. Hence, rather than be reduced to a subject-object of pity and

---

47. "Bought and bossed" is a phrase popularized by Brooklyn congresswoman Shirley Chisholm who worked briefly with white democratic bosses to leverage her election as the first Black congresswoman in NY, and later in 1972, the first Black woman presidential candidate representing a major party. Charlene Mitchell, who recruited Angela Davis into and mentored Davis as a leader in the Communist Party USA, ran for US president on the CPUSA ticket in 1968.

compassion, she became politically engaged and thus problematic to liberals and sideliners who watched the devastation as a spectacle but never engaged to stop it.

Garner's greatest contributions to political movements were heart-driven intellectualism and fierce opposition to hustlers and handmaidens of the state and corporate media that could increase their ratings through performative "care" coverage that monetizes anti-Black dishonor and death. When Garner jumped off the political-media merry-go-round of conventional electoral politics in which progressives and antifascists would logically vote for the Democratic Party, she emerged as a political doula and guerrilla intellectual. The "guerrilla" intellect came from the streets and its mobilizations and risk-taking that went beyond spectator politics and mourning. The mobilizing of protests on streets produced multi-racial radical and ethical factions that converged to make concrete demands from the state to quell predatory policing. Activism moved from protest to movement making and into diverse forms of marronage. Cadres were multiethnic and multiracial and cut across class lines. Although some dismissed her foray into electoral politics as "conventional," her 2016 endorsement of Bernie Sanders as he primaried Hillary Clinton startled and alarmed the political establishment. Garner represented autonomous, creative, and courageous communities that resisted conventional politics and advocacy democracy in which elites lead liberalism and advocate for the mass (akin to the US being a representative democracy—hence the electoral college determines presidential elections not majority vote).

With collectives, Garner produced skeletal frameworks for resistance to predatory policing, violence, and poverty. She grew into a movement organizer who would defy influential financial-political networks, corporate media, and mayors, governors, and Presidents (Obama and Trump). Working with radical maroon communities, Garner refused celebrity status—she functioned with high visibility mostly as an "anti-celebrity" due to her lack of performative politics. Garner avoided cooptation while remaining wary if not outspoken concerning the absorption of high-profile "movement leaders" into heavily funded nonprofits and surrogacies for the Democratic Party. As powerful state-aligned networks found it increasingly difficult to co-opt or corrupt her into a conventional caretaker role or a hustle in which victimization was a symbolic register for virtue and valor, Garner became more sophisticated about manipulation. Interactions with mainstream media sharpened her skills. Abrasive, she became a skilled street fighter and political player. Her "wild cards" included guerrilla theater leveraged to critique conservatism, DNC liberalism, mainstream media, and police propaganda.

Within her doula work, Erica Garner contemplated and coordinated on the terrain of electoral politics. Her doula labor moves from local, through state, to national politics. She would push past the DNC and Democratic Party that had created "Mothers of the Movement" from among other impacted Black families. Garner pushed forward toward "democratic socialist," radicalism, and antiracist confrontations with predatory policing. After months of being sought out by the media, and in some ways led to echoes of its political positions of respectful criticism and hopeful reforms, she became seasoned at avoiding the managerial mainstream and liberal media. This transformation did not take place immediately, as one sees in the media's attempts to paint a more subdued portrait of Erica Garner. As Malcolm X noted: "The media's the most powerful entity on earth. They have the power to make the innocent guilty and to make the guilty innocent, and that's power. Because they control the minds of the masses."[48]

MEDIA PORTRAITS: INTRODUCING ERICA GARNER TO THE PUBLIC

In terms of media politics, CNN can be described as more centrist and the *Guardian* as more liberal. That CNN is US-based, and so liable to offend its sponsors and viewers who are pro-American is not an issue for the British-based *Guardian*. Interviews that are on-camera and live lack a certain depth that print interviews offer. The latter allow the interviewee to be off-stage and not distracted by knowledge that (hundreds of) thousands would be scrutinizing their appearance, voice, and perspectives. The "privacy" of a recording that will be transferred into print, with a gap between the making of the interview and the ed-

---

48. Malcolm X, cited in Janice Gassam Asare, "The Pervasiveness of Racism and Bias in the Media," *Forbes*, February 28, 2022, https://www.forbes.com/sites/janicegassam/2022/02/28/the-pervasiveness-of-racism-and-bias-in-the-media/?sh=258991e12cc4.

iting process to focus and streamline the narrative, allows the speaker time to reflect rather than answer rapid-fire questions with a narrative shaped by a host interested in ratings more so than a journalist seeking facts and reflections.

Erica Garner's December 4, 2014, interview with (now former) CNN host Don Lemon took place less than five months after the murder of her father. Lemon's interview marks the relative "beginning" of Erica Garner's national recognition in mainstream media.[49] Compared to her later interviews, Garner's encounter with Lemon reveals a progressive twenty-four-year-old not yet evolved into a militant activist. The first-born child, Eric Garner's daughter was navigating raw grief in front of a prime-time audience as she grappled with a response to the NYPD's execution of her father. Lemon's interview focuses on the individual not the communal, as he avoided discussion of the material conditions that led to a movement for Black lives and against police violence.

When Lemon (fired from CNN in 2023 due to his gender bias) asked Erica Garner, "How do you manage to pull yourself together like this and be so strong in the midst of this tragedy?" she was candid about her vulnerability: "How do I pull myself together? Some days it's like I don't know *how* I keep it together." Garner also pointed to her young daughter and siblings as a key motivator for her activism. She maintained that it was necessary for her "to be the leader" and show strength to younger family members so that they could model her strengths as youths. For the elders, there was more levity. Erica Garner asserted that her mother, Esaw Snipes, managed her pain and to "keep her days full of laughter and around family."

When Lemon asked if he could play the video of her father's homicide, Garner agreed, stating that she was "used to it now." She had screened the disturbing footage multiple times in order to comprehend the details of the police homicide of Eric Garner. As Erica Garner described it: "I just wanted to see what happened . . . who did it, who did what, who was standing where." She also acknowledged that constant screening of the video clip on various media platforms was eroding her health: "I watched it over and over again   to the

49. "Erica Garner full interview with Don Lemon at CNN—12/4/2014," December 30, 2017, https://www.youtube.com/watch?v=voAWMnvLUm4.

point where I was talking to the TV, I was like, 'Get off of him, stop, don't touch him no more, what are you talking to him for?' Really just ad-libbing what people should've said, or his [Officer Pantaleo's] coworkers should have said, 'Alright, get up buddy, you [are] overdoing it already.'"

Responding to Lemon asking her opinion on the grand jury decision not to charge Pantaleo, Garner states that she expected the grand jury verdict would go against the family's wishes. The video should have been sufficient for a conviction, she maintained, and noted that advocacy for body cameras did not provide justice for her father. NYPD cameras did not capture the crime on film. Ramsey Orta did so by taking footage on his cell phone and later sharing it with the Garner family. During her CNN interview, Erica Garner questions the power of technology as protection for civilians: "[W]e got the video and my father dies on video. . . . My dad died on national TV, on a camera. He still ain't get justice. So, what's justice gonna do with these body cameras but promote more killing?" The LAPD were exonerated after brutally beating Rodney King on March 3, 1991 despite a civilian, George Holliday, filming the beating from his balcony and sending the footage to a local news station so that the public could be informed. The 2014 Supreme Court ruling expanded cell phone privacy rights. Yet, as noted in Part I's reference to George Floyd's murder, cell phone cameras are not protections or stable defense within war resistance. Ossei-Owusu dismisses cell phones (let alone police body cameras) as the "the great equalizer."[50]

Lemon is not seeking strategies of war resistance against police predatory powers. A celebrity pundit and multimillionaire, he does not desperately need protections from state violence. His interest in social stability and reconciliation that reassures his audience that the democracy is cohesive and caring means that he has to address the "race" issue without analyzing anti-Black violence in the democracy. Referring to Governor Cuomo's statement about the diversity of protesters rallying against the NYPD Garner murder, Erica Garner observes that police murders of civilians "is not a Black and white issue" but a "national crisis." She remarks that the protesters include whites,

---

50. See Bill Mears, "Supreme Court: Police need warrant to search cell phones," CNN, June 25, 2014, https://www.cnn.com/2014/06/25/justice/supreme-court-cell-phones/.

Asians, and "different people from different nations and different parts of the world" who demonstrated their shared shock and rage after screening the video of Eric Garner being choked to death. Stating that she "greatly appreciate[s]" the public's horror over the horrific killing of her father, she welcomes the national and global solidarity: "It's like a sense of 'I'm not the only one that feels this way.'"

Attempting to get Erica Garner to clarify that the struggle is "not a Black and white issue," Lemon pointedly asks: "Do you think it's a racial issue?" Garner downplays white supremacy in this first major media interview:

> I really doubt it. It was about the officer's pride, it was about my father being 6 feet, 4 inches and 350 pounds and he wanted to be the top cop that brings this big man down. . . . I mean, my father wasn't even doing anything. He wasn't really doing nothing, he didn't have no gun, he didn't run, he didn't smack him [the cop]. Nothing.

Reinforcing the perception of cross-racial unity, appealing to conservatives' and liberals' need to assert that Eric Garner did not die due to *racist* policing, a structural feature of US democracy, Lemon offers a follow up to confirm that Erica Garner is not making a specific charge that identifies the motive for police brutality as being racially driven: "A lot of people would be surprised because you know, this is being made out to be a racial issue, and you're saying you don't think it's about race." Erica Garner responds: "Being that my father was Black and the officer was white, that's different races, but as far as this situation . . . .Ah [sighs] I can't really say that it's a Black and white issue." After Lemon hums approvingly, Garner continues: "It's about, you know, the police officer. Abusing their power." Lemon, again, hums with affirmation. As the interview moves toward a close, the conversation shifts to national protests. The media personality deemphasizes anti-Black racism, deracializes the crime and the protests, and asks Erica Garner for her final comments on the spreading protests and her father, and her emergence as a grassroots leader. "You're saying it's not about race. But what do you want the world to know about your father? What do you think he'd want the world to know?" Evoking the Southern civil rights movement, Erica Garner replies that her father "would be very proud at the way these protests are going, without being violent, without burning stuff down." She emphasizes the torturous homicide and the peaceful protests: "He'd just want them to know, that, he died in a horrible way. A horrible way. . . . [Ramsey Orta gave] that video to the world, I think he would be very proud at the way these protests are going, without being violent, without burning stuff down, looting and all that. There's better ways to handle the problem."[51]

The month after the CNN interview, *The Guardian* published UK journalist Elizabeth Day's interview with Erica Garner. This interview offers a more in-depth and personal portrait. Erica Garner becomes not just a victim, generalized with the repetition of Black vulnerability to family loss, poverty, lynching, and police brutality. Rather, she is defined as a member of an extended family, a recipient of and contributor to Black family and culture as a barricade to a general and generalized hostile society. *The Guardian* interview describes how Erica Garner lived on the sixteenth floor of a Brooklyn high-rise with her husband, Hester, and their five-year-old daughter, Alyssa. In the corner of the living room a black-and-white photo shows a striking Black woman in a Victorian dress who Garner identifies as her great-grandmother, the daughter of an enslaved African.

The narrative shares that Garner grew up in Brooklyn in a family that lacked resources because of poverty and health issues, such as asthma, that plagued their father, Eric Garner. Yet, his daughter notes his temporary jobs, e.g., in the NYC Department of Parks & Recreation, that he was unable to maintain due to health issues, and she describes how Eric Garner was devoted to his children. According to his eldest child, he remained engaged with his children and grandchildren regardless of his health status and whether or not he lived with them. Erica Garner shares that she was closer to her father than to her mother, because it was her father who took on the domestic duties of child rearing, such as taking his children to and picking them up from school. It was her father who was the familial Captive Maternal caretaker. *The Guardian*'s snapshot of Erica Garner's personal life provides images that "humanize" Eric Garner to its largely white, middle-class European readership.

---

51. For all quoted material above, see "Erica Garner full interview with Don Lemon at CNN— 12/4/2014."

The interview shifts from the domestic sphere to the public sphere of protests against police violence. On the afternoon of Martin Luther King Day in 2015, across the river from Erica Garner-Snipes' Brooklyn apartment, hundreds gathered in Manhattan's Union Square before heading uptown by foot to demonstrate in front of the United Nations buildings, as Erica Garner repeatedly shouts: "I can't breathe!" while marching with her "support group." Describing her increasing feeling of ease in political public speaking, Erica Garner demonstrates her growing skills, she offers pointed soundbites to the media. Nonetheless, she confides to the journalist that she is concerned about the ramifications of public protests against the police. She especially worries about the safety of her two younger brothers:

> I don't want them to be targeted by the cops. I am angry but that's not going to solve anything. I'd rather be angry on a march and channel it with all those people and project it in my voice. Because now people are looking to me, so I have to keep pressing on for my father and end the cycle of violence. You can't fight violence with violence. You'll either get killed or go to jail.

Garner recalls her family's instructions: "It was always: 'You're the oldest, lead by example.'" When Day asks: "What her father would say to her" if he could communicate with her, Erica Garner answers: "That he's proud of me. That he knew I could do it." Offering spiritual and philosophical reflections, Garner shares: "I believe in justice. It will take a long time but it's gonna come."[52] Her language patterns that of Dr. Rev. King, who in a speech given days before his April 4, 1968 assassination, stated: "We shall overcome because the arc of the moral universe is long but it bends toward justice."[53]

Garner also shares with the journalist the poignant story of how she first heard of her father's homicide. On Thursday, July 17, 2014, riding a subway train from Queens to Staten Island, she received a phone call from her aunt who told her that her father had "stopped

52. Elizabeth Day, "Erica Garner Snipes: 'I believe in justice. It will take a long time but it's gonna come,'" *Guardian*, January 25, 2015, https://www.theguardian.com/us-news/2015/jan/25/eric-garner-erica-garner-snipes-justice-will-take-a-long-time-police-violence.
53. Dr. Martin Luther King, Jr., "Remaining Awake Through a Great Revolution," speech given at the National Cathedral, March 31, 1968, https://www.si.edu/spotlight/mlk?page=4&iframe=true.

breathing." Garner describes her confusion: "I didn't know what that meant. . . . I know he has asthma," she adds, slipping unthinkingly into the present tense, "So is he in hospital?"[54] When the train passed through a tunnel, connection was lost. Erica Garner began crying. Passengers in the train car who had overheard the conversation spontaneously began to pray. Garner recalls: "They prayed for me right there and then. . . . They said everything was going to be OK."[55] By the time she reached her grandmother's house in Staten Island, news of her father's death was circulating on national media. The prayer circle of community of fellow passengers comforting Erica Garner were likely from similar backgrounds and classes. Taking public transit from Queens to Staten Island rather than a private car offered the possibility of community, even if temporarily, to connect and offer care. Erica Garner then describes how departing from the train and having her first glimpse of the raw video of her father's homicide was traumatic:

> I just remember staring at the TV and saying 'Get off of him! Please move!' I was screaming at the TV as if I was there. All I can see on that video is my dad just trying to live for his kids, just fighting for us. You can hear his voice get muffled and high-pitched. It sounds like he was scared. Really scared. He wasn't fighting the police. He was fighting to breathe.[56]

Ten days after a Ferguson, Missouri grand jury refused to indict Darren Wilson (the white police officer who shot and killed unarmed Black eighteen-year-old Michael Brown), a Staten Island grand jury cited insufficient evidence to indict Daniel Pantaleo. Following the media announcing the secret grand juries' refusals to indict, NYC streets erupted. The two verdicts, so close together, sparked a wave of protests across the US. News coverage around the globe followed. In an attempt to stem the unrest, the US Justice Department under the Obama administration launched a civil rights investigation into Garner's death.

This was a refrain. It would sound, for activists, like a song stuck on repeat. The cries for justice from a daughter-mother doula never

---

54. Day, "Erica Garner-Snipes: 'I believe in justice.'"
55. Day, "Erica Garner-Snipes: 'I believe in justice.'"
56. Day, "Erica Garner-Snipes: 'I believe in justice.'"

skipped a beat. Rather than fall silent, Erica Garner became more vocal. She countered protesters' disappointments and government betrayals that diminished the value of her father's life and the atrocity of his death. Black lives did not matter to police forces, grand juries, government officials, and mainstream media. In the aftermath of the secret grand jury in Staten Island, journalists sold stories and "ambulance chasers"—attorneys and celebrities—followed the impacted families, held press conferences, and appeared before cameras. The year 2014 would spark the rise of movement-makers morphing into movement-millionaires.

CARETAKER

Captive Maternal functions range from domestic caretaking to political war resistance. The first stage of caretaking is the one most familiar to individuals or communities with lineages of captivity deflected by intense care for survivors. Birth and death doulas find that feminized care easily becomes a bottomless pit of exhaustion and triage unless one manages to deliver maternal self-care, and receive reciprocal care from families, communities, and movements. Doulas are largely viewed as feminine or female caretakers to pregnant women or reproductive people. The Alliance for Black Doulas for Black Mamas facilitates Black women's access to social, emotional, and educational support. As professionally trained doulas, they work to provide emotional, physical, and educational support for mothers and families. This is a key goal—given racial bias in the medical industry and its destabilization of Black health outcomes—to improve Black women's maternal and birth outcomes. Their strategies and healthcare interventions focus on social, emotional, and educational support. Without receiving care for frustration, depression, and illness, the premature death of a parent or a child through medical neglect and predatory violence becomes more prevalent. These strategies for biological birth can be replicated for political birth or freedom movements. In varied arenas, from birthing or medical centers to mass movements, caretakers are embattled.[57]

---

57. "Alliance for Black Doulas for Black Mamas (ABDBM)," University of North Carolina School of Medicine, https://www.med.unc.edu/fammed/service-to-the-community/abdbm/.

Erica Garner, as a political doula, did not restrict her organizing to NYC or Staten Island. She travelled to Missouri in order to participate in the protests in Ferguson, following media coverage on Brown's murder by Ferguson police, just weeks after Eric Garner's murder by police. Eric Garner's death attracted little media attention until the rebellion in Ferguson. Months later, the video of his death and eleven gasps of "I can't breathe" were shared around the world. At twenty-four years old, Erica Garner suddenly became the image of protests against police brutality. She routinely appeared on local and national television, and received requests to speak at universities, high schools, churches, and conferences. She wryly noted: "People have been calling me an activist overnight." More than "an activist overnight" in the public's eye, Garner was transforming into an intellectual guerilla and street fighter. After the Grand Jury exonerated Pantaleo in December 2014, protesters poured into the streets of New York City. News cameras came out for coverage and higher ratings, and to get sound bites. The NYPD came out for other reasons. The Garner family and their early supporters also "hit the streets." Specifically, the street where Eric Garner was killed in Staten Island, one month after his death. Erica Garner shared her feelings with the public, that she needed to march. When asked by some "When will you stop marching? What do you want from marching?" her response would be: "He was my father. I will always march."[58]

Organizers planned so that working-class people could participate every Tuesday and Thursday at 6:00 p.m., after the usual working hours. The majority of the protestors did not live in Staten Island. Garner describes her procedure: wait for an hour as protestors disembarked every fifteen minutes from the ferries from Manhattan, then march to the Supreme Court and the local police precinct. After the march, Erica Garner would lead a vigil and tribute, and walk to the spot on Bay Street—which became a shrine—where the NYPD killed her father. Sometimes thousands would attend the march and vigil, other times, only a few. The lack of consistent large numbers likely reflected the difficulties of reaching Staten Island. Most marchers took the subway to the southern tip of Manhattan, stood in line to

---

58. Davina Sutton, "Erica Garner Will Not Stop Marching," *NBC News*, March 30, 2015, https://www.nbcnews.com/news/nbcblk/erica-garner-will-not-stop-marching-n327941.

board the ferry, crossed, and marched to the designated shrine or precinct. Returning home would likely have been exhausting as well. The costs could mount for those without a steady and sufficient income. The marches were taking place in "hostile territories." Staten Island, considered to be the most conservative of the five boroughs populated by 8.5 million New Yorkers, is known as the home of a number of NYPD members and supporters. For Staten Island residents who were reluctant to protest or publicly critique the NYPD, Erica Garner reported that she would demand: "Speak up! This happened in your neighborhood. My dad was the guy that you see every day."[59] Only after months of marching, according to Garner, did significant numbers of New Yorkers begin to support the protest movement.

Police harassment followed the increasing visibility of the protests. An NYPD computer was used to change Eric Garner's *Wikipedia* page to disparage the deceased. Erica Garner publicly criticized Police Commissioner Bill Bratton for not disciplining the culprit. Determined to shape the narrative and meaning of her father's homicide, correcting false perceptions that Eric Garner died from a preexisting condition such as a heart attack or respiratory failure, Erica Garner constantly referenced the video of the homicide, declaring: "He was jumped. He was murdered for no reason at all. The cops had been bothering him for a long time."[60] Garner asserted that the NYPD used other techniques to control the narrative, such as intimidating protesters from traveling on the ferry to marching in Staten Island. Police trailed protesters in "unmarked cars" and barricaded the Supreme Court steps. The marches continued for a year, each Tuesday and Thursday at 6:00 p.m.[61]

Advocating fiercely for justice following her father's 2014 death, Erica Garner became familiar with how organizing for justice is traumatic in a violent nation and world. Those who organize are suffering and more vulnerable to negative health outcomes due to grief and stress. Constant mobilization might stave off or deepen depression. Fidelity becomes an extension of precarity, and mortality rates among caretakers in zones of violence and state warfare remain high. Caretaking is the priority, even at the expense of one's own self, which is

---

59. Sutton, "Erica Garner Will Not Stop Marching."
60. Sutton, "Erica Garner Will Not Stop Marching."
61. Sutton, "Erica Garner Will Not Stop Marching."

not a choice for the captive, it is often a necessity if the captive and community are to survive and eventually struggle to thrive. Resources help, but under capitalism and imperialism, resources are not equitably distributed. The impoverished and the working class remain the most vulnerable to police violence and the violence of incarceration.

Lacking a college degree and conventional politics, Erica Garner did not have affluent or influential networks. Her best resources were over-policed Black communities, largely working class and laborers, and radical-minded students and organizers. She could not be bought or leveraged as an icon through industrial progressivism and professional politicians. In the span of only two years, 2014–2016, Garner became an architect of transformative "new bones" abolitionism, leaving a significant imprint on political thought and activism. Because her confrontational tactics were deemed not "respectable," she became overlooked or forgotten after her death.

As a "disruptor," Garner sought transformative change through critique and confrontation. She challenged powerful politicians and bureaucracies—the NYC mayor and the governor, as well as two US presidents—and all officials who refused to meet the needs of working-class and poor communities. Like many well-known academic abolitionists, Garner too sought the nexus between historical Black rebellions and contemporary movements, but without the well-funded platforms that promote more idealistic, or visionary, yet still conventional politics as the evolutionary path for radical goals. Garner's "unruly hope" distanced her from elite corridors of power shaped by academia, nonprofit corporations, and progressive media.[62]

Erica Garner was publicly respectful to, but not necessarily aligned with, all advocay formations and Black women who had lost loved ones to police or white supremacist violence. Organized formations such as "Say Her Name," "M4BL," and "Mothers of the Movement" were all, to some degree, tied to the Democratic Party and Hillary Clinton's presidential campaign. Garner never trusted government to provide social justice. Hence, her activism was uncivil and persistent. Delivering cutting critiques of liberal politicians—whom radicals viewed as ob-

---

62. Jeff Shantz, "The Captive Maternal and Abolitionism: A Tribute to Erica Garner," Social Justice Centre, March 11, 2018, https://www.thesocialjusticecentre.org/blog/2018/3/11/the-captive-maternal-and-abolitionism-a-tribute-to-erica-garner.

structionists—Erica Garner alienated loyalists to a Democratic mayor, governor, and president who presented themselves as concerned progressive politicians. Those who sided with institutional political power tended to reject Garner as too abrasive and disruptive. A radicalizing Captive Maternal, Garner's references to the Black Panther Party as a prototype for struggle were not performative gestures of radicalism.

Lacking mainstream allies left her vulnerable to some but visible to supportive radicals. In some ways, her bold, righteous politics reflected the older Samaria Rice, who had lost her twelve-year-old son Tamir when a Cleveland police officer shot and killed the child. Although Erica Garner's platforms were originally small rickety stages built by un(der)funded outsiders—and delivered in the streets with her weekly die-ins in honor of her father—her militancy and that of her cadre helped spark a movement that abided by a Manichean divide between police violence and US democracy versus Black security and freedom. Longevity was not on her side. It remains to be seen whether, with the passage of years, this democracy, with or without decorum, can achieve the benchmark of her ethical demands.

Seeking forms of self-protection against police and predatory violence, she began to reference the Black Panther Party's tenets, including its original title: "Black Panther Party for Self-Defense." Self-protection, familial-protection, and communal-protection require emotional, physical, psychological shields and the capacity to warn predators or those engaged in predatory behavior that there are consequences to gratuitous violence. Radical defense is built on protective love and the sanctity of life. It is also, for some, built on honor.

In *Slavery and Social Death*, Orlando Patterson writes of slavery as an institution that has replicated itself over millennia, and how slavery is not only about exploitation, it is also about expendability and dishonor.[63] Severed natality means one loses family members, parents, and children under the routinization of state and police violence, and the violations of civilians raised in a violent culture. In the face of continued and protected (through police unions and legalism) brutal violation, dishonor, death by the state and police, Erica Garner argued that there should be consequences. Defunding the police was one approach, but it did not address the scope of the problem as it does not

---

63. Patterson, *Slavery and Social Death*.

ask, "who controls the violence?" At times, accounting of public funds becomes a shell game for governments funded by taxpayers who cannot rank or control expenditures, while corporations and the extremely wealthy often underpay their taxes.

Protesters had routinely chanted: "INDICT! CONVICT! SEND THESE KILLER COPS TO JAIL! THE WHOLE DAMN SYSTEM IS GUILTY AS HELL!" Demonstrating with fierce *glee* against a violent policing, those marching in NYC streets expressed their—sadness, rage, and depression. Through their outrage they demanded "justice" and autonomy from state bureaucracy and violence.[64]

Familial loss awakened Erica Garner's militancy. A young, single mother when her father died, Erica Garner fought to collect herself and repurpose herself following the tragedy. She had lived with her grandmother and spent some time in foster care as a youth. She had navigated personal circumstances as an outlier in a city controlled by billionaires and bureaucrats. She then mutated into a rebel. Garner was associated with BLM as a young leader when the movement emerged following George Zimmerman's 2013 acquittal for Trayvon Martin's murder. The following year, police officers killed unarmed Eric Garner, Michael Brown, and Tamir Rice. That violence dominated and drove media news cycles. From the death of her father in July 2014 to her own death in December 2017, Garner became a highly visible disruptor of conventional politics and abolition. By the time of the 2016 presidential election, her political position and backing of an "outsider" senator garnered international recognition for an alternative to the leadership of nonprofits, academics, and politicians.

As manifestos or calls to power, the common refrains in Erica Garner's speeches and videos are: "Enough is enough" and "No negotiations." Her political ethics centered on uncompromised commitments to the working class and poor, and those brutalized and killed by police violence. On July 7, 2016 she reflects on Alton Sterling's police murder, after the US Department of Justice exonerated the Baton Rouge police officer who killed Sterling during a traffic stop.[65] She begins by

---

64. This is powerfully noted by Ominira Mars' critique of hope. See James, *In Pursuit of Revolutionary Love*, xv–xviii.

65. The white officers stated that they would kill him if he moved, before they shot the African American man eight times. "Alton Sterling: New footage emerges of the lead up to 2016 police shooting," *BBC News*, March 31, 2018, https://www.youtube.com/watch?v=01r606Sx-

stating that she had been seeking "self-care" by absenting herself from marches, protests, and speeches based on her belief in democracy. However, the murder of Sterling in Louisiana propelled her to make political pleas for communities to issue demands to politicians. She recounts how she went "quiet for a few months for self-care" after nearly two years of protests, marches, and advocacy against violent policing. Garner shares that at the time she thought "justice was a real thing that could be achieved," only to learn that "this system is set up to protect the killers and criminalize the innocent." Garner describes her heart as broken by seeing the murder of an innocent man and his mourning family. She then categorically rejects the continuing collection of video tapes of police murders without a clear strategy to confront police violence. Garner demands that we move beyond reliance on video tapes and faux reconciliations that fail to deter police murders while advocating that all parties do the "'let's hold hands and have a conversation stuff.'" Garner asserts: "I/We got demands."[66] She then pointedly details those demands:

> In memory of Alton Sterling, Eric Garner, and too many others murdered by police. I call for every law maker in New York to pledge to vote to make Governor Cuomo's Special Prosecutor permanent. I call on all Black voters in New York to refuse to vote for any candidate that does not vote for this legislation no matter if it makes it to the floor for a vote or not. No Special Prosecutor, no vote. Period. I call on every law maker in NYC that claims to stand with Black lives to pledge to support the Right to Know act to support transparency in policing. I also call on you to support anti choke hold legislation. I call on ALL Black voters in NYC to refuse to vote for any candidates that don't support these bills. There is no reason that they don't pass in the city that claims to be democratic. I call on every congress person that protested on the floor last week to also protest on the floor to eliminate funding for programs that provide military-grade weapons to our local police departments and schools. They need to prove that their fight isn't just for show, and this is something that they can do

---

WCk; "Federal Officials Close Investigation into Death of Alton Sterling," US Department of Justice, May 3, 2017, https://www.justice.gov/opa/pr/federal-officials-close-investigation-death-alton-sterling.

66. See Erica Garner, "My latest thoughts on Alton Sterling," July 7, 2016, https://web.archive.org/web/20170503011718/http:/www.officialericagarner.com/2016/07/07/my-latest-thoughts-on-alton-sterling/.

right now. I call on any candidate for president to address what their DOJ would look like. They need to address why so many people don't get charged and they need to explain what they would do to address that. It has been two years since Eric Garner was killed on video and the DOJ and all of the resources of the federal government have still failed to conclude their so-called investigation.

Finally, I call on any candidate for president that values Black lives to end the federal 1033 Program that provides our local police and schools with drones, tanks, and M16 weapons. This can and should be done by executive order. I beg the Black community to support any candidates that pledge to support these things. I beg of you to FORCE democrats to appreciate your loyalty more if any of them refuse to support Black lives by refusing to vote for them. Period. No negotiations.

The "no negotiations" stance is not expressed by nonprofits funded to be abolition centers. The "no negotiations" stance is a movement away from caring carceral constructs and advocacy, and toward war resistance. Garner's tweets mobilized people as a potential force to resist in order to save their lives in a bid for autonomous zones of marronage, rather than conform in order to maintain their lives under the control of police forces and fear of police executioners.

NAVIGATING NYC WITH TACTICAL TWEETS

Within three years after the Don Lemon CNN interview, Erica Garner displayed considerable media and political organizing skills. Her "tactical tweets" were piercing and poetic and politically damaging. There would be a constant barrage of tweets strategically levied at public officials who obstructed justice toward her father, her family, and society in general.

Erica Garner engaged in creative and impactful organizing. Her growing realization that mass media and law enforcement were conjoined twins, sharing the heartbeat and pulse of a racist republic, meant that without a publicist or media consultant, or the backing of media networks and powerful political allies (other than the mass of protesting activists), that she would have to create and maintain her own analytical narratives pointing towards social justice. As her political lenses gained clarity, she began to verbally express her emotions and stronger critiques of the political-economic order that utilized and protected policing as we know it. Erica Garner called attention to the fact that the same corporate sponsors who fund the police unions, who reinforce police violence, are the same corporations who fund and fuel the various media outlets that citizens rely upon for informed news and perspectives.

The politics weren't correct, and she wasn't interested in being politically correct. Garner wanted politicians, police, and the masses to know how she felt: uncensored, raw, and uncut, and she wanted them to share her outrage and move forward toward tangible reforms and control of police violence. Turning to social media she crafted and weaponized a skill in which rhetoric laced with righteous rage and called individuals, bureaucracies, and governments to accountability. Erica Garner's tweets though were more salacious than headlines and newsroom journalism seeking ratings.

Some of her most pugilistic pronouncements included verbal evisceration of NYC's Italian American Mayor, Bill de Blasio, who was married to a Black woman and had two Black children:

> Just cause you love Black pussy don't mean you love Black lives . . . cc @ BilldeBlasio.[67]

A range of statements from Erica Garner's personal blog and tweets drove media headlines and fueled tweets. New York City papers appeared to delight in her brash attacks on an increasingly unpopular mayor. For instance, a September 8, 2016 *New York Daily News* headline blared: "Eric Garner's daughter blasts Mayor de Blasio."[68] Inside the paper, the journalist wrote: "The daughter of Eric Garner blasted Mayor de Blasio Thursday for not releasing disciplinary records on the cop whose chokehold led to her father's death."[69] Garner and activists pleaded and petitioned that the conduct files of the primary

---

67. Erica Garner (@es_snipes), Twitter post, September 8, 2016, 4:32 p.m., https://twitter.com/es_snipes/status/773982350854062080?lang=en.

68. Denis Slattery, "Eric Garner's daughter blasts Mayor de Blasio: 'Just cause you love black p---y don't mean you love black lives,'" *New York Daily News*, September 8, 2016, https://www.nydailynews.com/new-york/manhattan/erica-garner-blasts-de-blasio-withholding-record-article-1.2784073.

69. Slattery, "Eric Garner's daughter blasts Mayor de Blasio."

NYPD officer who killed Eric Garner be opened for public scrutiny. As earlier noted, the CCRB, a city agency, appealed a judge's order to release Pantaleo's records and thus alienated activists and advocates for NYPD accountability. Mayor de Blasio and the NYPD claimed that New York State law 50-a prevented him from releasing disciplinary records (the law was repealed in 2020). Protections afforded to Pantaleo outraged police reformers and militant activists alike, and of course, the Garner family specifically.

A state law largely ignored over the last thirty years suddenly became a hot button. Governor Andrew Cuomo (a centrist Democrat), opposed to de Blasio (a more progressive Democrat), used the conflict to disparage the mayor. Governor Cuomo claimed that the "law never stopped the release of similar files in the past"[70] and that for "many years the NYPD disclosed the information."[71] Those assertions seemed disingenuous at best. Erica Garner tweeted a photo of the article, with text attacking the governor, the mayor, as well as the former First Lady Senator Hillary Clinton, then-frontrunner Democratic presidential candidate:

> Cuomo is a bitch! So is DeBlasio! They be pimpin' Black lives for votes too . . . JUST LIKE #HILLARY![72]

In Garner's view, and in the views of many who found the politicians reprehensible or prone to bad faith, elected politicians were co-conspirators in predatory policing. Another tweet flew at its target:

> Cuomo and De Blasio can only agree on one thing and that is covering up this modern-day lynching by their henchman![73]

Pinpointing the white mayor's Black son, Dante—signaling that any family could be fair game in public debate and conflict—Garner blasted:

---

70. Slattery, "Eric Garner's daughter blasts Mayor de Blasio."

71. Andrew Cuomo, quoted in Slattery, "Eric Garner's daughter blasts Mayor de Blasio."

72. Erica Garner (@es_snipes), Twitter post, September 8, 2016, 4:28 p.m., https://twitter.com/es_snipes/status/773981373589626881 (also quoted in Slattery, "Eric Garner's daughter blasts Mayor de Blasio").

73. Erica Garner (@es_snipes), Twitter post, September 8, 2016, 4:29 p.m., https://twitter.com/es_snipes/status/773981576187170816 (also quoted in Slattery, "Eric Garner's daughter blasts Mayor de Blasio").

*The thing that kills me is that DeBlasio is raising a Black man. . . . This
is the example. . . . My dad lays down and rolls over for white supremacy.*[74]

Despite her powerful activism and radical autonomy for social justice, Erica Garner's despair grew. She acknowledged that her various
choices or option to seek justice for her father had largely failed. She
found that she had "hit a dead end" and was experiencing collective
trauma as she met other families impacted and devastated by police
murders. She reflects: "Reality set in: I live within a system that regularly kills Black people. My will to fight started to fade."[75] Garner identifies "grief" as the primary culprit for what she considered to be her
fading agency. Families grappled with and at times felt defeated by
grief, but family members compulsively observed and replayed the
deaths of loved ones. For Erica Garner, the search for the meaning of
her father's murder could not find closure: "I'm constantly reading
articles and doing the research on my dad's case. But I'm not taking
care of me."[76]

Captive Maternals engaged in political confrontations suffer increased precarity and diminished health. Garner suffered from the
lack of material and emotional resources.[77] Eric Garner's death at the
hands of the NYPD was embedded in a history of police dishonoring
Black communities and families. In an interview where she discusses
her personal struggles, Erica Garner publicly shared that her three-
year-old niece "bashed a boy in the head with a book at school and said
that 'I'm angry the cops killed my grandfather. That's the reason why
I did it.'"[78]

---

74. Erica Garner (@es_snipes), Twitter, September 8, 2016, 4:30 p.m., https://twitter.com/
es_snipes/status/773981960993591296 (also quoted in Slattery, "Eric Garner's daughter
blasts Mayor de Blasio").
75. Erica Garner and Kemi Alabi, "Conflict can destroy movements. We need to fight the
system, not each other," *Guardian*, December 9, 2015, https://www.theguardian.com/com-
mentisfree/2015/dec/09/erica-garner-conflict-can-destroy-movements-fight-the-system.
76. Erica Garner, quoted in Amy Goodman and Denis Moynihan, "Erica Garner: Rest in
Peace . . . and Justice," *Democracy Now!*, January 4, 2018, https://www.democracynow.
org/2018/1/4/erica_garner_rest_in_peace_and.
77. Vivian Wang, "Erica Garner, Activist and Daughter of Eric Garner, Dies at 27," *New
York Times*, December 30, 2017, https://www.nytimes.com/2017/12/30/nyregion/erica-gar-
ner-dead.html.
78. Erica Garner, "This is Trauma: Erica Garner & Ramsey Orta on Coping with the Aftermath of a Police Killing, Pt. 2 (Web Exclusive, video), *Democracy Now!*, January 12, 2016,
https://www.democracynow.org/2016/1/12/this_is_trauma_erica_garner_ramsey.

SOLIDARITY WITH BALTIMORE FOR FREDDIE GRAY

Obama signed an executive order for the creation of the President's Task Force on 21st Century Policing on December 18, 2014, following the Ferguson, Missouri shooting and killing of eighteen-year-old unarmed Michael Brown by police officer Darren Wilson. Michael Brown's death occurred the same year as Eric Garner's, Tamir Rice's, and Walter Scott's murders.

On April 12, 2015, Baltimore police severed Freddie Gray's spine while he was in custody and shackled in their van during a "rough ride." Seven days later, on April 19, 2015, Gray died while in a coma. President Obama, the Commander-in-Chief, informed the public that he could not "federalize" police forces.[79] Nonetheless, reactionaries and white nationalists continued to post or state on their platforms that POTUS planned to federalize or place local police under his control. Media reports of Baltimore students rioting after school on Monday, April 27, 2015—the day of Freddie Gray's funeral, which also saw widespread riots across the city—failed to note what teachers, administrators, and students themselves witnessed: militarized riot police forcing students off buses, blocking subway travel, and refusing to let students leave Frederick Douglass High School for home.[80]

In May, a student's handwritten missive to the alternative press explained that when police commandeered their transportation, corralled, and intimidated them, students reasoned that rather than turn their anger on each other, they would turn it against the police. Just as with media narrative of the gang threat, media outlets uncritically accepted the predator-teen threat, increasing public sympathy for police. Governor Larry Hogan outlined the military campaign, with Baltimore divided into sectors cleared by police and secured by the National Guard. The mayor set a curfew, lifted only after police indictments.

Meanwhile, underreported by the press, gangs called truces as Black clergy and community leaders walked the streets with members of the Nation of Islam, serving as moving shields between rioters/rebels, police, and property. This apparent inversion of the 1971 Attica

79. Maya Rhodan, "President Obama Says There is 'No Excuse' for Violence in Baltimore," *Time*, April 28, 2015, https://time.com/3838611/president-obama-baltimore-riots-violence/.
80. James Fenton and Erica L. Green, "Baltimore Rioting Kicked Off with Rumors of 'Purge,'" *Baltimore Sun*, April 27, 2015, https://www.baltimoresun.com/news/crime/bs-md-ci-freddie-gray-violence-chronology-20150427-story.html.

rebellion—in which Black and Brown prisoners mistakenly believed that National Guard troops would not shoot through white prison guards used as shields—revealed these leaders' comprehension of the agency, grief, and rage (as well as venal opportunism) of their burning communities. Leaders maintained discipline by keeping everyone within the community, sharing criticisms of police violence and containment strategies. For his part, President Obama condemned Baltimore "thugs" and acknowledged his inability to control police, even as he called for a national movement addressing the needs of impoverished children.[81]

Erica Garner traveled to West Baltimore to attend Freddie Gray's funeral in 2015. She observed the uprisings with concern and encouragement for the protesters:

National guard been activated in Baltimore it only gets wors[e] from here.[82]

Why do police respond to anger over police violence with more police.[83]

Baltimore PD CAUGHT HIDING IN ALLEY BECAREFUL [sic]*!!!*[84]

A day later, on April 29, 2015, she was back in New York City, protesting with comrades in a Solidarity for Baltimore march in Union Square, where contingents also faced "[h]eavy police presence . . . helicopters and lots of people . . . barricades."[85] The NYPD eventually

---

81. President Obama states, "The overwhelming majority of the community in Baltimore I think have handled this appropriately, expressing real concern and outrage over the possibility that our laws were not applied evenly in the case of Mr. Gray, and that accountability needs to exist. And I think we have to give them credit. My understanding is, is you've got some of the same organizers now going back into these communities to try to clean up in the aftermath of a handful of criminals and thugs who tore up the place." See "Remarks by Barack Obama and Prime Minister Abe of Japan in Joint Press Conference," The White House Office of the Press Secretary, April 28, 2015, https://obamawhitehouse.archives.gov/the-press-office/2015/04/28/remarks-president-obama-and-prime-minister-abe-japan-joint-press-confere.

82. Erica Garner (@es_snipes), Twitter post, April 27, 2015, 6:24 p.m., https://twitter.com/es_snipes/status/592816551730008064.

83. Erica Garner (@es_snipes), Twitter post, April 27, 2015, 7:08 p.m., https://twitter.com/es_snipes/status/592827698042576896.

84. Erica Garner (@es_snipes), Twitter post, April 27, 2015, 7:30 p.m., https://twitter.com/es_snipes/status/592833222830067713.

85. Erica Garner (@es_snipes), Twitter post, April 29, 2015, 6:23 p.m., https://twitter.com/es_snipes/status/593541256845914112.

halted the peaceful march. Meanwhile, the National Guard presence was escalating in Baltimore. National media offered one-sided reportage of chaos and accounts of (non)protesters "looting" and inflicting violence on cops. It did not equally cover the violence of the National Guard against civilians or the historical violence of Baltimore police against civilians, as typified by Gray's death by severed spine while in police custody.

Newly appointed US Attorney General Loretta Lynch condemned protesters' violence against Baltimore police and property.[86] Validating what she described as "legitimate peaceful protesters," Lynch raised the possibility of a Department of Justice investigation into Freddie Gray's death, an offer that the city accepted the following week. But Lynch's predecessor, Eric Holder, Jr. rejected Baltimore Mayor Stephanie Rawlings-Blake and Police Commissioner Anthony Batts' calls for a federal investigation after *The Baltimore Sun* published an exposé on police brutality.[87] Instead, the Department of Justice settled on a collaborative review of the police department, in keeping with President Obama's Community Oriented Policing Services initiative. Even as police continued to violate Black communities, Attorney General Lynch instructed "the Baltimore community" to adhere to nonviolence. Police aggression was seen as necessary, protected by bureaucracy, unions, and laws such as Maryland's Law Enforcement Officers' Bill of Rights. The National Guard had terrorized school-aged Black children protesting in Baltimore. The president and attorney general referred to protesters, including children, writ large as "thugs." Later Obama and Lynch walked back the name-calling, castigation, and dismissal. Activists noted that before the mistrial was announced police showed up in force with riot gear to protect businesses. By December 2015, Garner's analyses had severed from liberal ideologies and the standard radical liberalism of well-funded BLM chapters.

Garner tweeted an image that squarely rejected the prioritization of private property in the wake of civilians murdered by police forces:

---

86. Loretta Lynch, "Statement by Attorney General Lynch on the Situation in Baltimore," US Department of Justice, April 27, 2015, https://www.justice.gov/opa/pr/statement-attorney-general-lynch-situation-baltimore.

87. Mark Puente, "Undue Force," *Baltimore Sun*, September 28, 2014, http://data.baltimoresun.com/news/police-settlements/.

I do not mourn broken windows. I mourn broken necks. #FreddieGray
FREDDIEGRAY.[88]

In response to this tweet, a (white, male-appearing) Twitter user responded with a screen shot and the message: "Hey @CNN, before you put @es-snipes back on TV, why don't you ask her to explain this picture she tweeted?" In a direct tweet to Garner, he writes: "Okay, but first let me say I am sorry for your loss and pray for your family," and then asks Garner, "But how do you mourn what's going on in Baltimore?" Erica Garner replied:

> *In my response my message is clear as day the answer to police brutality isn't bringing in more cops....*[89]
>> *would you cry over a broken window or would you more likely fix it....*[90]
>
> *but we do cry over our loved ones being killed by cops never did I once say they are justified for rioting or violence....*[91]
>> *how they control people who are supposed to be free when....*[92]
>
> *no one is hold [sic] these killer cops accountable....*[93]
>> *the time for change is now wished they did it differently but all i can say is i understand....*[94]
>> *violence is never the answer ... better jobs accountability being able to go to the store without being stopped by police....*[95]
>> *better schools better neighborhoods housing ... our youth are scared*

88. Bipartisan Report (@Bipartisanism), Twitter post, April 28, 2015, 12:51 a.m., https://twitter.com/bipartisanism/status/592914072955301888.
89. Erica Garner (@es_snipes), Twitter post, April 28, 2015, 4:01 a.m., https://twitter.com/es_snipes/status/592961813442101248.
90. Erica Garner (@es_snipes), Twitter post, April 28, 2015, 4:02 a.m., https://twitter.com/es_snipes/status/592961984674582528.
91. Erica Garner (@es_snipes), Twitter post, April 28, 2015, 4:03 a.m., https://twitter.com/es_snipes/status/592962325939892224.
92. Erica Garner (@es_snipes), Twitter post, April 28, 2015, 4:04 a.m., https://twitter.com/es_snipes/status/592962650046386176.
93. Erica Garner (@es_snipes), Twitter post, April 28, 2015, 4:07 a.m., https://twitter.com/es_snipes/status/592963252331622400.
94. Erica Garner (@es_snipes), Twitter post, April 28, 2015, 4:05 a.m., https://twitter.com/es_snipes/status/592962865172246528
95. Erica Garner (@es_snipes), Twitter post, April 28, 2015, 4:08 a.m., https://twitter.com/es_snipes/status/592963595102756866.

of becoming the next [victim] *of these systematic. . . .*[96]

killings no hope in the future fair opportunity how when the education systems put u in zoned schools and spend more. . . .[97]

money on special education than the talented and gifted programs and charter [p]*ublic schools. . . .*[98]

kids in the streets throwing rocks while officers have guns riot gear and tear gas for kids!!! My heart goes out. . . .[99]

#alllivesmatter #blacklivesmatter a building doesn't have more value over a human life you can rebuild you cant [sic] *bring. . . .*[100]

the dead back. . . .[101]

i wasted enough time answering ya questions have a good night n u figure out why they picked up rocks, not guns. . . .[102]

instead of writing me try writing someone who can actually change this without killing kids. . . .[103]

not one cop is dead but answer this . . . how many police killings have its [sic] *been in the last year alone.*[104]

The Twitter user appeared to be challenging Garner as a legitimate member of the liberal mainstream—or an extension of the liberal voice of BLM—roles that were foisted upon her after the CNN interview with Don Lemon, when she rose to national fame as a "daddy's girl" crying out for "peaceful protests" and downplaying white supremacy. But that interview was in 2014. A year later, Garner had dis-

96. Erica Garner (@es_snipes), Twitter post, April 28, 2015, 4:09 a.m., https://twitter.com/es_snipes/status/592963901140180992.

97. Erica Garner (@es_snipes), Twitter post, April 28, 2015, 4:11 a.m., https://twitter.com/es_snipes/status/592964379290787840.

98. Erica Garner (@es_snipes), Twitter post, April 28, 2015, 4:12 a.m., https://twitter.com/es_snipes/status/592964614515752960.

99. Erica Garner (@es_snipes), Twitter post, April 28, 2015, 4:13 a.m., https://twitter.com/es_snipes/status/592964904841273345.

100. Erica Garner (@es_snipes), Twitter post, April 28, 2015, 4:16 a.m., https://twitter.com/es_snipes/status/592965594871390208.

101. Erica Garner (@es_snipes), Twitter post, April 28, 2015, 4:16 a.m., https://twitter.com/es_snipes/status/592965640878759937.

102. Erica Garner (@es_snipes), Twitter post, April 28, 2015, 4:20 a.m., https://twitter.com/es_snipes/status/592966714045931520.

103. Erica Garner (@es_snipes), Twitter post, April 28, 2015, 4:23 a.m., https://twitter.com/es_snipes/status/592967358991474688.

104. Erica Garner (@es_snipes), Twitter post, April 28, 2015, 4:26 a.m., https://twitter.com/es_snipes/status/592968124611358720.

cerned the difference between politics that deliver and politics which were performative or rhetorical. The former would be punished by dominant interests and state players; the latter would be compensated by centrist-liberal nonprofits, politicians, and corporations seeking to burnish their images as caring entities.

Garner increasingly demanded material support for liberation struggles against predatory policing. Her Twitter responses highlight the lack of power that civilians wield: police "control people who are supposed to be free when"[105] "none . . . hold these killer cops accountable."[106] After organizing in multiple cities where police murdered Blacks with impunity, Erica Garner and other activists pushed past political protests into mass movements with the capacity to shut down cities and "business as usual."

WHITE ALLIES QUERY ERICA GARNER'S STATUS
AS A CAPTIVE MATERNAL

On February 8, 2020, a Canadian colleague, let's call them "T," sent me extensive email queries about identifying the Captive Maternal with Erica Garner's agency. Their queries included: "What Erica Garner 'does' for the theory of the Captive Maternal?" and "Does Garner exceed theorizing?" My responses attempt to "make sense" of Garner's activism as legible within the analytic of the Captive Maternal. The paradigm continues to mystify or alienate some. Addressing the queries of a white ally with more privilege than Garner or myself may or may not clarify the analyses.

As a Captive Maternal, Erica Garner mutated from victim of a personal and familial tragedy to a vanguard member of a political movement. Her political demands for adequate, rather than cosmetic remedies to quell state violence and terror, were fueled by personal grief over the loss of a loved one. Yet her caretaking expanded to demand accountability and safety for the public from state predation. Her politics originated with civil rights liberalism, but she went be-

---

105. Erica Garner (@es_snipes), Twitter post, April 28, 2015, 4:04 a.m., https://twitter.com/es_snipes/status/592962650046386176.
106. Erica Garner (@es_snipes), Twitter post, April 28, 2015, 4:07 a.m., https://twitter.com/es_snipes/status/592963252331622400.

yond the politics embraced by "Mothers of the Movement," parents of Black children, such as Trayvon Martin and Sandra Bland, slain by police forces and white vigilantes. Those mothers campaigned for 2016 presidential candidate Hillary Clinton who, as a state feminist, was/is pro-police forces and advocates for capitalism and imperialism. Erica Garner backed Clinton's opponent, democratic socialist Bernie Sanders.[107] The discernible growth in her political evolution went beyond electoral politics, and beyond liberal and state politics. Garner understood the importance of politics and of healing, care, and comfort. Conventional training and therapy seemed insufficient for her chosen task, and political performances appeared to be a distraction and deflection from state violence.

T's response to my sketch of the Captive Maternal as an imprint on Erica Garner was to question whether I had departed from the political norm: "The strategic guide to radical politics is a kind of incitement to organize differently." The often-received query about the Captive Maternal is about the relationship between the figure and organizing, and if the Captive Maternal as a concept is disruptive of necessary organizing. In fact, I believe the Captive Maternal has to be a lover as well as an analyst, strategist, organizer, and war resister. The Captive Maternal on the upper levels or registers of rebellion against state warfare will destabilize conventional politics and the (petit) bourgeois who refuse confrontation with state/police power, as well as the compradors, handlers as betrayers of freedom movements. The fierce Captive Maternals that I have met are skilled organizers and intellectuals who focus their care on nonelites, the oppressed, the "wretched of the earth." They remain difficult to brand. Still, one can identify them as rebels who are not being paid for staging protests or movements as "rebellions."

---

107. On a February 2020 podcast, Bernie Sanders' 2020 National Press Secretary Briahna Joy Gray analyzes the smear campaigns against the Sanders campaign by mainstream media that promoted the imago of the "vicious Bernie bros." Attacks on Sanders came from millionaire CNN commentator Chuck Todd, Secretary of State Madeline Albright, and feminist Gloria Steinem. Gray, a Black woman attacked by Black women liberals opposing Sanders primarying Clinton, joked about the hashtag "Trust Black Women," as she notes that she was not trusted by Black women politically aligned with former presidential female candidates Amy Klobuchar, Elizabeth Warren, Hillary Clinton. See Roqayah Chamseddine and Kumars Salehi, "Episode 161: Organizer in Chief," *Delete Your Account* (podcast), February 13, 2020, https://deleteyouraccount.libsyn.com/page/4/size/25.

Most people view themselves through their identity not their function outside the personal family or for-profit or nonprofit employment sector. Functioning to tackle empire, rather just talking about it, represents the latter stages of marronage and war resistance. We can demonstrate our personal morality by asking "how can I support this family victim of state violence?" When T asks "how can I support Erica Garner?" what comes to mind is to provide what she asked for: turnouts at demonstrations with principled politics that challenge the duopoly (The Garner Way Foundation is now run by Gwen Carr. Private donations are charity). The public payouts after police murder kin are usually culled from taxpayers, not the police unions that often defend officers charged with murders by progressive or impacted sectors of the public.

Charity, of course, does not stop the war, and being taxed to pay for domestic and foreign warfare drains the public coffers for health care, public schools, environmental restoration, clean water, affordable housing, etc. Charity or personal morality is not an ethical strategy to dismantle predatory policing. The state is unethical so it will not dismantle or derail predatory policing. Its laws and enforcers will destabilize or counter war resistance plans that have efficacy. They will counter war resistance through grants, buyouts, propaganda, sentimentalizing performances, hagiography, celebrity culture, academia, religion, and public grief and memorials. For example, less than a year after Eric Garner was killed by the NYPD in 2015, white supremacist, neo-Nazi Dylann Roof killed nine Black people and injured another at the Charleston, South Carolina Emanuel African Methodist Episcopal Church, after he joined their midday Bible study. President Barack Obama gave the eulogy of Emanuel AME Church's senior pastor, State Senator Clementa C. Pinckney. The President sang *Amazing Grace* at the funeral. Many, including POTUS, teared up at the emotionally rich service. Yet, in the following days, weeks, and year, Obama failed to mandate his administration to develop a war resistance plan for white nationalist terrorists (the January 6, 2021 capitol insurrection reveals how far into extremism—when abetted by a president and embedded in police and military forces—such terrorists will go). Support becomes "resistance" only when one/the collective moves past the stages of conflicted or celebratory caretaker (Roof is on death row which some view as a "win.").

As a white ally, T raises more queries: "Does Erica even want my support?" Of course, I cannot speak for Erica Garner. However, that seems somewhat odd, but probably a routine question posed to Black radicals resisting state violence. As a member of a "race" of people who for centuries were/are colonized, maimed, hunted, trafficked, exploited for labor, rape, and psychotic pleasures, my response is "Yes." Yet, I wrote back: "Do you plan to support a freedom movement or just the performance of one?" Garner, her communities, the nation, and international struggles, wanted and want help. Whether or not privileged classes or sectors provide aid, to what degree and with what strings attached if any, poses other queries for consideration. A lot of people never even bother to ask if solidarity is requested. Some or indifferent others are without dialogue, already in the protest, march, maroon camp, donating time, effort, funds. Some protest and are arrested. Others protest and are murdered by an eighteen-year-old, Kyle Rittenhouse, who—backed by white nationalist funders, President Trump, and police forces—walks after shooting three white males and killing two at a Black Lives Matter protest.

Before, alongside, and after Erica Garner, there are constant waves of struggle against predatory forces that humiliate, abuse, impoverish, imprison, and kill. Erica Garner and communities of marchers and protesters gave and received advice, motivation, strategies, and spirituality. All focused on and developed an appetite for rebellion and resistance to state violence. Hundreds and thousands marched and protested. She refused steerage into conventional politics or moneymaking organizations that monetized Black death—disproportionately meted out against poor and working-class people. Garner never became a movement millionaire. Erica Garner's tweets—political critiques and some ribald condemnations of politicians—called for mobilization and marronage. Her calls to show up and resist did not follow a script or prescription written by a presidential task force or a large nonprofit or academic conference.

CONCLUSION

Erica Garner's language and critiques were not ambiguous. She rejected conventional politics as a zone of betrayal, distraction, and cooptation that worked to siphon off the energies of community-based movements serving the impoverished and working classes. Erica Garner's caretaking and activism marked her as a Captive Maternal who navigated multiple stages of engagement: family care, protest, movement organizing, marronage with small cadres, and war resistance. Through her constant battles with the NYPD, the city, state, and federal leadership and bureaucracies, she built movements to honor her father and others slain by predatory policing. That stage morphed into war resistance as Erica Garner regularly confronted the police during protests to alert the public about the necessity of controlling their predatory violence. Many remain fearful of waging the battles in which she participated, in order to quell police and state violence. The catalyst that brought her into fierce political battles for nearly four years was the police execution of her father, Eric Garner, on Bay Street, Staten Island. Trauma led to transformation best described by the prophetic Howard Thurman's lessons from his mother: faith and awareness can overcome fear and "transform it into power to strive, to achieve, and not to yield."

CHAPTER 6

CAMPAIGNING FOR BERNIE AND AGAINST THE DNC

TOWN HALL: CONFRONTING CO-OPTATION NATION

In July of 2016, Bernie Sanders challenged Hillary Clinton for the Democratic Party nomination. Meanwhile, Donald Trump was securing the Republican nomination as a white nationalist cheering police violence. Two years after her father's death, ABC network producers invited Erica Garner to participate in President Obama's televised town hall. The July 2016 program was to showcase both the tragedy and victimization of Black families and communities as well as the merits of US policing. Her involvement was meant to present her quiet support for a conciliatory view of police power and a narrative of Black acquiescence to predatory policing and presidential powers as a virtue.

Toward the end of the forum, the host directs President Obama and the audience to the testimony of a Black mother from Dallas, Shetamia Taylor (though she was unnamed in the broadcast), who had been attending a protest with her two sons when she was shot in the leg and "rescued" by police. The Black mother and her young son close the town hall with a prime-time rebuttal to the politics of refusal that Garner embraced. They offer to the public a role reversal of Erica and Eric Garner, as daughter and father. Her eldest son, a Black middle-schooler named Jermar, tells Obama, and the national audience, that he aspires to *become* a policeman in order to "make the world a better place," even though "some police officers make mistakes." Eclipsing the sharp critiques of Erica Garner, Jermar becomes the stand-in or model for Black youth leadership. The town hall's selection and sequence of speakers creates a "choreography" of narratives that gradually align with, and recenter US state, police, and presidential power:

> **ABC town hall host:** And here's that mother, and what she told the nation.

> **Shetamia:** [Crying with fear and gratitude] I said, yes sir, I'm hit in my leg and that officer jumped on top of me and covered me and my son and they just . . . they stayed there with us, and I saw another officer [crying] saw another officer get shot . . . .

> **ABC town hall host:** Jermar, I would just ask that you stand up for a moment. If you wouldn't mind, would you just share with the President your plans now, given what's happened these last few days.

> **Jermar:** I wanted [sic] to be a police officer when I get older, and that, the reason I want to be a police officer is that I want to try to make this world a better place as much as I can. . . . I want to tell kids and adults that not all police officers are bad. Some police officers make mistakes. And that's just what I want to tell people.[1]

Erica Garner stormed out of the town hall in protest, claiming that she was manipulated into attending the nationally televised event, where she was promised and then denied the chance to speak, but not before interrupting the taping, and confronting Obama directly in a brief dialogue just offstage. Garner later recounted: "I had to stage a walkout by myself." She added: "And I went out there and I had to yell, scream, and eventually I was able to speak to the President. It's a shame as Black people that we have to scream, yell, and become belligerent to have our voices heard."[2]

The exchange was recorded, though most of the dialogue has been lost or shielded from the public. Garner stands angled toward Obama, as his security service detail looms behind her. Erica Garner's protest was omitted from the ABC video of the town hall. Video of her

---

1. "President Obama and the People Town Hall: A National Conversation," *ABC News*, July 15, 2016, https://www.youtube.com/watch?v=sNZvIgAoDIc.

2. Erica Garner, video featured in Lilly Workneh, "Eric Garner's Daughter Says ABC News Silenced Her During Race Symposium with Obama," July 14, 2016, *HuffPost*, https://www.huffpost.com/entry/erica-garner-abc-obama_n_57881eee0e4b03fc3ee5031e9.

interrupting the program appears to have been edited out and erased from the archive. I remember a clip which briefly appeared, of Garner with President Obama and Chief of Staff Valerie Jarrett. Obama first chides Garner for storming out, catches himself and then states that he is sorry for the loss of her father as he shakes her hand. POTUS then returns to his initial mandate for public civility and cautionary admonishment to Erica Garner: rebellion and rudeness are not how one conducts proactive politics in this democracy.

In the official version that appears in print text, President Obama was unaware of ABC's agreement to allow Garner to ask questions during the session,[3] but offers reassurances and condolences:

> But I promise you, people are hearing it, and I wouldn't be spending all this time here if I wasn't concerned about it. But I have to make sure that we don't get in a situation in which there's a perception that in any way these [NYPD] guys' investigations are being influenced. But I just want to say that respectfully, but I am sorry for your loss and I. . . .[4]

Erica Garner interrupts softly to ask the President about the federal 1033 Program that provides military weapons to local police departments. She says, "I do have one question. What are you going to do about the 1033 Program?" President Obama responds, "Well, we already—well, we have already implemented it [inaudible]. We already reformed it, and we can provide you information about that, okay?"[5] Obama is referencing an announcement he made in May 2016 to restrict police from obtaining certain military equipment.

The details are unclear. However, the spin control that followed Erica Garner's indignation about how a presidential town hall, which was supposed to be about justice, became reconciliation without justice, was clear in its political implications. Erica Garner's protest was omitted from the ABC video of the town hall. Video of her interrupt-

---

3. "Harris said Obama then left the meeting, but his senior adviser, Valerie Jarrett, continued speaking with Garner. Jarrett said Obama didn't know about ABC's agreement to allow Garner to ask her questions during the session, according to Harris," Workneh, "Eric Garner's Daughter Says ABC News Silenced Her."

4. Barack Obama, video in Workneh, "Eric Garner's Daughter Says ABC News Silenced Her."

5. Erica Garner and Barack Obama, video in Workneh, "Eric Garner's Daughter Says ABC News Silenced Her."

ing the taping appears to have been edited out and erased from the archive.

After the town hall event, the spontaneous encounter between recordings of Erica Garner and Barack Obama, which was also recorded by a number of people including those who aligned with or had befriended Erica Garner, in the hall behind the stage appeared online.[6] Reporting on the interaction between Obama and Garner, *Essence* noted:

> Erica did get the chance to speak with President Obama briefly backstage after voicing her displeasure with the way things were handled, but she maintains her belief that she was used by ABC to exploit Black pain and grief. In a video provided exclusively to *Huffington Post*, President Obama gave a pointed response to Erica's question about the federal investigation into her father's death and what's being done on the legislative end to improve policing policies . . . . Erica also shared that she initially had plans to stay home and prepare for the upcoming anniversary of her father's death on Sunday, but rearranged her plans to attend the town hall at ABC's request. 'Not once did they mention Eric Garner or acknowledge the family,' she said. 'I say we rise up and say enough is enough.'[7]

Erica Garner's Instagram response details her confrontation with President Obama. The full video of Obama and Garner, which was provided exclusively to *Huffington Post,* was not linked to the article. The conversation between POTUS and the rebel is taken from a video by Garner's political ally and advisor Reggie Harris, who made it available "exclusively" for view, but not publication, to *Huffington Post.*[8]

---

6. A recorded excerpt of the Garner-Obama encounter outside of the town hall event is linked to the pinned tweet of Erica Garner's friend and advisor Blackstar Flower, who also managed Erica Garner's Twitter account. See video in Workneh, "Eric Garner's Daughter Says ABC News Silenced Her."

7. Rachaell Davis, "Eric Garner's Daughter Says ABC News Silenced Her at President Obama's Televised Town Hall Meeting," *Essence*, October 27, 2020, https://www.essence.com/news/eric-garners-daughter-abc-news-silenced-her-town-hall/.

8. The author recalls a brief clip taken down from the internet in which Obama gently chastises Erica Garner about her demeanor before offering her condolences for her father's death. *Huffington Post* released an edited video of the encounter, without Obama's brief chastisement about Erica Garner needing to use "appropriate" political tactics, with the language of "that's just not how things are done."

The article provides an excerpt of their interaction, in which Garner informs *Huffington Post*: "ABC is using Black lives as a rating and to get paid. They guaranteed me that I would be asking the president direct questions about what's going on. I was lied to." According to Harris, the head of Disney, ABC's parent company, considered Garner "a major political figure" and specifically asked for her to attend the town hall. While most video records of Erica Garner's interaction with Obama seem to have disappeared from the Internet, her 2016 Instagram video remains.[9]

Shouting, Garner exposed the ploy that became normative: bait by saying she could *raise a policy question* for substantive discussion only to reduce her to a mute figure of Black abjection in a photo op. Loudly berating the gathering while being whisked away through the hallways, Garner boldly evidenced her sadness, sense of betrayal, and outrage. Being silenced and manipulated by establishment leaders of the Democratic Party was the emotional condition that Garner faced in her advocacy. What the town hall debacle reveals is an important transformation in the Captive Maternal's life. Erica Garner's wavering uncertainty back in her 2014 interview with Don Lemon interview had now solidified into fierce advocacy:

> So, I'm back at the train station, and y'all know I had to turn the fuck up right, on ABC. These motherfuckers want to use Black lives and railroad and lie and tell me that I will be able to speak with the President today, and that was bullshit. I told them, I wouldn't be coming on that show if I wouldn't be able to ask my question to the President. I had to turn the fuck up and curse them motherfuckers out.
>
> I walked out in the middle of taping, had everyone going crazy, screaming out. And I got to speak with the President. It's a shame that Black people have to go out and speak [loud], and yell, just to get their voices heard. All I wanted to know from the President was why was it taking so long in my dad's case, and what're you going to do about the militarized police department. This is a shame. ABC, fuck you.

---

9. See Erica Garner (@miss_garner2U), Instagram post, July 14, 2016, https://www.instagram.com/p/BH235Cehj-8/?utm_source=ig_embed&utm_campaign=embed_video_watch_again. The Instagram video does not show the interaction with President Obama.

"ABC, fuck you" brings clarity and relief to those who might have otherwise thought their expletives towards mainstream media and mainstream progressives were an infraction or an incivility toward the "good people who care." With growing frustration, Erica Garner met with and petitioned politicians to investigate the NYPD. Her rhetorical warfare with Mayor Bill de Blasio included verbal vulgarity. She disparaged Governor Andrew Cuomo. She yelled protests at President Obama's televised town hall on race and policing.

The archived CNN piece on the town hall mostly functioned as containment and clean-up on behalf of the conglomerate and administration.[10] Erica Garner's grief and fury were apparent. On tape, she could be heard exiting the town hall, yelling: "I was railroaded! I was railroaded by ABC on the two-year anniversary of my father's death!" Television pool tape recorded her as saying: "They liars. They got us all the way down here." According to *Essence*, BLM cofounder Patrisse Cullors agreed with Erica Garner and echoed Erica's sentiments, describing the town hall as "one of the worst experiences you could've put families [of police brutality victims] through. . . . It was all about apologizing about the cops, it was just a mess. . . . It felt like a lovefest for cops. The entire show was about respectability politics. It was so staged and so curated."[11]

The media clean-up or spin worked to mute her outrage and contain its impact on the public. *ABC News* issued a statement that said President Obama spoke with Garner following the event and that the news agency "took an extra thirty minutes to get to as many people as we could during the town hall." The network's statement also reiterated that "the President spoke to several people after the event ended, including at length with Erica Garner." White House Press Secretary Josh Earnest released a statement confirming that the President spoke with Garner. "After the ABC-hosted town hall that was taped this afternoon, the President had a brief opportunity to visit with Erica Garner who was upset that she didn't get called on to ask a question." Sugges-

10. Rachaell Davis, "Eric Garner's Daughter Says ABC News Silenced Her at President Obama's Televised Town Hall Meeting," *Essence*, October 27, 2020, https://www.essence.com/news/eric-garners-daughter-abc-news-silenced-her-town-hall/.
11. Davis, "Eric Garner's Daughter Says ABC News Silenced Her."

tively, the press was informed that Erica Garner maintained that she had been "railroaded" by *ABC News*.[12]

GUERRILLA INTELLECTUAL CAMPAIGN STRATEGIST

Ruptures in conventional politics appeared early in 2016 when Erica Garner conceived a striking, unsolicited campaign ad for Senator Bernie Sanders' primary campaign against Hillary Clinton, entitled *It's Not Over*. Focusing on police violence and murder of Black people, the campaign ad addressed a range, and reached a register rarely seen in politicking for electoral victories, particularly the presidency of the United States. Garner's political imagination in *It's Not Over* helped propel me to attend campaign meetings and rallies, volunteer, and donate to the Sanders campaign. I even sat in crowded church pews or performance halls to hear Sanders speak. But more importantly, it had helped motivate me to watch and hear from those who were mobilized by shared beliefs in justice and containment of the "1 percent" and predatory policing.

As Erica Garner campaigned for democratic socialist Bernie Sanders in 2016, "realistic" liberals, progressives, radicals, prominent Black figures, masculinists, and feminists overtly or covertly campaigned for Barack Obama's heir apparent Hillary Clinton. In 2020, they would mobilize for Obama's Vice President Joe Biden, and Biden's VP Kamala Harris. The structure of US democracy is bent as unrepresentative. Senator Biden's state of Delaware, with a population of two million, is allotted two seats in the Senate. Senator Harris' state of California, with a population of twenty million, is allotted two seats in the Senate. Harris was a prosecutor prior to being elected a senator. She harassed and persecuted working-class and poor parents who could not successfully force their children to attend schools that alienated or harmed them. Once children were designated "truants," their parents were liable for fees, child removal through foster care, or incarceration.

Erica Garner's favorable visibility in liberal politics shrank as she became more politically combative and helped Sanders in his run

---

12. Dylan Byers, "Eric Garner's daughter says she was 'railroaded' by ABC," *CNN Business*, July 14, 2016, https://money.cnn.com/2016/07/14/media/erica-garner-abc-townhall/.

against Hillary Clinton. Her politics were not assimilable to mainstream tastes and she consistently challenged the authority of all executive branches at the national, state, and city levels. Her targets included President Obama, New York Governor Andrew Cuomo, and New York City Mayor Bill de Blasio—all of whom she condemned with vulgarities for caring too little about Black people. After Erica Garner's death, journalist Ben Norton wrote: "New York City Mayor de Blasio was one of the most shameless figures trying to co-opt Erica Garner's memory—even though Erica had relentlessly criticized de Blasio and the impunity he has guaranteed for police who kill Black people."[13]

A political "wild card"—as were the Panthers' social programs, armed self-defense, and militarism—Garner's street-based leadership was often deemed too loud, unruly, and impractical for mainstream abolitionism. A rebel, Garner appeared sporadically on varied platforms, largely using them to denounce the prevalence of conventional politics and coalitions in abolitionist movements. Garner avidly turned her ire on the Democratic Party and bluntly criticized powerful politicians. She repeatedly mourned, criticized, and raged against the NYPD homicides, and the city failing to hold police accountable. At every level of executive power—presidential, gubernatorial, and mayoral, there were betrayals.

Garner's radicalism organically differentiated itself from liberalism, and managerial, or advocacy democracy. Garner's personal loss of her father led her to militancy that linked Black victimization with Black rebellion and street protests. Her militancy was an expression of her community, her cadre, and her grief. Months after her father's death, without funding or platforms, Garner gained media attention by staging demonstrations at the exact site where Pantaleo killed her dad. There were no platforms, networks—other than street and underground—to leverage her critique of the NYPD as an organized "gang" of "killer cops." So, she used her body in die-ins with the chant "I Can't Breathe!" at the site where her father had been killed. Garner sought the support of Al Sharpton, whose National Action Network (NAN) brought three busloads of protestors to Staten Island. Conflicts with

---

13. Ben Norton, "Erica Garner was a revolutionary. Don't let neoliberal Democrats whitewash and exploit her," December 30, 2017, https://bennorton.com/erica-garner-revolutionary-neo-liberal-democrats-whitewash/.

NAN and other organizations existed, yet Garner continued to organize, and the splinter groups NYC Shut It Down and Millions March emerged. Negative or conservative press featured Garner criticizing Sharpton, yet the street protests grew. Garner confronted elected officials and filed a Freedom of Information Law (FOIL) request for civilian complaints against Pantaleo (the NYPD and the mayor blocked the release of those civilian review files).

Erica Garner's political rebellion against police violence and government culpability was gritty, on the asphalt, and loving as in *Agape*, imbuing her with a political will that could drive one to the brink. From her New York City Housing Authority (NYCHA) apartment, Ms. Garner, a mother and bereaved daughter, wielded authority and worked as a tactician and strategist against the wealthiest and most powerful police force in the United States. Without glamor, political prestige, or celebrity, she came of political age in the years marked by the rise of the Black Lives Matter movement—what Mellon Foundation CEO Elizabeth Alexander called in her April 2022 New York Public Library talk the "Trayvon Generation." That era yielded a model for challenging liberal activists whose tepid politics were fastened to, and courted by, capitalist interests.

In a 2015 *Guardian* piece, four months after her father's murder, and two years before her own premature death, Garner noted the warping effect of advocacy democracy fueled by philanthropist money and the cultivation of a managerial class. Speaking in relation to her own experience organizing, she declared:

> Conflict can destroy movements. The need for funding turns allies into competitors scrambling for the spotlight. Media-ordained spokespeople co-opt the work of grassroots leaders. From tactical differences to infiltrator sabotage, internal struggles plague social change work—present movements against police brutality included. But for months after my father's homicide, I didn't quite feel part of a movement at all. My family and a few locals rallied in Staten Island every Tuesday and Thursday; for hours, we would protest as passersby went on with their lives like they didn't even see us standing there.[14]

---

14. Erica Garner and Kemi Alabi, "Conflict can destroy movements. We need to fight the system, not each other," *Guardian*, December 9, 2015, https://www.theguardian.com/com

Buttressed by the exorbitant capital circulating in what some have dubbed the nonprofit industrial complex, these activists made an effigy of radical politics, and exploited political organizing to launch lucrative careers, acquire agents, sign book deals, pontificate on panels, win grants and funding, and enshrine themselves firmly, and ineradicably, in the capitalist class they sometimes, conveniently, claim to oppose. Samaria Rice, the mother of Tamir Rice, referred to liberal activists profiting off police killing Black people as "hustling Black death."[15] Markedly different from such activists, Erica Garner did not profit in her battles against the NYPD.

Unlike those who position liberalism as an extension of radical, working-class struggle, Garner's political critiques were pointed and clear. Her callouts to politicians and political organizations that betrayed struggling Black communities were uncivil for their antiradical postures. "Rudeness" was a jarring contrast to abolitionist speech emanating from the academy and well-funded nonprofits. Garner was channeling the discourse and tactics of the lumpen proletariat about which Marx wrote, at times dismissively. Ideologies deemed too radical by the mainstream can be popularized if the "rabble" is persuasive, persistent, and material reality is analyzed without filters. Speaking for the dispossessed and violated, Erica Garner became a media "magnet," while loudly defending her family and her father's memory.

"IT'S NOT OVER"

Garner had on occasion entertained the idea of running for office, tweeting: "If I run . . . [it's] because the #democrats there have failed us."[16] Erica Garner briefly contemplated a run for Congress against Daniel Donovan, in Staten Island's 11th district. Donovan was a former district attorney. He was appointed by Governor Cuomo to convene the grand jury for the Eric Garner homicide. That grand jury sealed all testimony and refused to indict Daniel Pantaleo for the July 2014 death of Eric Garner. For Erica Garner, Donovan's pro-cop stance used

mentisfree/2015/dec/09/erica-garner-conflict-can-destroy-movements-fight-the-system.

15. Samaria Rice, quoted in Perry, "Stop Hustling Black Death."

16. Erica Garner (@es_snipes), Twitter post, December 31, 2015, 11:46 a.m., https://twitter.com/es_snipes/status/682603864034570241.

her father's death to buttress his political career. Garner considered running against Donovan in the 11th district but changed her mind: "I think what would be best is if I organize the people in Staten Island to vote and be involved in the voting process."

Donovan and the grand jury's refusal to indict Pantaleo might have increased Garner's incentive to support Senator Bernie Sanders. Yet, she had already made a character assessment of the Vermonter (and former Brooklynite) in terms of his character. First Erica Garner researched Sanders' political stances, then she contacted him to offer her services to his campaign. Garner succinctly states in the interview why Sanders, and not Clinton, Obama's pick, should lead the Democratic Party: "I felt compelled after [seeing] his history with civil rights. He cares. He's zero tolerance on police brutality . . . he's a spiritual person and he gets it.[17] The journalist who is near Garner, amused, writes: "So she did what any millennial would do: she tweeted at him. That tweet led to some calls, and ultimately to Garner joining Bernie Sanders on the campaign trail."[18] Campaigning for Sanders outside of New York, Garner introduced him at his February 16, 2016 rally at the University of South Carolina (USC). There, when she reached out to shake the senator's hand, he hugged her instead. Both Bernie and Jane Sanders showed interest in the Garner family as more than a political endorsement. Of the USC event, Erica Garner observed: "He stopped and spoke with my daughter, and his wife thanked me . . . and told me to keep up the fight."[19]

The "wrenching endorsement video for Sanders . . . viewed more than 750,000 times" was also one of the most striking and novel political ads in presidential politics (as discussed shortly).[20] Front-runner Hillary Clinton, her husband former president Bill Clinton, President Obama, and the DNC were surprised that Sanders could successfully primary Clinton and distance her (more accurately, her *rhetoric*) from billionaire donors. Initially, Sanders was considered laughable because the DNC had large donors, loyalists, professional politicians, and people on payroll. Young voters and people who did not generally

17. Chaédria LaBouvier, "Police Brutality, Bernie, and Me: Erica Garner Tells Her Story," *Elle*, March 21, 2016, https://www.elle.com/culture/career-politics/a35000/erica-garner-profile/.
18. LaBouvier, "Police Brutality, Bernie, and Me."
19. LaBouvier, "Police Brutality, Bernie, and Me."
20. LaBouvier, "Police Brutality, Bernie, and Me."

vote, who wanted structural changes in the democracy, gravitated toward the Sanders campaign. It vociferously protested billionaire and
corporate control over public finance and government abetting corporate interest through theft of decent wages, and absence of universal
healthcare, social infrastructure, and resources for the poor, working
and middle classes. When Sanders accepted the support of Erica Garner, police predation became a central tenet of Bernie's presidential
campaign. Working with Sanders organizers, Garner was trained in
canvassing, speaking at town halls, participating in phone banks,
holding one-on-one conversations within the community, and giving
media interviews.

Garner pitched the concept of an ad to the Sanders campaign that
would directly confront racist police violence. Garner conceived, directed, and narrated "It's Not Over," which pundits and activists described
as the most compelling campaign ad in 2016. In a 2016 *National Public Radio* interview, Garner explained her support for Sanders: "He's
been, basically, a protester his whole career. He's not scared to go up
against the systematic racism that exists in America today."[21] Garner's
powerful campaign video for Bernie Sanders—a democratic socialist
who had argued in 2012 that Obama should be "primaried" to push
him toward progressive reforms—was a key rupture and offered an
alternative to conventional democratic candidates. Garner's social media comments before and after the 2016 election made it clear to the
public, however, that both parties had failed.

After the 2016 presidential victory, Garner was dismissive of the
DNC as "high net worth democrats [who] deconstruct the election . . .
they are no allies of mine."[22] She asserted that Blacks were neither true
Democrats nor Republicans: "WE are Black in America which means
we will NEVER be American. Cant u tell 300 yrs later?"[23] During the
Democratic primary elections, her critique of capitalism was front
and center: "when i think about capitalism i think about slavery, share
cropping, bank scandal wall street donors . . . #HillaryClinton's peo-

21. "Daughter Of Late Eric Garner Endorses Bernie Sanders," NPR Weekend Edition with
Rachel Martin, February 14, 2016, https://www.npr.org/2016/02/14/466720663/daugh-
ter-of-late-eric-garner-endorses-bernie-sanders.
22. Erica Garner (@es_snipes), Twitter post, November 22, 2016, 10:03 a.m., https://twitter.
com/es_snipes/status/801078657422794753.
23. Erica Garner (@es_snipes), Twitter post, February 6, 2017, 10:43 a.m., https://twitter.
com/es_snipes/status/828630150698786816.

ple."[24] Pointing to the communal care or Captive Maternal aspects of the Panthers, she tweeted: "The Panthers were a threat because they had the largest 'school lunch' program in the nation."[25] The fact that Panthers were uniformly depicted as terrorists—even those framed or acting in self-defense—was included in Garner's analysis: "#Hillary on the death penalty—must be reserved for terrorists . . . remember they called the Panthers enemies of the state #DemDebate."[26] Unruly hope and despair were seen as liabilities by those who could adjust to unspoken but established guidelines for acceptable protest. Even the most prominent Black mothers who had lost children to police or vigilante violence deflected their rage away from Democratic officials who did not deliver tangible gains against police violence.

When activists took over the Seattle stage at a campaign rally in August 2015, they derailed presidential candidate Bernie Sanders' plan to speak. Sanders relinquished the stage and left the event without addressing the crowd (much to the ire of some of his white supporters).[27] Yet, Erica Garner approved of the intervention and disruption: "We got to hold our elected officials accountable. If he's not going to talk about our issues, he shouldn't talk at all."[28] Yet, Erica Garner would later create one of the most striking political campaign ads in a presidential race for Senator Sanders. By the time Erica Garner had endorsed Sanders with the ad "It's Not Over," the campaign had "evolved" enough to make him worthy of Garner's endorsement and the striking political ad she created. Former Hollywood producer Harvey Weinstein offered to counter Erica Garner's "It's Not Over" for the Clinton campaign— the Clinton campaign declined the offer.[29]

24. Erica Garner (@es_snipes), Twitter post, October 13, 2015, 9:07 p.m., https://twitter.com/es_snipes/status/654101076069584896.

25. Erica Garner (@es_snipes), Twitter post, December 12, 2017, 10:12 p.m., https://twitter.com/es_snipes/status/937882336649023488.

26. Erica Garner (@es_snipes), Twitter post, February 4, 2016, 10:41 p.m., https://twitter.com/es_snipes/status/695452100508037120.

27. Tanya Basu, "Black Lives Matter Activists Disrupt Bernie Sanders Speech," *Time Magazine*, August 9, 2015, https://time.com/3989917/black-lives-matter-protest-bernie-sanders-seattle/.

28. Bob D'Angelo, "Erica Garner Rips Clinton Campaign for Emails about Her Father's Death," *Dayton Daily News*, October 29, 2016, https://www.daytondailynews.com/news/national/erica-garner-rips-clinton-campaign-for-emails-about-her-father-death/AvEp67c3CcN-sQMjL5KxtSN/."

29. Goodman and Moynihan, "Erica Garner: Rest in Peace . . . and Justice."

In "It's Not Over," Erica Garner refers to Martin Luther King, Jr. and Rosa Parks. Both King and Parks were shunned by petit-bourgeois Blacks and white philanthropic foundations when they found them becoming too radical. In "It's Not Over," Erica Garner tells her seven-year-old daughter that "Mommy is an activist." The type of activist she refers to is the radical who challenges racism, capitalism, and officialdom with condemnation and curses, not petitions and pleas. As an abolitionist shaped by new bones and Captive Maternals, Erica Garner never steered her agency into compromised zones.

The impressive political advertisement conceived and designed by Erica Garner for the 2016 Bernie Sanders presidential campaign was an unusual sensation at the start of a contentious presidential primary season. Less than five minutes long, its brilliant political narrative is undergirded with fierce emotional intelligence. The ad went viral and was covered by mainstream media outlets such as *The New York Times* and *The Washington Post*, even though mainstream media rejected Sanders' candidacy and his denunciations of the "1 percent" or "billionaire class." The ad—which remains a catalyst for countless tributes to Erica Garner, reflections on antiracist democratic socialism, and the assertion of political rights not to be terrorized by anti-Blackness and police forces—reflects Erica Garner's political contributions, activism, and caretaking.[30]

Donald Trump, meanwhile, built his electoral base with reactionary "law and order," pro-police, anti-BLM rhetoric, and funding. Movement leaders became surrogates for the standard bearers of the Democratic Party, deflecting critiques of Hillary's abysmal track record on race and policing. All became political surrogates for the DNC and Hillary Clinton's 2016 presidential campaign; they also collectively garnered millions of dollars from (non)profit corporate donors. When Garner endorsed Sanders for president in 2016, she contributed to the insurgent's challenge against a DNC led by Obama and Hillary and Bill Clinton.

In the campaign ad, Sanders appears at the very end. In a rousing campaign speech, he asserts that "when a police officer breaks the law" by killing an unarmed Black person, then "that officer must be

---

30. Erica Garner (dir.), "It's Not Over" [03:56 campaign ad for Bernie Sanders], February 11, 2016, https://www.youtube.com/watch?v=Syln8IkOIqc.

held accountable."[31] Sanders' remedy to police violence was the boldest among all presidential candidates in the major parties. In the video, Garner narrates her journey into activism after police executed her father. She addresses both the camera and her young daughter, Alyssa. Garner talks with her daughter about Black lives and struggles, walks her daughter to elementary school, and takes to the streets to join mass protests. She depicts Captive Maternal functions of nurturing and stabilizing family and of sharing life, love, and struggles. For instance, when Garner tells her young daughter about civil rights ancestor Rosa Parks, she introduces the child to her inheritance: "This is what Mommy is. I'm an activist."[32] Protest highlighted what was stolen from the Garner family—and what the family would wrestle back: dignity, commitment to reconstitution, family, demands for justice, and that police be held accountable for their crimes. In October 2016, media reported that DC Leaks released hacked emails revealing that Hollywood mogul Harvey Weinstein (convicted in 2020 for rape) had approached Clinton campaign manager Robby Mook, urging him to focus on the Sandy Hook school shooting and Sanders' stance on gun rights, in order to counter the impact of Garner's ad. Mook responded with enthusiasm.[33]

Erica Garner's abolitionism was distinct and, for some, threatening. She crafted her own image and advocacy, without establishment mentorship or management. Her contributions were singular. Garner's confrontational street theater, especially die-ins on city streets that blocked traffic, rattled and infuriated the NYPD. She criticized the Democratic Party as hypocritical in its concern for Black well-being in the face of constant racism, violent policing, and poverty. Combative with police officials, rank-and-file officers, and Democratic Party officials who offered condolences, but few, if any, effective policies for redress. Garner's truth-telling was rejected by Democratic politicians and pundits who resented radicals who would not stay within the DNC "big tent." Yet she stabilized her capacity for criticism by focusing on the needs of her family and communities: "Even with my own heart-

31. Garner, "It's Not Over."
32. Garner, "It's Not Over."
33. Zaid Jilani, "Harvey Weinstein urged Clinton campaign to silence Sanders's Black Lives Matter Message," *Intercept*, October 7, 2016, https://theintercept.com/2016/10/07/harvey-weinstein-urged-clinton-campaign-to-silence-sanderss-black-lives-matter-message/.

break, when I demand justice, it's never just for Eric Garner. It's for my daughter; it's for the next generation of African Americans."[34] With the function of a Captive Maternal; that is, "Mommy is an activist" means that the mother enacts practices that do not just change society or social order, but the world.

Garner's ire and despair over the Democratic Party increased after Trump's victory. "Who is organizing to put these corporate democrats the fuck up out of your community?"[35] For Garner, the Democrats failed to win the presidency because they had failed to enforce ethical policing in Black and Brown communities: "My dad was killed under democrats and had democrats in a liberal city cover it up."[36] Disparaging the Democratic Party and the Congressional Black Caucus in tweets, Garner evokes the unethical policing practices used against the BPP as highly relevant: "i wonder sometimes are we setting ourselves up to be stamped out like the panthers."[37] Given how a segment of white nationalists and police forces (represented at the January 6, 2021 insurrection at the US Capitol) have expanded their aggression we might wish to reflect on how Trump's supporters rose up as anti-BLM, although the politics of BLM were varied and not always consistent with the needs of the mass and the poor.

BLACK WOMEN SPLINTER IN THE 2016 PRESIDENTIAL ELECTION

An iconic abolitionist admonished Black progressives and radicals to vote for "her"—Hillary Clinton—in September 2016 while Erica Garner was campaigning for Hillary Clinton's antithesis, DSA's choice Bernie Sanders, a democratic socialist. During the Cold War, Angela Davis had run in a third party twice, as a CPUSA vice presidential candidate with Gus Hall. Davis' policies aligned with the CPUSA un-

34. Erica Garner, "Black lives like my father's should matter. That's why I'm endorsing Bernie Sanders," *Washington Post*, January 29, 2016, https://www.washingtonpost.com/posteverything/wp/2016/01/29/black-lives-like-my-fathers-should-matter-in-america-thats-why-im-endorsing-bernie-sanders/.
35. Erica Garner (@es_snipes), Twitter post, February 6, 2017, 1:29 p.m., https://twitter.com/es_snipes/status/828672099849940992.
36. Erica Garner (@es_snipes), Twitter post, January 22, 2016, 3:07 a.m., https://twitter.com/es_snipes/status/690445743954513920.
37. Erica Garner (@es_snipes), Twitter post, September 12, 2016, 11:33 a.m., https://twitter.com/es_snipes/status/775356633144635392.

til the Soviet Union disintegrated and the Cold War, in theory, ended. Sanders' politics were aligned with the liberalism of FDR's New Deal mandates during the Depression which sought to meet the basic needs of the people with decent work wages, food, and some forms of safety nets so that they would not mobilize to end capitalism as the alternative to hunger, misery, and premature death. By 2016, Davis and Sanders—who are only a few years apart in age—had switched positions. Davis was now campaigning for centrist liberals fending off socialism and communism, and Sanders was advocating for democratic socialism as a form of "socialist lite."

Activists had castigated Hillary Clinton's "super predator" labeling of Black children and the then-First Lady's implicit support of Bill Clinton's 1996 Omnibus Crime Bill. By 2016, however, Clinton had embraced and leveraged Black feminists as campaign supporters for her centrist police reforms and iconic embodiment of feminist leadership in government. In a 2016 interview, Davis expressed support for some of Sanders' policies. Clinton was forced to adopt $15 per hour minimum wage along with the democratic socialist candidates' other policies in order to bolster her appeal to the working class and sectors of the middle class. Davis stated that she prioritized "independent, more radical politics," such as tuition-free public education and single-payer or universal healthcare. These policies were supported and aggressively advocated by Sanders, not Clinton.

It was Sanders' progressivism that led Erica Garner to support him. Yet, Davis critiqued Sanders' positions on mass incarceration: "there are larger questions about the prison industrial complex that have not been sufficiently raised. We not only need to bring about an end to mass incarceration, we need to question the racism that is embedded in the whole history of punishment in this country."[38] Elsewhere, Davis would assert that Sanders "seemed to be just learning how to incorporate a critique of racism."[39] There is no record of Davis and Garner having a conversation about why, as Black wom-

---

38. Angela Davis, quoted in Sheryl Huggins Salomon, "Angela Davis Talks Black Liberation, History and the Contemporary Vision," *Ebony*, February 17, 2016, https://www.ebony.com/angela-davis-black-liberation-interview/.

39. Angela Davis, quoted in Maya Dukmasova, "Advice from Angela Davis in the aftermath of the election," *Chicago Reader*, November 17, 2016, https://chicagoreader.com/blogs/advice-from-angela-davis-in-the-aftermath-of-the-election/. Also see Margaret Sullivan, "Were Changes to Sanders Article 'Stealth Editing'"? *New York Times*, March 17, 2016, https://

en progressives, they were backing candidates in conflict with each other during the 2016 primary. Garner trusted Sanders on his "racial politics" in terms of addressing predatory policing. Davis disparaged Sanders' capacity for addressing racism.

Historical data complicates the narrative of Sanders as naïve or a novice in terms of confronting anti-Black racism or white supremacy. While an undergrad at the University of Chicago, Sanders participated in a 1963 school boycott on behalf of 200,000 mostly Black children, who with their parents protested the use of trailers on the South Side and the West Side of Chicago to keep Black students from integrating white public schools with empty desks and the capacity for more students.[40] Sanders later marched with Martin Luther King, Jr. Reverend King had lived for months in a Chicago tenement with Coretta Scott King to gain experiential knowledge for the "poor people's campaign."[41] Yet the narrative that Sanders was naïve or actively complicit in white supremacy (presumably more so than Clinton) persisted.

Despite Sanders' history of antiracist *activism*, Davis suggested that the senator take a "crash course on intersectionality."[42] The concept of intersectionality (discussed earlier in terms of Black feminism) appears to supplant actual activism for Black freedom (see the analysis below of Barbara Smith who would support Sanders). Sanders' organizing with Black families led to his arrest as an undergrad at the University of Chicago. He protested for integrated school resources —at a time when Davis, a minoritized but privileged student at Brandeis, was a non-activist student studying studying culture and literature in France. The intersectional lens through which Davis finds Sanders lacking itself lacks vectors for *ideology and political commitment*. Risk-taking *alliances* are tied not just to ideas or concepts, but to working-class and impoverished laborers, i.e., such alliances require

archive.nytimes.com/publiceditor.blogs.nytimes.com/2016/03/17/new-york-times-bernie-sanders-coverage-public-editor/.

40. Carol Felsenthal, "The Story Behind Bernie Sanders's 1963 Arrest," *Chicago Magazine*, March 15, 2016, https://www.chicagomag.com/chicago-magazine/felsenthal-files/march-2016/bernie-sanders-arrest-kartemquin-1963/.

41. The photo of Sanders' arrest by aggressive police was printed on 2020 election swag T-shirts for his campaign.

42. Dukmasova, "Advice from Angela Davis in the aftermath of the election."

discernible stages of development besides labels of "progressivism," "Marxist," and "Black radical tradition."

How nonelites share peerage with elites is not often discussed or decided in ways that favor the most radical and rooted in workers' communities. Angela Davis, in an interview with civil rights leader Julian Bond, defined Barack Obama as part of the "Black radical tradition," without establishing a standard relevant in objective narratives about historical struggles. His election as the first Black POTUS is historical. However, one would not celebrate Supreme Court Justice Clarence Thomas as the successor of former NAACP attorney Thurgood Marshall, without specifying what antiracist and anticapitalist laws or policies were stabilized for the larger communities in need or under siege. "Black pride" and "Black evidence" are not a foundation for resisting predatory structures and presidents, especially war hawks who expand AFRICOM, and refuse to release political prisoners. The repression and allegiance are part of warfare.

The Obama administration prosecuted more whistleblowers under the Espionage Act than previous administrations combined. While offering no clemency for Edward Snowden, Obama commuted the sentence of Chelsea Manning (who as a middle-class, white, trans woman was serving in the US Army as an intelligence analyst, and released documents on government malfeasance to mitigate war crimes. (The US is trying to extradite Julian Assange for publishing those documents in Wikileaks.) No Black rebel defending their communities against poverty and police violence has ever been pardoned or received clemency by a US president. It was during the Obama administration that Assata Shakur's bounty was doubled to $2 million. Davis wrote the foreword to Shakur's memoir but there is little evidence that while campaigning for Obama the former political prisoner raised the issue of incarcerated political prisoners.

Well-known Black women, such as Erica Garner, supported Sanders' presidential campaign. Black feminist lesbian educator and cofounder of the Combahee River Collective—which formed the concept "identity politics"—Barbara Smith, also endorsed Bernie Sanders:

> Of all of the people who are running, Bernie Sanders is the person whose political commitment most closely reflects and aligns with political commitments that I've had throughout my life. He has a

much deeper understanding of . . . why we have injustice and inequality and oppression and discrimination. . . . He [has] the most
incisive, sharpest understanding of where all that comes from.[43]

When Sanders ran for the second time in 2020, National Press Secretary for the Sanders campaign, Briahna Joy Gray, referring to Barbara Smith, informed media that the Sanders campaign is "enormously
proud to have earned the endorsement of one of the preeminent black
feminist activists in American history."[44] Although some Black feminists criticized Sanders for not having an analysis of racism, Smith asserts that the contemporary concept of "identity politics" substantially
differs from Combahee River Collective's "race, class, gender, and sexuality platform and analysis," formed decades ago:

> When we use the term 'identity politics,' we are actually asserting
> that black women had a right to determine our own political agen-
> das. We, as black women, we actually had a right to create political
> priorities and agendas and actions and solutions based in our experi-
> ences in having these simultaneous identities—that included other
> identities via the working class, gay, lesbian, bisexual, etc. So that's
> what we meant by it. That didn't mean we didn't care about other
> people's situations of injustice. We absolutely did not mean that we
> would work with people who were only identical to ourselves. We
> did not mean that. We strongly believed in coalitions and working
> with people across various identities on common problems. I think
> that the Sanders campaign and the candidate himself are absolutely
> consistent with what we meant by identity politics.[45]

Hence, working with Sanders to meet the material needs of impoverished and working-class communities was a coalition or an alliance.
For Smith, Sanders was aligned with the needs of working class and
impoverished Black women and Captive Maternals who sought to protect themselves, their kin, and their communities.

---

43. Barbara Smith quoted in Terrell Jermaine Starr, "Barbara Smith, Who Helped Coin the
Term 'Identity Politics,' Endorses Bernie Sanders," *The Root*, February 3, 2020, https://www.
theroot.com/barbara-smith-who-helped-coin-the-term-identity-politi-1841419291.
44. Briahna Joy Gray, quoted in Starr, "Barbara Smith Endorses Bernie Sanders."
45. Smith, quoted in Starr, "Barbara Smith Endorses Bernie Sanders."

DNC CHEAP SEATS

In July 2016, I found myself in Philadelphia, at the Wells Fargo Convention Center—named for the bank that had defrauded mostly Black and Latinxs homeowners. I received the tickets to the Democratic National Convention from the National Women's Political Caucus (NWPC). As I shifted in a cramped seat, I gazed around at the expansive sports arena named after a bank that had preyed upon families headed by women of color and dispossessed them of their primary assets, their homes, through their predatory lending processes. The DNC had not been deeply invested in antiracism until the recent uprisings. In fact, Bill Clinton had chastised young Black protesters, and Hillary had informed them that they were not pragmatic—a note that Black elites, monied or aspirational, would sing to the press when Clinton would lose the electoral college, but garner two million more votes than Trump. The fact that Sanders had primaried the establishment's heir-apparent, and Obama's own personal choice, was evidently the problem.

I sat in the cheap seats of the rafters that first night and noted the vagaries in the performances orchestrated for the DNC. Activists challenged the DNC from the left; the range of emotional and analytical expressions and demands for a just world were extensive. This was when few people thought that Donald Trump—who was not taken seriously by the DNC at the time—could get elected to the presidency of the United States (a representative democracy determines presidents by the electoral college not by popular vote). I watched former president Bill Clinton—who had helped fuel mass incarceration with the 1994 Omnibus Crime Bill—walk on stage and be booed (mostly by the Bernie contingent).

Later that evening, the "Mothers of the Movement"—as surrogates for Hillary Rodham Clinton—appeared on stage to cheers and applause. Among the Black parents-turned-activists whose unarmed children had been killed by police or died in police custody, were: Sybrina Fulton, mother of Trayvon Martin; Geneva Reed-Veal, mother of Sandra Bland; Lesley McSpadden, mother of Michael Brown; Lucy McBath (now a congresswoman), mother of Jordan Davis; and Gwen

Carr, Erica Garner's paternal grandmother.[46] (Although Carr participated in campaign appearances for Clinton, Garner herself remained adamant that only one presidential candidate, an outlier and opponent to Clinton, seriously embraced reforms to quell predatory policing and imprisonment.)

Witnessing them was painful. Their loss was keen, and listening to them speak, the proximity to their family sorrow, was uncomfortable for those who watched. Yet it was also strange to view them with matching corsages and color-coordinated outfits with shades of maroon, crimson, and cream. The mothers waded into a Clinton campaign, not so much directed against the "insurgent" Donald Trump as against Bernie Sanders' populism. "It's Not Over"—Garner's campaign ad for Sanders—would in fact be over in the early days of the convention.

On a distinct evening, First Lady Michelle Obama spoke about how she woke up each morning with her two beautiful Black girls in a White House built by Black slaves. The crowd roared at that remarkable achievement—more remarkable, apparently, than stopping police violence, poverty, militarism, and feminicide. Some Black, white, and people of color had flourished under Obama, but largely only those who were already among the affluent. More jobs were created, but they were part-time and lower paid. Police and military abuses were exposed by activists and whistleblowers (prosecuted by the state); banking, finance, and military elites, despite crises and malfeasance, were largely protected.

Later, in the hotel room, I watched on television Reverend William Barber's moving speech from the DNC podium, and his warning that those with hardened hearts must soften and work for the poor and not use "religion to camouflage meanness."[47] Barber seemed to refuse to indict and demand more from both the Democratic Party and Republican Party (as well as from Independents). The DNC had invited him to recruit Christian or ethical voters. Yet, in a misrepresentation of the material world—and the Clintons who had added hundreds

---

46. Eric Bradner and Eugene Scott, "'Mothers of the Movement' makes case for Hillary Clinton," *CNN*, July 26, 2016, https://www.cnn.com/2016/07/26/politics/mothers-movement-dnc-hillary-clinton/index.html.
47. Reverend William Barber, "FULL: GET IT! Reverend William Barber – Democratic National Convention (LIVE)," ABC15 Arizona, https://www.youtube.com/watch?v=tbjhzI1g3EE.

of millionaires to their wealth out of office, in part with the support of nonprofits that some considered as preying upon Haiti—Barber maintained that Hillary Clinton "embraced our deepest moral values," and so we, as citizens, should embrace her.[48] Barber suggested a "revolutionary conservatism" (not as ideology or party affiliation) and gestured toward a code of ethics and spirituality, liberation, and love that could bridge the duopoly of the two dominant parties. Barber dictated that we must "shock this nation" for mercy and democracy and "fight for the heart of this nation." After the election—in which the electoral college, not the majority of votes determines the presidency—brutish rhetorical and physical brutality became the norm as the Trump administration promoted white nationalism, defended white nationalist terrorists, and sought to bar those south of the border, and refugees or immigrants from African "sh*t-hole countries"[49] from entry into the US. The siege of the Capitol on January 6, 2021, abetted and cheered on by Trump, was a dress rehearsal for fascism.

Five years earlier, in an emotional moment at the DNC, Sanders' supporters attempted to keep the senator "left," hoping he would run as an Independent. Garner's "It's Not Over" campaign for Sanders had expired. Sanders would concede to Clinton and, while standing on stage, be booed by former stalwart delegates and supporters who wanted no concession. They wanted succession from the DNC or to take it over and make it a people's party for the mass. At the time, I had thought that the task was simply to tell the truth to the best of our abilities without gaming it for perceived victories, protections, or opportunism. I imagined that truth-telling was a firewall or insurance policy against a future governance flexing the "rule by iron fist."[50] I was educated, and that largely happened because Erica Garner had pushed the contradictions into such public visibility that one could not ignore the betrayals. In 2023, Cornel West who had campaigned for Sanders would announce his candidacy for the US presidency. Unlike Sand-

---

48. Barber, "FULL: GET IT! Reverend William Barber – Democratic National Convention (LIVE)."

49. Ali Vitali, Kasie Hunt, and Frank Thorp V, "Trump referred to Haiti and African nations as 'shithole' countries," *NBC*, January 11, 2018, https://www.nbcnews.com/politics/whitehouse/trump-referred-haiti-african-countries-shithole-nations-n836946.

50. I expand on this notion in a dialogue with Ahmad Greene-Hayes; see Ahmad Greene-Hayes and Joy James, "Cracking the Codes of Black Power Struggles: Hacking, Hacked, and Black Lives Matter," *The Black Scholar* 47, no. 3 (August 1, 2017): 68–78.

ers, West would denounce the Democratic and Republican Parties and run as an independent third party-candidate seeking the Green Party endorsement. Sanders would back President Joe Biden's second term and with that endorsement reform the duopoly.

HACKING THE DNC

The BLM slogan became part of the Democratic Party, steered by corporate elites and professional politicians. As that slogan became a performance that functioned as a silencing mechanism,[51] it became more difficult to hear the songs and chants of Erica Garner and her communities of resisters. "Sabotage" suggests that capitalism and neoliberalism embed inside Black liberation movements. If that is the case, exploitation, is a fixed feature that has to be constantly uprooted in order to clearly speak of a freedom movement under destabilizing conditions?

BLM and other activist organizations appear as a catalyst for confrontations with institutional, interpersonal, and internalized violence. Yet, there are significant differences between hacking white supremacy and heteropatriarchy, and being hacked in ways that allow a liberation movement to be hijacked. For example, the continued rollout of Black Lives Matter luminaries that became prominent spokespersons and pundits for police murders of largely Black working-poor and impoverished classes, mystified segments of the public who witnessed the rise of "movement millionaires." Police reforms would have largely been stalled or decimated, as hundreds of millions of payout dollars through grants, nonprofits, and for-profit corporations, flooded the "movement" market along with academic and popular trade books. The desire to render Black feminist abolitionists from anonymity led some to promote celebrity.

The historical symbolism of racial progress imbued in the 2008 Democratic National Convention was renewed in 2016 when Hillary Clinton became the first woman nominee for president from a major party. After several years of sensational deaths of Black people through encounters with police or vigilantes during the Obama administra-

---

51. Greene-Hayes and James, "Cracking the Codes of Black Power Struggles."

tion, BLM protests and activism dominated the political arena. As it had been for the Kennedy and Obama administrations, race as an integration formula (which Derrick Bell warned of given "interest convergence") was a rusted conveyor belt into anti-Blackness, white nationalism, capitalism, and imperialism that would consistently derail democratic progress.

CONCLUSION

It is unlikely that Erica Garner believed a presidential election would lead to a remedy for predatory policing. Even if Sanders had won, the senator's liberal FDR policies would be consistently fought and undermined by Congress, the courts, corporations, and mainstream media (the *New York Times* editorial board was consistently hostile to Sanders' campaign). Garner did engineer resistance movements, one protected by a spiritual political phenomenon: Agape. Her low-tech "wild card" allows countless people to make courageous choices. Captive Maternal care and familial and communal love, buttressed by political will, do not demand or deliver permanent, tangible successes. We did not acheive justice for Eric Garner, Trayvon Martin, Sandra Bland, Bresha Meadows; in the absence of resurrections—millions remain incarcerated, exploited, and abused, thousands remain traumatized. The Agape amid Captive Maternals is a form of fidelity and devotion, not a fetishization of electoral politics. Even when they transition into ancestors, perhaps particularly when they reappear as ancestors, revolutionary lovers and rebels reproduce the norm as a mutation that is not fully controlled or encircled by state violence.[52]

---

52. Sections of this chapter first appeared in Ahmad Greene-Hayes and Joy James, "Cracking the Codes of Black Power Struggles," *The Black Scholar*, August 1, 2017, 47:3, 68–78

Chapter 7

CAPTIVE (AFTER)LIVES

The only thing I can say is that she was a warrior. She fought the good fight. This is just the first fight in 27 years she lost.

—Esaw Snipes

From 2014 to 2017, Erica Garner repeatedly—at times ritualistically—informed the public that Daniel Pantaleo and other NYPD officers applied a chokehold to her father's neck, and the weight that compressed his chest restricted his breathing. His plea, eleven times, of "I can't breathe" was ineffective in getting them to release him so that he could breathe. Erica Garner and activists in NYC and beyond routinely would chant "Murderer!" and "Guilty as hell!" at police forces. Yet, Pantaleo did not need to rely on abolitionists to ensure that he would never be incarcerated. The state and the police unions—as with the unions for correctional officers in jails and prisons—had long embedded protective policies within the very structure of policing. Pantaleo was never prosecuted and imprisoned for participating in a collective homicide or murder. He was only fired when the NYPD police commissioner James O'Neill terminated his employment. O'Neill then retired into lucrative employment in private security industries, reportedly becoming a senior vice president and global head of security for Visa credit cards. The press quotes O'Neill on August 5, 2019: "Had I been in Officer Pantaleo's situation, I may have made similar mistakes. And had I made those mistakes, I wish I would've used the arrival of backup officers to give the situation more time to make that arrest. . . . And I wished I would've released my grip before it became a chokehold." Essentially co-blaming Garner for his homicide, he is also quoted as saying: "Every time I watch that video, I say to myself, as I'm sure all of you do, 'Mr. Garner, don't do it. Comply. Officer Pantaleo, don't do it. . . . But none of us can take back our decisions, most especially when they lead to the death of another human being."[1]

The commissioner retired, vilified by his (white) rank-and-file NYPD and the Police Benevolent Association, but well compensated as he entered the private sector as a security expert. Campaigning for president, Mayor Bill de Blasio denounced racist violence from police and reassured agitated activists who called on him to use his executive powers to fire Pantaleo that, although he would not directly act, justice would be served.[2]

SISTER MAROONS

Erica Garner agreed to an interview with writer and artist Chaédria LaBouvier. The interview was published March 21, 2016, in *Elle*. This interview is likely the most insightful and complex interview that Erica Garner ever granted to the press. Perhaps because she knew that LaBouvier's brother, Clinton Allen, was murdered by Dallas police officers, she was more candid and reflective in her dialogue with LaBouvier.[3] This personal pain of losing a family member to police murder creates recognition and bonds, linkages within a political family that emerges within struggles against death, movements triggered by state killings of their beloved. LaBouvier interviewed Garner "in a Mexican diner in an un-gentrified patch of Williamsburg near her home." When told that her looks favor her father, Garner replies: "I'm my father's twin, no doubt."

1. See Andrew Siff, Jonathan Dienst, and Melissa Russo, "NYPD Commissioner Fires Officer Daniel Pantaleo Over Eric Garner's Death," *NBC*, August 5, 2019, https://www.nbc-newyork.com/news/local/nypd-commissioner-decision-fate-officer-involved-nyc-eric-garner-death-chokehold/1484829/.

2. Ashley Southall, Ali Watkins, and William K. Raushbaum, "Daniel Pantaleo, N.Y.P.D. Officer in Eric Garner's Death, Should Be Fired, Judge Says," *New York Times*, August 2, 2019, https://www.nytimes.com/2019/08/02/nyregion/pantaleo-garner.html.

3. See Collette Flanagan, "Dallas Police Killed My Unarmed Son: Their Brutality is a Global Problem," ACLU, July 13, 2020, https://www.aclu.org/news/criminal-law-reform/dallas-police-killed-my-unarmed-son-their-brutality-is-a-global-problem.

The candor and openness with LaBouvier, a Black Cuban artist, reveals a bonding, as LaBouvier recounts: "she's telling me, within five minutes of our meeting, about The Video—the recording of the final two minutes and forty-nine seconds of her father's life." Garner tells LaBouvier that she watches the death of her father not as a daughter, but as an analyst looking at a "case study." She has watched the clip "hundreds of times." As an analyst, Garner weekly checked her father's *Wikipedia* page. That "horrific death" or killing became manageable but the image of him lifeless on the gurney with his eyes looking into the camera is the most disturbing." The video allowed the rare "chance to actually see their loved one die [or dead] right in front of them . . . and everyone is watching."[4]

At age twenty-five, lacking wealth and an Ivy League pedigree, Erica Garner had created a singular presidential electoral ad, campaigned throughout the US for an "outsider" primarying the establishment, organized mass die-ins on NYC streets, and battled predatory policing. Garner challenged a massive and lethal organization that existed for a century and a half, at the time of her birth. Established in 1845, now the largest US police department, the NYPD has approximately 36,008 full-time active officers and 19,000 civilian employees.[5] (Following the NYPD, the Chicago Police Department is one-third the size.) The 2023 NYPD budget exceeds $10.8 billion.[6] The excessive budget, according to Emily Drabinski, who heads NYC libraries, will be paid through slashing $100 million from the City's budget for public libraries, as police are used to suppress all forms of dissenting cultures, including LGBTQ+ protests against reactionaries and white nationalists.[7]

Weekly Staten Island rallies and die-ins on Tuesdays and Thursdays lasted for more than a year, with Erica Garner and devoted cadres who made the trek by subway and ferry, to stand or lay beside

4. LaBouvier, "Police Brutality, Bernie, and Me."
5. "Current NYPD Members of Service," Data Transparency Initiative, Civilian Complaint Review Board, https://www.nyc.gov/site/ccrb/policy/data-transparency-initiative-mos.page.
6. "Six Fast Facts about the NYPD's Preliminary FY2023 Budget," *CITY BUDGET* blog, March 18, 2022, https://cbcny.org/research/six-fast-facts-about-nypds-preliminary-fy2023-budget.
7. Emily Drabinski, "Essential to the Public: Libraries at the End of the World," NIA Project, Bard College, March 21, 2003, https://www.youtube.com/watch?v=DcPEEy6bBfo. Drabinski asserts that there are 1,800 schools in NYC but only 300 certified librarians.

Erica Garner outside the Victory Boulevard bodega where her father died. Comfortable with LaBouvier, Garner revealed her emotional intelligence and spirituality and how loving protections radiate beyond death: "I can feel him there." Eric Garner, her father, functioned as an ancestral presence and stabilizer for his daughter who confided to the journalist: "I definitely feel him with me, protecting me."[8] It was intimacy with family, and so familiarity with love as a practice, the writer states, that led Garner to remain fearless as she confronted police, some in intimidating riot gear, to a standstill or stare off. Erica Garner, with cadres, routinely stopped traffic by laying her body in the street. Cadres also disrupted subway travel. Bringing the metropolis to a halt, they disrupted Gotham's routine of the work and wealth hustle (nannies, maids, door(wo)men take public transportation).

Erica Garner affirmed to LaBouvier that she evolved in order to be devoted to social justice: "I've absolutely discovered what I want to do with my life. Before, I was just kind of aimless, not sure what I was going to be doing. Now I know."[9] Yet, she notes that mothering and caretaking for her personal family remained a constant effort and stressor. Garner informed the *Elle* journalist that her then six-year-old daughter, Alyssa, "runs out of the room when she sees" on a television clip her grandfather being asphyxiated by NYPD or "them tackling Pop Pop."[10] She also shared that it was difficult to be a mother, daughter, and potential partner once the gawkers for Black-death gawkers turned her father's homicide and memory into a celebrity symbol dominated by the news and negotiations over the $5.9 million settlement following wrongful death at the hands of the NYPD (the taxpayers paid for the settlement of course):

> There were a lot of lawyers. Protests. Interviews. Lawyers. Juggling motherhood alone. Trying to date when your name renders more than 2 million search results on Google. 'I'd like to date someone that can understand and not be starstruck,' she says. She tells me the story of a guy she briefly dated who would accompany her to press conferences but essentially perform for the camera with exaggerated displays of 'shyness.' She slips into a story of an ex who sued her for

8. LaBouvier, "Police Brutality, Bernie, and Me."
9. LaBouvier, "Police Brutality, Bernie, and Me."
10. Erica Garner, quoted in LaBouvier, "Police Brutality, Bernie, and Me."

a bag that he left at her place. 'It's difficult to date people sometimes without them looking for the settlement.'[11]

Her memories of her father are fond, and fixed on the comfort, care, and indulgence that he gave her: "I was a Daddy's girl. We never heard 'No.' If I needed something, my father provided. If he couldn't do it right then, he'd say, 'Give me time, but he never said 'No.'" What LaBouvier calls "the transition into adulthood" is a struggle that Erica Garner wrestles with on a regular basis. Without romanticism or judgment, LaBouvier views the Garner family through a clear lens:

> Her family is close, loving, and unhappy in the way all families are, and traumatized in a way that most never will be. Almost none of them show up to her rallies and protests. Navigating adulthood with those kinds of wounds and pressures makes it easy to forget that Garner was only 23 when she lost her father. If young Black kids have to grow up faster and savvier than most because their lives depend on it, Garner might very well be middle-aged in Living While Black years.[12]

When LaBouvier asks about her day, Garner responds "normal"; the writer then asks for clarification. Erica Garner offers a thoughtful response: "My day is normal until I'm around people that I don't know or that don't know me."[13] Outside of community care, reality becomes more tense and fraught. One of the few journalists recognizing themselves as emotionally connected to Erica Garner, LaBouvier sees how Garner is misconstrued as "a large Black woman who answers a question brusquely and is perceived as 'angry,' rather than as young, hurting, and vulnerable." Through the interview, conversations between two young Black women who had beloved family members killed by predatory police, LaBouvier writes that Garner "vacillates between the aggressive fearlessness of a young Black woman who knows she can't depend on the world to protect her and the vulnerability of a young Black woman who acknowledges how unprotected she is." This is the shared experience of Black people, with the specific vulnerabilities of

---

11. LaBouvier, "Police Brutality, Bernie, and Me."
12. LaBouvier, "Police Brutality, Bernie, and Me."
13. LaBouvier, "Police Brutality, Bernie, and Me."

young Black women. LaBouvier is seeking answers just as Garner is. So, the writer is pushed into a reflection of self-care and self-identity with her encounter with Erica which becomes a collective conversation and musing of multiple Black families who had the lives of loved ones stolen by police power:

> I'm one of the people asking Garner questions, too—'How does it feel to share the most devastating thing that's happened to you with the world?'; 'Do you feel defined by this?'—because I'm asking myself too. I'm hoping that she has answers for me, for Ramarley Graham's mom, for India Kager's mom, and the too-long list of Black women I know who are left after their children have become the victims of police brutality, feeling their way through the new normals that will always feel like warped universes. Garner seems to know this and volleys back a time or two, 'Well, how was it for you?' We're all looking for answers.[14]

On their way back to the subway, the two women stop at a bodega for Erica Garner to buy a loosie. LaBouvier and Garner both recognized their bold gesture as Black women who lost family to predatory policing but would still defy the police apparatus. The NYPD had falsely accused Eric Garner of selling loose cigarettes as they harassed and attempted to arrest him, and then killed Mr. Garner.[15] His defiant daughter, accompanied by another Captive Maternal, exerted will and Agape—offering an homage to the slain, beloved departed, still connected to the living through the afterlife.

STRUGGLING

In an interview with Ben Dixon, Erica Garner acknowledged that she was struggling: "This thing, it beats you down. The system beats you down to where you can't win."[16] Referencing the lack of sufficient mental health services for grief and exhaustion, she raised the issue of

---

14. LaBouvier, "Police Brutality, Bernie, and Me."

15. LaBouvier, "Police Brutality, Bernie, and Me."

16. A clip of this interview is included in Benjamin Dixon's tweet where he wrote: "Listen to Erica Garner (@es_snipes) as she spoke about the stresses of the struggle. This was just three weeks ago in an interview with me, @RebeccAzor, and @Russian_Starr. Erica was fierce and committed. I'm going to remember all of that PLUS her smile at the end of this

childhood trauma, which receives less attention despite the fact Black women have become the face of movements. Of course, adults are not the only ones impacted or offering care. In her conversations with others, Erica Garner would observe how her seven-year-old daughter expressed solidarity and care for her mother. In the Garner apartment, Erica's daughter Alyssa would turn her back to the television whenever news flashes used the images of her grandfather being choked to death. Thus, the (grand)father became a symbol or stand-in for Black death or murder during police encounters. Watching and making eye contact with her mother, the child would only turn back to the television after the news report and footage of their (grand)father dying disappeared and cartoons appeared. The child's need to comfort the maternal outweighed her desire for entertainment and play. In brief moments of solidarity and care, the child became the Captive Maternal to the parent as she engaged her mother in conversation to check on her feelings. Four generations of Garners protested and grieved in different ways: Gwen Carr, Esaw Garner, Erica Garner, Alyssa.

Erica Garner's exhaustion and despair led not to suicide but to physical breakdown and collapse. An asthma attack precipitated a major heart attack that, in turn, precipitated brain damage and a medically induced coma on December 23, 2017. Her first heart attacked occurred earlier in 2017, during or after the birth of her son, Eric. Stressors, including poverty, racism, grief, depression, and rage at political compromises that devalued the life of her father, and others lost to police violence or devastated by incarceration, were constant during her brief lifetime. There is no digital record or horrific chronicle of Erica Garner's death. However, Erica bitterly complained that she had to watch her father's murder over and over again on news footage as his primary killer, Daniel Pantaleo, received exoneration, promotion, and pay increases at a desk job in a local Staten Island precinct. Her life was nevertheless violently, prematurely, and unnecessarily taken.

It is unclear if the public hospital to which she was taken provided the best of care which she so desperately needed. She died at Brooklyn's Woodhull Medical and Mental Health Center one week later. At the age of twenty-seven, she left behind two sisters, two broth-

---

clip." Benjamin Dixon (@BenjaminPDixon), Twitter post, December 28, 2017, 12:44 p.m., https://twitter.com/benjaminpdixon/status/946436687588192257.

ers, her grandmother Gwen Carr and mother Esaw Snipes-Garner, and her own two children, seven-year-old Alyssa (who appears in the Sanders ad) and four-month-old Eric (her father's namesake). Garner transitioned from being a loving mother and dutiful daughter into a revolutionary lover—a grief-stricken protester/movement-maker/maroon fighting against homicidal violence. Her legacy offered political leadership that shaped and inspired a call-and-response that rocked NYC streets and subways and radiated into state and national politics. Garner's "BLM" politics proved to be more closely aligned to a Black Liberation Movement than to funded elites, celebrities, and elected officials.

The 2016 philanthropic donations of hundreds of millions, if not billions, of dollars for a Black-led movement for Black lives included dozens of organizations, yet that financial support never reached Erica Garner.[17] The radical Captive Maternal lacking fame and wealth—two days before her death—shared on *Democracy Now!* her vulnerability to collapse:

> When you deal with grief. When you talk about grief and you talk about how regular families deal with it, you know, families have problems. Trouble coping with that. Mental health is very important. Black families that's on public assistance [can't get] therapy at $300 an hour, and I don't think that's fair how are we supposed to cope with this if we don't have someone to talk to, someone professional to talk to. I'm constantly reading articles and doing the research on my dad's case, but I'm not taking care of me.[18]

Although New York City had settled in 2015 with Eric Garner's family for $5.9 million, the city failed or refused to distribute the funds until *after* Erica Garner's death. For activist and journalist Kirsten West Savali, Garner was politically unique: "Erica stood, unshakable, as an emerging, powerful voice of the radical Black left. . . . Erica Garner was

---

17. Karen Ferguson, "The Perils of Liberal Philanthropy," *Jacobin,* November 26, 2018, https://jacobin.com/2018/11/black-lives-matter-ford-foundation-black-power-mcgeorge-bundy.

18. Erica Garner, "Anti- Police Brutality Activist Erica Garner in Her Own Words on *Democracy Now!*," December 28, 2017, https://www.democracynow.org/2017/12/28/erica_garner_in_her_own_words.

an intentional revolutionary."[19] In January 2018, Erica Garner's close friend and political ally, Reggie Harris, noted:

> Erica was not a born activist. She was a daddy's girl and she loved hard. She was a mother, a sister, and a loyal friend. Activism was a tactic she saw as the best way to seek justice for her father, Eric Garner. In the end, after Erica put her entire life into this fight, not only for herself but for everyone Black, she got no changes. . . . She got empty words and promises. . . . De Blasio called himself a progressive but sided with the police unions. . . . Cuomo . . . appoint[ed] a special prosecutor, but only for one year. . . . Erica took her fight all the way to a Democratic White House to no avail.
>
> The stresses of fighting for three years became too much for one person to bear. The fact that her death took place mere weeks after she took a year off, and a few months after having her child, is not lost.[20]

National Public Radio journalist Rachel Martin spoke with Kirsten West Savali about her article "Erica Garner: I'm In This Fight Forever."[21] Published in the Black publication *The Root*, the article started with a sound bite from Garner: "I'm in this fight forever. And no matter how long it takes twenty years from now, I—we deserve justice . . . it's hard, but you got to keep on. You got to keep the name out there because people will forget." Savali recalled that Garner felt that "she didn't have a choice" but to protest on behalf of her father. For Savali, Garner "wanted to make sure that she walked in the tradition of people like Martin Luther King and like Malcolm X . . . Ida B. Wells . . . Fannie Lou Hamer" in order to "be that voice for people who were not only marginalized but who were actively being occupied in their own communities."[22] Referring to Garner as "an intentional revolutionary," Savali asserted that Erica Garner "did not just stumble into anything."

---

19. Kirsten West Savali, "Erica Garner: 'I'm in This Fight Forever,'" *The Root*, December 31, 2017. [*The Root* retracted this article on June 12, 2018.]

20. Reggie Harris, "Garner Way Political Director: Erica Garner 'Put Her Entire Life in This Fight,'" *Time*, January 3, 2018, https://time.com/5086625/erica-garner-obituary/.

21. See "Remembering Anti-Police Brutality Activist Erica Garner, Who Died at 27," NPR, January 2, 2018, https://www.npr.org/2018/01/02/575028106/remembering-anti-police-brutality-activist-erica-garner-who-died-at-27.

22. Savali, "Erica Garner: 'I'm in This Fight Forever.'"

She was "very clear-eyed" about her goals—justice for her father and marginalized people "targeted by the police state."

For Martin, Erica Garner "took on a lot of high-profile Democrats" who would have benefitted from an alliance with her because adjacent to her militancy would have positioned them as "radicals" for social justice. High-profile elected politicians who sought to sway or pacify Garner included: President Barack Obama, Governor Andrew Cuomo, NYC Mayor Bill de Blasio, and Senator Hillary Clinton. Agreeing with Erica Garner's critique of the Democratic Party, Savali asserted that President Obama "was very tepid when it came to talking about police brutality and state violence." Salvi also noted that Mayor de Blasio had refused to release Daniel Pantaleo's disciplinary record which showed that the officer was a serial offender of civil rights. When Martin concluded the interview by stating that Erica Garner "wanted a more aggressive" response to injustice, Savali corrected the host, stating that what Erica Garner wanted was "a more authentic response."

FUNERAL

Journalist Angela Helm described the January 8, 2018 funeral for Erica Garner, held at Harlem's First Corinthian Baptist Church, as "more like a production than a homegoing ceremony for the twenty-seven-year-old mother of two." Dignitaries, celebrities, entertainers, and politicians attended the funeral. Senator Bernie Sanders sent a letter to the family. Activists who could not get into the funeral fumed, while politicians and celebrities were announced as they arrived.[23] Activists who viewed him as an opportunist heckled Shaun King outside the services. The musician Common, who had met Erica Garner at a protest, attended the funeral alongside the father of slain teen Michael Brown. Michael Brown, Sr. told *The Root*: "The [Garner] family has been there with our family from day one. It was my duty to come out and show the family the love that they've shown us."

For Helm, Erica Garner was first and foremost, a young Black woman who became a prominent activist "by some stroke of tragic luck," while resisting "the random, pervasive nature of police brutal-

---

23. An altercation between family members temporarily cleared sections of the church.

ity in America."[24] Yet, the funeral at times was disappointing because honoring Erica Garner was not always central in the funeral proceedings. After the burial, *The Root* asserted that the white or mainstream press disparaged the Garner family's desire to speak only to Black journalists. Under the headline "The Caucasity of Outrage Because Erica Garner's Family Won't Talk to White Journalists," *The Root* journalist Michael Harriot penned a scathing assessment of mainstream news coverage of the funeral. Harriot described the falling of journalists' "white tears" as irrelevant and a distraction from Erica Garner's activism and death: "Caucasian tear ducts don't even open for black bodies. They only respond to the perceived oppression of white people." According to the writer, "salty faces" at Erica Garner's funeral only appeared after "Garner's family announced that they would give interviews and comments only to black journalists."[25]

The white journalists' response to a Black family that had lost two family members was outrage; perhaps in part because since Eric Garner's murder in 2014, white publications and media markets had generated income from publicizing Black death. At the funeral, journalists who had received bylines and perhaps a burgeoning readership lacked no decorum for privacy and intimacy within Black communities that cared for, and to some degree shared—despite class standing—the vulnerability of the Garner family. Privileged to meet with other Black journalists, with the family as an insider rather than an outsider, *The Root* ridicules white grievance blocked from content to generate more repetitive narratives about Black death:

> The outcry was immediate and deafening. Some rummaged through knapsacks filled with privilege and fake outrage to find the right words to describe their self-righteous indignation. They made it about *themselves* and played the 'reverse racism' card. They bemoaned the decision as discriminatory . . . [and] pivoted from Erica Garner's death and spoke of how the family had lost their "respect." Their counterargument was: 'Shouldn't Erica Garner's kin talk to

---

24. Angela Helm, "Erica Garner's Funeral Was Marred by a Family Dispute, but Her Unapologetic Warrior Spirit Could Not Be Diminished," *The Root*, January 9, 2018, https://www.theroot.com/erica-garner-s-funeral-was-marred-by-a-family-dispute-b-1821899747.

25. Michael Harriot, "The Caucasity of Outrage Because Erica Garner's Family Won't Talk to White Journalists," *The Root*, January 4, 2018, https://www.theroot.com/the-caucasity-of-outrage-because-erica-garners-family-w-1821752347.

any qualified journalist, regardless of skin color? Isn't their request against everything Erica Garner fought for? If a journalist covers social justice, why should color matter?"[26]

Harriot acknowledges that some of the queries might have been legitimate but insists that Black journalists are likely "more familiar with the cultural dynamic of the grieving process." Harriot then points to political narcissism, noting the "collective Caucasian clutching of pearls" as incensed white journalists, blinded by self-interest, ignore or refuse to acknowledge that Black journalists talking with the family might bring more comfort to the Garners.[27] For Harriot, those most likely to incorrectly address the life and death of Erica Garner would be those who refuse to "respect the wishes of a grieving family." (This author takes note and is not seeking to write a biography on Garner, filtered through the lens of her family, friends, and comrades, but writes as a political theorist focused on her contributions in the public sphere of politics, not in the familial or social spheres.)

CONCLUSION

Esaw Snipes-Garner's eulogy for her daughter provided the final words about her at the funeral: "She was born at seven-and-a-half months, four pounds, eleven ounces, but she proved to be a giant." According to Harriot, Snipes-Garner would "beg Erica" not to protest at the twice-weekly vigils that continued for a year. Erica Garner traveled from Brooklyn, "trudging out to the Staten Island Ferry station, thick with commuters, rain or shine, to bring light to the nonindictment of the police officer who held her father in that fatal chokehold; a man still employed with the New York City Police Department." Harriot writes that Snipes-Garner reminded Erica Garner that she had two children and repeatedly asked her to put her own health before political struggle, adding: "I can't take care of these kids." (The children are now likely raised by their grandmother, Snipes-Garner.) Erica's mother affirmed her daughter's choices, declaring at the funeral that "[Erica]

---

26. Harriot, "The Caucasity of Outrage."
27. Harriot, "The Caucasity of Outrage."

lived on her own terms. And she died on her own terms." The mother celebrated the daughter's strategic courage and took pride in how her eldest child shut down New York's eight-lane Verrazano Bridge that connected Staten Island to Brooklyn. Erica Garner had reported to her mother that the NYPD was afraid to arrest her despite breaking traffic laws in order to protest the murder of her father. With admiration for the feats of a daughter whose resistance was more militant than that of her family, community, city, and nation, Esaw Snipes-Garner observed: "She did it by herself. Eight lanes of traffic. She said, 'I can't breathe.'"

Part III

Figure 4: An FTP child activist in Atlanta, GA distributes food to elders, 2022. Photo by Shawne "H2O" Bailey.

CHAPTER 8

POLICE VIOLENCE AND THE
LIMITS OF LEGALISM

Following the 2015 police killing of Freddie Gray in Baltimore, Obama's Attorney General Loretta Lynch promised the public that the state and society would become ethical and stable structures supporting all citizens: "We can restore both trust and faith, not only in our laws but also in those who enforce them."[1] Theorists Jared Sexton and Frank Wilderson III assert that civil society as a stable and beneficial enterprise exists only for those bodies that do not "magnetize bullets."[2]

Policing in the United States is officially regulated by three levels of governance: federal, state, and local or city. On the national level, the director of the Central Intelligence Agency (CIA) and the head of the Federal Bureau of Investigation (FBI) directly or through their superior—e.g., for the FBI, the Attorney General—report to the President of the United States (POTUS), as does the Secretary of the Department of Homeland Security who oversees Immigration and Customs Enforcement (ICE). Under combined federal and state control since 1933, National Guard commanders receive instructions and ethical mandates from their governor and/or POTUS. On the local level, police forces are directed by executive branches or "chiefs." City mayors appoint and oversee their chiefs of police. From 1790s Caroli-

---

1. Loretta Lynch, "Statement by Attorney General Lynch on the Situation in Baltimore," Office of Public Affairs, US Department of Justice, April 27, 2015, https://www.justice.gov/opa/pr/statement-attorney-general-lynch-situation-baltimore.
2. See Frank Wilderson III, "Gramsci's Black Marx: Whither the Slave in Civil Society," *Social Identities* 9, no. 2 (2003): 225–240.

na plantations' use of slave catchers to the 2014 killing of Eric Garner, 2018 police murder of Botham Jean in Dallas, and 2019 police murder of Atatiana Jefferson in Fort Worth, police violence remains mired in controversy and tragedy in US democracy, particularly in Black communities.

It has been extremely difficult, if not impossible, to regulate US policing with enforceable ethical standards to mitigate excessive force and violence disproportionately inflicted on Black, Indigenous, impoverished, queer, or differently abled people. The political demand for ethics to be operational throughout the nation requires a strategy that leverages the power of nonelites to shift the current political system. Elected officials cannot standardize nonracist/antiracist procedures into police structures because they do not control police forces. The limited protections garnered through the mid-twentieth-century civil rights movements have been eviscerated over the last half century, most notably so with the erosion of voting rights protections, the right to abortions without campaigns to bring homicide charges or incarceration or executions. Reforms and advocacy led by professional elites rarely tap the violent surges of state violence arrayed disproportionately against Black/Brown/Indigenous and working-class and impoverished communities—those most vulnerable to police malfeasance.

The focus on police reform and ethical mandates usually scrutinizes local or city police actions. The majority of people are surveilled, disciplined, and punished by local police—for example, the NYPD monitors subway fare evasion as "quality-of-life" infractions that increase data and fees collections that disproportionately target Black/Brown low-income communities. Although protests, flash mobs, die-ins, social media, and therapy allow an outlet for ethical people confronting predatory policing, the depth and breadth of political strategies are to quell police terror. In 2016, demanding that Hillary Clinton take personal responsibility for lobbying to pass President Bill Clinton's 1994 Omnibus Crime Bill that fueled mass incarceration, was a protest not a war resistance strategy. A key task of the Captive Maternal is not to get lost in repetitive political or symbolic acts that do not offer access to the Achilles heels of predatory policing.

This challenge is not restricted to US capitalism and imperialism, or US domestic and foreign policies. Dismantling genocidal practices is a global politics, a form of international solidarity and cooperation. Of course, the work of US leaders means that US local and international police forces and military formations murder civilians at home and abroad on a regular basis. For example, AFRICOM drone strikes kill civilians on the African continent and destabilize Indigenous cultures and political economies that stabilize communities. ICE deportations of Haitians and Africans reflect Obama-Biden, Trump-Pence, and the Biden-Harris administrations' relationships with Haiti for decades. Most people are overwhelmed by family needs, to struggle and study on discussions about domestic care, in the home and in the nation, inevitably reference internationalism and human rights, which is defined on a global level even as civil rights remain unsecured within the US. There is no real restitution from the state because it cannot resurrect a murdered loved one. More recently, impacted families—from George Floyd to Tyre Nichols—note that anti-Black violence can be administered by non-Blacks and Blacks.

MOVING TARGETS

The homicides of Black Americans by deputized whites, or white police, include the slayings of: Sean Bell, Oscar Grant, Trayvon Martin, Akai Gurley, Eric Garner, Michael Brown, Yvette Smith, Aiyana Stanley-Jones, Tamir Rice, John Crawford, Rekia Boyd, Miriam Carey, Tanisha Anderson, Walter Scott, and Tarika Wilson, who died holding her fourteen-month-old son, Sincere, who was also shot but survived.[3] Police predatory violence kills unarmed children and adults.

Police have not been held accountable for these homicides by their departments, unions, district attorneys, grand juries, and sizable segments of the public. It is that lack of accountability before the law (federal investigations still pending) for criminal acts by police that incites outrage. That rage was recently expressed in youth, female, and

3. Mary M. Chapman and Susan Saulny, "Tragedy in Detroit, With Reality TV Crew in Tow," *New York Times*, May 21, 2010, https://www.nytimes.com/2010/05/22/us/22detroit.html; Ashley Goudeau, "Twin sister of woman killed by Bastrop County deputy grateful for indictment," *KVUE ABC*, June 18, 2014, https://www.kvue.com/article/news/local/twin-sister-of-woman-killed-by-bastrop-county-deputy-grateful-for-indictment/269-260120896.

queer Black leadership followed by tens of thousands of multiracial, diverse protestors and organizers chanting "Black Lives Matter!"

The protestors and families of those slain emerged as national spokespersons against torture and police violence. They could either deflect attention from formal civil rights leadership privy to state-corporate power or meld into those formations.[4] Disparate sites of torture, dishonor, and disappearance have forced diverse people around the globe to huddle closer—to do more than scrutinize laws and policies that reward police violence with immunity and money.

Police are not inherently protectors of the poor, working class, or those racially fashioned for dishonor. Some are surprised or even stunned by predatory policing, likely because they believe in law and police forces as protectors of civil society. Officers do not routinely "go rogue" in wealthy, white communities because those communities have the economic and political resources to discipline them. Yet, they are routinely roguish and lethal in Black, Brown, and Indigenous communities, and among the working class, the poor, the unhoused, queer, and incarcerated.

Police are technically public employees. They work—*in theory*—for us. In reality, they work for the state, which taxes us for militarism and militarized policing, and for their expansion and investment portfolios. We obey police forces ostensibly for our own "safety" and that of the general good. In reality, we obey police forces because we fear police forces. That fear becomes a form of accumulation for anti-Black and anti-civilian militarized policing. Community members disappearing into jails, prisons, psych wards, or graves is the norm. Police forces are supported by politicians, and unions have immunity from myriad crimes. Thus, they routinely act with impunity.

As Commander-in-Chief, Obama ramped up drone strikes in Africa after President George Bush created AFRICOM to militarize the African continent in the interests of US foreign policy and control. Obama's Black Homeland Security executive Jeh Johnson authorized secret surveillance of #BLM, while downplaying white supremacist

---

4. Stephanie Clifford, "Brooklyn Grand Jury to Examine Akai Gurley Shooting Death," *New York Times*, December 5, 2014, https://www.nytimes.com/2014/12/06/nyregion/brooklyn-grand-jury-to-examine-akai-gurley-shooting-death.html; Richard A. Oppel, Jr., "Police Shooting of Tamir Rice Is Ruled a Homicide," *New York Times*, December 12, 2014, https://www.nytimes.com/2014/12/13/us/police-shooting-of-tamir-rice-is-ruled-a-homicide.html.

domestic *terrorism*. No US president has publicly prioritized the necessity of neutralizing white nationalist (mass) killers. Emboldened by the election of Donald Trump, and the "forever [imperial] wars," vets following the illegal invasion of Iraq, under pretense or deception, sold to the public that Iraq was manufacturing weapons of mass destruction. White nationalist vigilantes became empowered and emerged from the underground to foster domestic civil wars largely waged against Africans/Blacks, Indigenous, Muslims, Palestinians, the undocumented, impoverished, queered, and feminized.

GOTHAM

In 2020, the largest police force in the United States, the New York Police Department, had a $6 billion annual budget. The $1 billion "defund the police" demand by activists and concerned citizens resulted in the New York City Council doing creative accounting. The budget meeting was set for 8:00 p.m. on June 30, 2020. It began about 9:40 p.m. with a contentious session. The budget was passed July 1, 2020, just after midnight. Protestors camped out in front of City Hall booed when City Council speaker Corey Johnson shared the details. New York City moved about $300 million back to the Department of Education (DOE). For years it had loaned money to the NYPD for school police.[5] Speaker Johnson stated that the passage of the budget was not a "day of celebration . . . [but] a time of necessity."

Protestors reacted with frustration, anger, and resolution to continue social justice activism. The adopted fiscal year 2021 budget for New York City showed an over $420 million cut to the NYPD and a $44 million cut to the Department of Corrections (DOC). At the time of the vote, Speaker Johnson asserted that more than $880 million was cut from the NYPD. Mayor de Blasio cited $1 billion. Critics, however, argued that the budget was "smoke and mirrors," citing the City Council's cancellation of the July 2020 cadet training, while main-

---

5. Christopher Robbins, Jake Offenhartz, and Gwynne Hogan, "NYC Budget Updates: City Council Passes 'Heart-Wrenching' Budget, 32–17," *Gothamist*, June 30, 2020, https://gothamist.com/news/nyc-budget-updates-de-blasio-announces-agreement-tweaks-nypd.

taining the October 2020 training for newly minted officers.[6] Cuts to police overtime written in the budget might be fictitious. Citizens Budget Commissioner Andrew Rein stated: "Reducing police overtime by almost $300 million is highly unlikely given the weak history of overtime management."

In 2019, when there were no mass deaths from COVID-19 or mass deployment of police to intimidate or kettle protestors, the NYPD exceeded its overtime budget by $130 million. Given the overtime and pending lawsuits against the NYPD for documented acts of police brutality against peaceful protests, police-related costs would soar in 2020. No hiring freeze was imposed on the NYPD. Its counterterrorism unit remained fully funded despite NYC Public Advocate Jumaane Williams' and progressive City Council members' demands to limit the budget.[7] Substantial cuts were made to the DOE and social services for the impoverished and working class. However, over $400 million was put back into youth summer programs and employment (allegedly taken from the NYPD budget). The NYC FY23 budget totaled $106 billion with $5,771,499 for policing; for FY24, approximately $107 billion was allocated with $5,552,252 for policing according to the Mayor's Office of Management and Budget.

NYPD ON "TRIAL": POST-COP RIOT HEARINGS

Police accountability was never seriously addressed by Mayor Bill de Blasio and NYPD Commissioner Dermot Shea. Both consistently denied that police brutality, malfeasance, and systemic racism were structural problems. Many were left incredulous as police denials continued, despite cell phone footage that captured cops in riots and mass arrests against peaceful protesters following the death of George Floyd and other civilians trapped by racial and economic inequities and mounting deaths during the pandemic.[8] Following the Floyd

---

6. "City Council Changes as Adopted Schedules A and B to the Fiscal Year 2021 Expense and Contract Budget Resolutions," https://www1.nyc.gov/assets/omb/downloads/pdf/adopt20-expreso.pdf.

7. Robbins, Offenhartz, and Hogan, "NYC Budget Updates: City Council Passes 'Heart-Wrenching' Budget, 32–17."

8. Allison McCann, Blacki Migliozzi, Andy Newman, Larry Buchanan, and Aaron Byrd, "N.Y.P.D. Says It Used Restraint During Protests. Here's What the Videos Show," *New York Times*,

protests, New York State Attorney General Letitia James held virtual public hearings to reassure the public. James chose as one of her co-moderators, Obama's former AG, Loretta Lynch. James, protestors, and press documented the NYPD's assaults and beatings of peaceful protestors, its practices of working to "kettle" or confine protestors, and the indiscriminate use of mace/pepper spray.

Officers drove police squad cars into crowds, placing protestors into crowded filthy cells with urine, feces, and mold on the floors. Reports state that the NYPD also crowded protesters into cells without Personal Protective Equipment (PPE), such as masks, and even confiscated masks.[9] Aggressive arrests of activists continued after demonstrations subsided.[10] Most recently, officers used helicopters/drones, police dogs, and tactical squads. What was not present was a warrant for a Black protest leader who allegedly chanted in a megaphone too close to an officer's ear. As noted by white activists during the NYC public hearings, police attacks and arrests disproportionately target Black, nonviolent protesters.

During testimony, NYPD Commissioner Shea denied that abuse was widespread.[11] In 2019, NYC taxpayers paid $69 million in compensation for lawsuits against police abuses/homicides and false imprisonment.[12] Those funds could have been used for food and housing security, child/family wellness, education, parks, and medical care. Yet under current austerity measures and varied forms of abandonment, New Yorkers have dealt with over 23,000 deaths in the city, a million jobs lost, and long food lines outside of churches. These traumas and

July 14, 2020, https://www.nytimes.com/interactive/2020/07/14/nyregion/nypd-george-floyd-protests.html.

9. Sydney Pereira and Gwynne Hogan, "NYPD's Historic Mass Arrest Campaign During George Floyd Protests Was Mostly For Low-Level Offenses," *Gothamist*, June 10, 2020, https://gothamist.com/news/nypds-historic-mass-arrest-campaign-during-george-floyd-protests-was-mostly-low-level-offenses.

10. Jake Offenhartz, Christopher Robbins, and Jen Chung, "The NYPD Banged on a Black Lives Matter Organizer's Door, Shut Down His Street, Stayed For 5 Hours, Then Left," *Gothamist*, August 7, 2020, https://gothamist.com/news/nypd-banged-black-lives-matter-organizers-door-shut-down-his-street-stayed-5-hours-then-left.

11. "AG James Releases Video of NYPD Commissioner Shea Testimony in Ongoing Investigation into Interactions Between Police and the Public," Office of the New York State Attorney General, June 22, 2020, https://ag.ny.gov/press-release/2020/ag-james-releases-video-nypd-commissioner-shea-testimony-ongoing-investigation.

12. Jake Offenhartz, "NYPD Misconduct Lawsuits Cost Taxpayers Nearly $69 Million Last Year," *Gothamist*, January 31, 2020, https://gothamist.com/news/nypd-misconduct-lawsuits-cost-taxpayers-nearly-69-million-last-year.

losses were, and are, disproportionately borne by Black and Brown communities that are treated as expendable "essential workers."

The least resourced communities grapple with the most violence. Mass media reported massive increases in the NYPD and claimed a stark rise in gun violence is due to the decay of "law and order" stemming from protests and bail reforms for the impoverished and BIPOC.[13] Investigative journalists challenged the facticity of police narratives.[14] Commissioner Shea and Mayor de Blasio made false claims that the decline in 68 percent police arrests was due to courts abdicating their duties during the pandemic. Journalists pointed out that virtual courts were open, and that arrests *preceded* court appearances. Police forces were deployed against largely peaceful protests, to quell their political and legal demands, rather than used to monitor criminal gangs and illegal gun possession. The NYPD vigorously defends itself against all allegations of misconduct and against any and all forms of reform.[15] Critics noted that the NYPD might be in violation of the Taylor Law for New York State public employees which addresses work stoppages or slowdowns.[16]

During the hearings on NYPD brutality against protestors, Commissioner Shea informed AG James that the passage of the New York State "Eric Garner Anti-Chokehold Act" was largely ineffective.[17] Shea stated that only the repeal of "50-a" laws, which shield police records, worried police unions.[18] Police unions, which function as protection franchises and PR firms, are now suing to block public access to police

---

13. Sydney Pereira, "49 People Shot in 72 Hours as Wave of Gun Violence Continues in NYC," *Gothamist*, August 16, 2020, https://gothamist.com/news/49-people-shot-72-hours-wave-gun-violence-continues-nyc.

14. Alan Feuer, "The Mayor Blames the Virus for Shootings. Here's What Crime Data Shows," *New York Times*, August 4, 2020, https://www.nytimes.com/2020/08/04/nyregion/nyc-shootings-coronavirus.html.

15. Christopher Robbins, "'Most of Our Powers Were Taken Away': NYPD Blames Reforms for Increase in Violent Crime," *Gothamist*, July 7, 2020, https://gothamist.com/news/most-our-powers-were-taken-away-nypd-blames-reforms-increase-violent-crime.

16. "New York State Public Employees' Fair Employment Act—The Taylor Law," New York State Office of Employee Relations, https://goer.ny.gov/new-york-state-public-employees-fair-employment-act-taylor-law.

17. "New York Lawmakers Pass Eric Garner Anti-Chokehold Act," *Scripps News*, July 10, 2020, https://www.youtube.com/watch?v=uPOGEItbmiY.

18. See "A guide to the 50-a, the most contentious state law on the books," *City & State New York*, https://www.cityandstateny.com/articles/policy/criminal-justice/reformers-look-to-repeal-or-reform-50a.html.

disciplinary records.[19] Some 4,000 of the 36,000 NYPD force have substantiated repetitive offenses against civilians. The NYPD and politicians continue to block or diminish substantive reforms. On August 17, 2020, ProPublica released data indicating that the NYPD routinely withholds evidence in police abuse cases.[20]

While Mayor de Blasio and the City apparently made no substantive cuts in the NYPD budget, the mayor did authorize cuts to the Civilian Complaint Review Board (CCRB), which was to be funded at a certain percentage relative to the NYPD budget.[21] The CCRB planned for staff layoffs, despite its needs for additional resources to handle the sharp increases in civilian complaints of NYPD abuses. Through the repeal of 50-a legislation, data on police brutality against civilians and peaceful protestors became available as police officers' files were shared with the public. The outcome of these legal maneuvers to protect civilians is cloudy. Through the standard operational system of protest politics, despite spikes in the volume of mass protests, predatory police officers largely remained in their jobs with few if any consequences (e.g., losing several vacation days or weeks).

POTUS-45, Donald Trump, filled the judicial vacancies that Obama assumed that Hillary Clinton would fill with centrist-liberals (Clinton did win the popular vote but that does not determine a presidential election). Trump appointed over one hundred ultraconservative/reactionary judges.[22] Pro-police politicians, prosecutors, attorney generals, and judges continue to limit or block substantive reforms and oppose amnesty and/or release for dissenters.

19. Ross Barkan, "How Did Police Unions Get So Powerful?," *The Nation*, July 2, 2020, https://www.thenation.com/article/society/police-unions-nypd-history/.

20. Eric Umansky and Mollie Simon, "The NYPD is Withholding Evidence from Investigations into Police Abuse," ProPublica, August 17, 2020, https://www.propublica.org/article/the-nypd-is-withholding-evidence-from-investigations-into-police-abuse?utm_source=The+Marshall+Project+Newsletter&utm_campaign=6842c85448-EMAIL_CAMPAIGN_2020_08_17_11_46&utm_medium=email&utm_term=0_5e02c-dad9d-6842c85448-174597336.

21. Josefa Velasquez, "Council Watchdog Calls for Close Look at NYPD Complaint Investigation Budget Cuts," *The City*, August 14, 2020, https://www.thecity.nyc/2020/8/14/21369521/council-watchdog-calls-for-close-look-at-nypd-complaint-investigation-budget-cuts.

22. Sara Reynolds, "Trump has appointed second-most federal judges through July 1 of a president's fourth year," *Ballotpedia News*, July 3, 2020, https://news.ballotpedia.org/2020/07/03/trump-has-appointed-second-most-federal-judges-through-july-1-of-a-presidents-fourth-year/.

THE LIMITS OF LEGALISM

Samaria Rice, the mother of twelve-year-old Tamir, killed by Cleveland police, became an open critic of Black feminist BLM leadership, and Tamika Mallory, for using her son's name in what Rice viewed as profiteering. Over several years, Rice "called out" Black Lives Matter, M4BL, political celebrities, entertainers, nonprofits, and writers that she perceived as accumulating wealth after the police murders of working-class or impoverished Blacks. With no attribution to a source,[23] *The Cut* printed the below quote which likely came from young Black organizers who provided emotional, journalistic, and economic aid to impacted families:

> Families of those who are killed by the police—and whose loved ones' deaths spark mass movements—continue to navigate political misrepresentation, battle zones of police repression, homelessness, and poverty, while Black "leadership" that has not been selected by the masses flourishes through celebrity status. These families must be provided the resources to sustain themselves, their families, and their work dedicated to building community infrastructure. . . . Stop celebrity activism; stop corporate investments that support lobbyists for this norm; put an end to the political-economy's parasitism on Black death and poverty.[24]

The quote is linked to organizing by Black anonymous activists, who raised funds for impacted families, while militantly denouncing well-funded nonprofits. Samaria Rice—as was the case with Erica Garner—became marginalized by Black liberals.[25] Rice refused to become

---

23. Content likely came from community-based organizing with Samaria Rice and Lisa Simpson, with activists Da'Shaun Harrison and Rebecca Ann Wilcox, and the request that Fred Hampton, Jr. (son of the slain Chicago Black Panther assassinated by the FBI and Chicago Police Department in a joint pre-dawn December 4, 1969 raid; the federal government issued a settlement to the impacted families) and author/academic Joy James. Rice and Simpson were seeking an audience with Patrisse Cullers, Melina Simpson, and Tamika Mallory to discuss accountability of funds raised in the names of their sons, or others, slain by police.

24. See Imani Perry, "Stop Hustling Black Death Samaria Rice is the mother of Tamir, not a 'mother of the movement,'" *The Cut*, May 24, 2021, https://www.thecut.com/article/samaria-rice-profile.html.

25. See Black Internationalist Unions, "Official Statement from Samaria Rice, mother of Tamir Rice, Lisa Simpson, mother of Richard Richer, and the Collective," *Abolition Journal*, March 28, 2021, https://abolitionjournal.org/official-statement-from-samaria-rice-mother-of-tamir-rice-lisa-simpson-mother-of-richard-richer-and-the-collective/.

one of the impacted families or "Mothers of the Movement" who became surrogates for Hillary Clinton.[26]

After six years of protesting her son's death, Samaria Rice petitioned and challenged the US Department of Justice (DOJ) on its 2020 decision to close the civil rights investigation into the murder of Tamir Rice by Timothy Loehmann (who was later fired after the execution). In 2022, Samaria Rice, Da'Shaun Harrison, and I wrote separate segments interpreting, or referencing, the DOJ's refusal to convene a grand jury in response to the Cleveland, Ohio police killing of Tamir Rice. The collective article begins with Harrison's "Overview and Analysis: The limitations of legalism in an anti-Black world," which notes that Samaria Rice sent letters to the DOJ on April 16, April 29, and June 1, 2021, requesting that the 2020 ruling be reversed and that the DOJ convene a federal grand jury. Assistant Attorney General for the Civil Rights Division, Kristen Clarke, a Black woman, met with Ms. Rice on October 27, 2021, in Washington, DC. A letter to the DOJ[27] from fifty legal scholars and attorneys arguing that the ruling to close the investigation is unconstitutional followed. The letter urged the department to consider that their interpretation of Section 242—a statute enacted as part of the Civil Rights Act of 1866—is unfounded, stating that the particulars of Tamir's case "arguably commands the convening of a federal grand jury and prosecution" of Timothy Loehmann. Legal experts had argued that a federal grand jury is mandated because the local grand jury was "tainted, defective, and aimed at providing a predetermined public exoneration, as opposed to a good faith deliberation based on a fair presentation of the facts."[28] Prominent attorneys from Harvard, Columbia, Yale, and NYU maintained in the letter: "Only an uncorrupted, fairly administered federal grand jury process can ensure justice and restore public confidence in the rule of

---

26. Filmmaker and social justice advocate Michael Moore and others have argued that the Democratic Party betraying working-class people and impoverished people, specifically the Flint, Michigan water crisis during the Obama administration diminished turnout for the Democrats.

27. Da'Shaun Harrison, Joy James, and Samaria Rice, "'Justifiable police homicide' and the ruse of American justice," *Scalawag*, March 8, 2022, https://scalawagmagazine.org/2022/03/doj-tamir-rice-civil-rights-investigation/#letter.

28. See Harrison, James, and Rice, "'Justifiable police homicide' and the ruse of American justice."

law, both of which have been substantially diminished by the actions of local officials and police officers in this case."[29]

The DOJ on January 28, 2022, rejected the arguments waged by prominent faculty at prestigious law schools, and refused requests to reopen the investigation. The DOJ response[30] was addressed to Ms. Rice and her lawyer. Assistant Attorney General Clarke stated that in order "to establish a violation" of Section 242 (excerpts follow), it must first be proven that former-officer Loehmann "acted willfully" or "with the specific intent to do something the law forbids." According to AAG Clarke, when Loehmann shot and killed the twelve-year-old, he was "not depriving Tamir of his constitutional rights." Thus, the consequence of the then-police officer shooting a gun at a child and killing him proved insufficient to prosecute under the civil rights Section 242 statute.

Harrison's *Scalawag* response asserts that "the law" is used as justification for murders "because the development and maintenance of this country required and requires anti-Black violence." In addition, for Harrison, the DOJ's rejection of the request to reopen this investigation reveals the limitations of "critical race theory—which has been given an ample amount of attention in recent months—with regard to its (in)ability to create 'justice' for Black subjects." Harrison asserts that both legal studies and critical race theory cannot "undo the violence of law and legality as a structure" that objectifies Black humanity. Given that those who signed the DOJ letter as "pioneering scholars in legal studies and critical race theory" were still rebuffed by the Biden administration, indicated to Harrison that scholars lack sufficient "power to sway the decision of the DOJ. Because "anti-Black legalism holds more power" over governance and "Black subjects can't be written into laws they were intentionally written out of."[31] In summation, the DOJ's website posts legal protections that do not materialize for the Black mass:

---

29. See Harrison, James, and Rice, "'Justifiable police homicide' and the ruse of American justice."
30. Harrison, James, and Rice, "'Justifiable police homicide' and the ruse of American justice."
31. Harrison, James, and Rice, "'Justifiable police homicide' and the ruse of American justice."

Section 242 of Title 18 makes it a crime for a person acting under color of any law to willfully deprive a person of a right or privilege protected by the Constitution or laws of the United States. . . . Persons acting under color of law within the meaning of this statute include police officers, prisons guards and other law enforcement officials, as well as judges, care providers in public health facilities, and others who are acting as public officials. It is not necessary that the crime be motivated by animus toward the race, color, religion, sex, handicap, familial status or national origin of the victim.[32]

Linking to the analyses of the Rice case, my contribution to "Justifiable police homicide and the Ruse of American Justice" describes a case covered by RSTV/BPM about Black families and communities' hypervulnerability to violent policing. In "Reflections" for *Scalawag*, I reference twelve-year-old Tamir Rice's murder as signifying waves of brutality and terror. Before and after Tamir's death, (legal) procedures further "justifiable police homicide" rulings/determinations which stabilize the escape hatch through which the state walks free. I reference a case discussed by Kalonji Changa on RSTV/BPM. On September 13, 2021, Georgia police killed twelve-year-old Leden Boykins when they allegedly performed a risky pursuit intervention technique (PIT) maneuver on the car in which he and a fourteen-year-old, with his father, sat defenseless while they began a desperate collective conversation with police dispatchers.[33]

Charlie Moore, the Black father of the fourteen-year-old, requested an onsite supervisor to control the police, who were endangering

---

32. TITLE 18, U.S.C., SECTION 242 reads: "Whoever, under color of any law, statute, ordinance, regulation, or custom, willfully subjects any person in any State, Territory, Commonwealth, Possession, or District to the deprivation of any rights, privileges, or immunities secured or protected by the Constitution or laws of the United States . . . shall be fined under this title or imprisoned not more than one year, or both; and if bodily injury results from the acts committed in violation of this section or if such acts include the use, attempted use, or threatened use of a dangerous weapon, explosives, or fire, shall be fined under this title or imprisoned not more than ten years, or both; and if death results from the acts committed in violation of this section or if such acts include kidnapping or an attempt to kidnap, aggravated sexual abuse, or an attempt to commit aggravated sexual abuse, or an attempt to kill, shall be fined under this title, or imprisoned for any term of years or for life, or both, or may be sentenced to death." "DEPRIVATION OF RIGHTS UNDER COLOR OF LAW," United States Department of Justice, https://www.justice.gov/crt/deprivation-rights-under-color-of-law#:~:text=Section%20242%20of%20Title%2018,laws%20of%20the%20United%20States.

33. "Deadly Force Behind the Wheel," *Washington Post*, August 23, 2020, https://www.washingtonpost.com/graphics/2020/investigations/pit-maneuver-police-deaths/.

the children. (Allegedly, police surrounded and smashed car windows next to the children in the parked car.) His response is standard: unable to de-escalate police violence, we ask for assistance from supervisors, civil rights laws, and attorneys general. Without the time to litigate or the conditions under which the vulnerability of Black life would be recognized, the father drove away, reportedly at a high speed, which was followed by a chase. The 911 conversations continued—leaving the family at the mercy of a police chase. Allegedly, police in squad cars rammed a civilian car. The car flipped over, and Leden died. The state incarcerated the parental driver, Charlie Moore, on felony murder charges for Leden's death.[34]

It was determined that Moore was driving under the influence (DUI) of alcohol and lacked a valid license. Leden's family petitioned for all camera footage and documents concerning the killing of their child with a precision immobilization technique (PIT maneuver). PITs are banned by police if children are in the targeted car. The family demanded a special prosecutor, as was the case in the Ahmaud Arbery investigation. Four officers repeatedly lied, stating that they did not know that there were children in the car. Officers used flashlights to look into the vehicle, and they would have seen two children. Georgia general orders do not allow the PIT maneuver, as noted in the dash cam. When the dispatcher stated that there were children in the car, the police officers said that if the car did not stop, the children would be in a ditch.[35]

On the same day in April 2021 that Derek Chauvin was to be sentenced for murdering George Floyd in Minnesota, Ohio police killed sixteen-year-old Ma'Khia Bryant. They fired four shots toward her as she threatened two girls with a knife during an altercation at a foster home.[36] Rather than watching the Chauvin verdict later that day, a Black father, Rayshawn Whiting went to the neighborhood protest for

---

34. "GA Police Murder 12 Year Old and Charge Father with the Crime!," *Black Power Media*, March 2, 2022, https://youtu.be/n_8HeXISt6k. Also see "911 calls released in crash that killed 12-year-old boy during chase with state trooper," 11Alive, September 14, 2021, https://www.youtube.com/watch?v=JfkoAg1KbwA.

35. Calls for special prosecutor 12-year-old's death in high-speed chase with Georgia State Patrol," https://www.youtube.com/watch?v=qO6kaQWwWpI.

36. Neil Vigdor and Bryan Pietsch, "Teenage Girl Is Fatally Shot by Police in Columbus, Officials Say," *New York Times*, October 11, 2021, https://www.nytimes.com/2021/04/20/us/columbus-ohio-shooting.html.

Ma'Khia. Describing our limited legalistic choices through the analogy of climate crises, he shared his emotional exhaustion with the media: "I've got daughters . . . I'm tired of it. I feel like a polar bear with the ice caps melting. We have nowhere to run. If we protect ourselves, we go to jail. If we don't, we die."

Neither the killings themselves nor the injustices surrounding Tamir Rice, Ma'Khia Bryant, and Leden Boykin's deaths are aberrations. We are taxed to pay for structures of state violence as well as ineffectual legalistic responses to violent police corruption. Our political strategies for protections will evolve in communal-democratic strategy sessions where we struggle to control predatory violence by containing the violators we fund.[37] Asking for Attorney General Carr in Georgia to "do his job," if not then the press conference and attorneys note that they would reach out to Kristen Clarke, Assistant District Attorney at the DOJ, the same attorney that Samaria Rice appealed to.

Environmental attorneys argued that one should not have to prove intent in a court of law concerning pollution and environmental devastation. It is irrelevant if someone *intended* to poison the water, air, and land. The fact that they committed such violations indicates that they are killing life. Individual or collective intent becomes irrelevant. The harm that follows the actions determines consequence and metrics for restitution and correction.

In "Final Words," Samaria Rice describes her meeting with AAG Clarke and two DOJ career attorneys in DC, on October 27, 2021. Ms. Rice, who asked for an indictment of the white police officers who killed twelve-year-old Tamir Rice as he played with a plastic toy gun, describes the DOJ as callous in its refusal to address statute 242, which it claimed would be difficult to challenge. Rice instructed the DOJ to test the difficulty of a challenge by actually doing one. She also asserted that what Loehmann was *thinking* about on November 22, 2014, when he shot Tamir, was irrelevant. Rather her "life has changed forever."[38] She makes a pointed query: "The DOJ breaks their

---

37. Alexis Hoag, "Derrick Bell's Interest Convergence and the Permanence of Racism: A Reflection on Resistance," *Harvard Law Review* (blog), August 24, 2020, https://blog.harvardlawreview.org/derrick-bells-interest-convergence-and-the-permanence-of-racism-a-reflection-on-resistance/.

38. See Harrison, James, and Rice, "'Justifiable police homicide' and the ruse of American justice."

own rules, so how do we get justice in a system like that?" The DOJ argued that the state had to prove that Loehmann "acted willfully," but the fired and disgraced police officer was sitting in the passenger seat of the squad car with his gun on his lap as his trainer Frank Garmback braked the police car only a few feet in front of Tamir. For Rice, it was the Cleveland police who created the danger—in hiring a police officer who had been fired from a previous post due to his recklessness and aggression. Rice wanted both officers "indicted and charged with first-degree murder, conspiracy, and the cover up of Tamir Rice's murder."[39]

Rice describes the prosecutors, who rose to the ranks of Assistant Attorney General and Vice President, respectively Kristen Clarke and Kamala Harris, as disappointments. "Two *Black women* in power and unwilling to support the needs of Black people, what a damn shame." Rice also denounces the Congressional Black Caucus as having "stood for nothing." Resonating with Erica Garner's analyses and declarations to the public, she lists the crimes of the state:

America is designed to fail Black and Brown people. You may think you are one of the white people with power, but you better double back and look in the mirror. A child can be killed in America and the American legal system will justify it. This system is broken from the inside out and it can't be fixed. No one will give us justice in the DOJ where they commit crimes of genocide, conspiracies, and the cover up of murders on American citizens—especially for Black and Brown people. I'm so disgusted with the DOJ, Democrats, Biden and all other presidential administrations. None of you all have ever done right by the people that put your sorry asses in office, and now I know they will not ever make it right.[40]

Referencing anti-Black genocide within the US, noting that justice is an impossible possibility for Black people writ large in the US, Rice instructs: "Save yourself, train your family . . . ."[41]

---

39. Harrison, James, and Rice, "'Justifiable police homicide' and the ruse of American justice."
40. Harrison, James, and Rice, "'Justifiable police homicide' and the ruse of American justice."
41. Harrison, James, and Rice, "'Justifiable police homicide' and the ruse of American justice."

CONCLUSION

Centrist and liberal politics do not create substantive change, they stabilize reforms that fail to address the deepest needs of the dishonored who are most vulnerable to predatory policing. If "non-reformist reforms" is an oxymoron, how best to strategize to confront and quell predatory police forces? The epistemology of the Captive Material requires material struggle. The data collection and analyses have already been offered. (One can search for excellent resource for analyses and critiques that keep us informed about laws, bureaucracies, prisons, and police forces.) Radical politics became increasingly dismissed if not demonized as an effective war resister appears, e.g., in Atlanta, Georgia to oppose "Cop City." Protests that prove too unruly and disruptive are penalized, at times by (radical) liberals and nonprofits, or coopted for adjacent radicalism. Erica Garner did not stop progressing past the early stages of protests. She became adept at war resistance and countering police formations and media manipulations. Neither the state nor the (nonprofit) corporations will stabilize funding for a freedom movement. Still, cadres focused on communities continue to give and receive care. The capacity to do so consistently requires marronage that cannot be bought, sold, or monetized by donors.

Despite physical, emotional, psychological exhaustion and structural violence, Captive Maternals continue to foster new communities of accountability, love, and labor. Some seem resigned, animated, or reserved in their duties. Perhaps the familiar becomes a form of comfort. As noted in the refrain of Boots Riley and the Coup's "The Guillotine": "We were in a war before we fought one."

CHAPTER 9

INTERNATIONAL ALLIANCES FOR HUMAN RIGHTS

Policing in America is not broken. The judicial system is not broken.
American society is not broken. All are functioning perfectly, doing
exactly what they have done since before some of this nation's most
prosperous slave-murdering robber-barons came together to consecrate
into statehood the mechanisms of their barbarism.
—Albert Burneko, "The American Justice System Is Not Broken"[1]

In *Truthout*, Marjorie Cohn covered the International Commission of Inquiry on Systemic Racist Police Violence Against People of African Descent in the United States, on January 18, 2020, Martin Luther King, Jr. Day. According to Cohn, the Commission of Inquiry, over eighteen days, reviewed nearly fifty cases "of unjustified police homicides" of Black people. Three principal organizations convened the hearings: the National Conference of Black Lawyers (NCBL), International Association of Democratic Lawyers (IADL), and the National Lawyers Guild (NLG). The Trump administration barred the UN Human Rights Council from establishing a commission to investigate US systemic racism and police brutality.[2] The Council ordered the

---

1. Albert Burneko, "The American Justice System Is Not Broken," *Deadspin*, December 3, 2014, https://deadspin.com/the-american-justice-system-is-not-broken-1666445407.
2. Marjorie Cohn, "After Trump Blocked UN Inquiry of Racist Violence, NGOs Are Conducting their Own," *Truthout*, December 22, 2020, https://truthout.org/articles/after-trump-blocked-un-inquiry-of-racist-violence-ngos-are-conducting-their-own/.

High Commissioner for Human Rights, Michelle Bachelet, to prepare a report about police violence against people of African descent, but not limited to the United States, by June 2021."[3]

GWEN CARR

The Inquiry addressed impacted families. Eric Garner's mother Gwen Carr addressed familial loss due to predatory police violence. She notes the "tens of thousands" of impacted families by police violence. Some of the cases are "high-profile," some are not, but Carr asserts that every case should be so. She describes how one "case is as bad as the next," and how impacted mothers on some days cannot leave their beds. Death through different forms of murder is rampant, according to Carr: "They kill us twice. First, the police, they murder in broad daylight, they murder us in the night when they don't think anyone's looking, then they murder us in the newspaper . . . [to] criminalize us."[4] Carr's testimony recounts her specific ordeal, of losing her son and the battle to stabilize and preserve her family:

> [In] the future when they hear the name 'Eric Garner,' I want them to say, because of his death, that the ones who came behind him got justice. His death was not in vain. I want them to say that his mother stood up for him, when she didn't even know what was going to happen to her. . . .
>
> Some of the mothers . . . on medication [or] . . . losing their mind. But I thank God that He let me keep my mind . . . [to] advocate for my son as well as yours and yours and yours. Until the day I die, this is what I'm going to do. . . . I have met so many mothers around the nation who I have never met before, so many people who have supported me, and now that you supported me, I support you.[5]

---

3. Marjorie Cohn, "Eric Garner's Mother Says We Must Push for Justice That Her Son Didn't Receive," *Truthout*, January 21, 2021, https://truthout.org/articles/eric-garners-mother-says-we-must-push-for-justice-that-her-son-didnt-receive/.
4. See transcript of the March 2021 International Commission of Inquiry, https://inquiry-commission.org/report/.
5. Gwen Carr, "International Commission of Inquiry – Hearing on the case of Eric Garner– January 18, 2021," https://inquirycommission.org/video-and-transcript-eric-garner-hearing-monday-january-18-international-commission-of-inquiry/.

In June 2020, an international coalition of hundreds of organizations and individuals requested that the United Nations Human Rights Council "convene a commission of inquiry" to investigate racism and racist police violence in the United States. The UN Human Rights Network, ACLU Human Rights Program, and grassroots organizations such as Mothers Against Police Brutality made the request which the UN declined. Instead, the UN requested the UN High Commissioner on Human Rights to prepare a report on racism. The National Conference of Black Lawyers, the National Lawyers Guild, and the International Association of Democratic Lawyers convened a "commission of inquiry to investigate systemic, widespread and grave violations of the rights of Black people by law enforcement in the US." Their report was to be shared with the UN High Commissioner and the public.

Responding to racial discrimination in the National Bar Association, the National Council of Black Lawyers had formed in 1968. By 2021, it was the leading organization in the 2021 hearings on police violence and brutality. The NCBL co-convened its commission on police violence and homicide against US civilians on January 18, 2021, coinciding with Martin Luther King, Jr. Day, and two years after the passage of the Eric Garner Law. This Commission of Inquiry stated that it did not seek to supplant UN obligations and its responsibility to adequately address racism and police violence in the US. However, it appears that the UN is largely aligned with or silent about US domestic and foreign policies and outsources its condemnations of US structural violence through military or police, to its working groups, committees, or commissions.

The International Commission of Inquiry on Systemic Racist Police Violence against People of African Descent (ICISRPVPAD) in the United States focuses on the investigations and reports that further the work of the High Commissioner. It is not clear what the "work of the High Commissioner" is in regards to confronting US predatory violence. The High Commissioner is not a Captive Maternal and, hence, is not marching toward a confrontation with the United States that hosts the UN in tony eastside neighborhoods in midtown Manhattan. Unsurprisingly, the Commission of Inquiry's investigation into anti-Black US police violence determined that murder cases of unarmed civilians were shaped or driven by systemic racism. The US Commission would agree and then recommend "accountability measures" to ensure legal accountability and protect vulnerable people.

HUMAN RIGHTS ATTORNEY JONATHAN MOORE

A longtime member of the NLG and IADL, Jonathan Moore had practiced civil rights law for some four decades before he represented the Garner family. Specializing in police violence against people of color, he began litigating against police violence in 1983 when Manhattan Transit Authority (MTA) police killed young Black graffiti artist Michael Stewart (1958–1983). Stewart was arrested for spraying or tagging a subway wall with spray paint. He was beaten by the transit police and taken to the hospital because he was comatose. Stewart was declared brain dead and died thirteen days after his arrest and encounter with the NYPD. He was said to have cuts and bruises all over his body. Thirty minutes elapsed between Stewart's arrest and hospitalization as comatose. The NYC coroner changed his findings of cause of death three times: from alcohol intoxication to spinal cord injury to blunt force trauma. The family hired a private autopsy that ruled that the artist had been strangled to death. However, the coroner would not supply Michael Stewart's eyes for confirmation (the families do not get to collect the body parts of their loved ones murdered by police forces). The six MTA police who were present at the beating and torture of Stewart were all acquitted. The Stewart family petitioned to have the chief medical examiner, Dr. Elliot Gross, fired. They were successful. The Stewart family received a $1.7 million settlement. Their battles instructed communities, artists,[6] in war resistance.

---

6. In 2019, Afro-Cuban artist-activist Chaédria LaBouvier, discussed in this book, was the first Black curator to organize a solo show at the Guggenheim, focused on Jean-Michel Basquiat. Basquiat's 1983 painting *The Death of Michael Stewart (Defacement)* shows ghoulish cops in blue coats and hats sporting fangs as they wield clubs. Michael Stewart's murder incited artists to express communal solidarity. Allies followed Basquiat's 1983 art: Keith Haring created *Michael Stewart—USA for Africa* (1985); Andy Warhol included a *New York Daily News* article on Stewart's death in a 1983 screen-printed "headline" painting.

LaBouvier's protest against institutional racist bias in the museum led to a June 23, 2020 letter signed by 200 curators which became a catalyst for changes within the Guggenheim Museum. See "Basquiat's 'Defacement': The Untold Story," https://www.guggenheim.org/exhibition/basquiats-defacement-the-untold-story.

After Stewart, multiple high-profile cases of Black people tortured or murdered by the NYPD followed. Working as a security guard in a club, in 1997, Abner Louima (1966–) was mistaken by a NYPD officer as someone he thought had hit him. Louima was beaten in the police car and later sodomized in a prison precinct with a broken broomstick by NYPD officer Justin Volpe. Convicted and then sentenced to thirty years in prison, Volpe was released six years early in June 2023. In 1999, Guinean student Amadou Diallo (1975–1999) was shot at forty-one times by an undercover NYPD unit, and hit nineteen times by plainclothes cops Sean Carroll, Richard Murphy, Edward McMellon, and Kenneth Boss, all of the members of the Street Crime Unit (which was later dismantled). Although a Bronx grand jury had indicted all of the officers, the trial was moved upstate to Albany, where they were acquitted. Diallo's parents received a $3 million settlement from New York City. Musician Bruce Springsteen composed the song "American Skin [41 Shots]" in his memory.

NYPD officers are known to alter the *Wikipedia* pages reporting police predatory violence, in order to change facts and make murders look heroic. Rarely are they seriously disciplined for stealth-editing and altering history in order to further predation and violence. Sean Bell (1983–2006) was murdered by undercover police after he left a Queens strip club in the early morning of his wedding with his bachelor party. NYPD shot fifty bullets at Bell and his two companions. They were injured, struck in the neck. Bell died, leaving behind his partner and daughters.

By the time he became the Garner family attorney, Jonathan Moore had litigated many cases where the police used excessive force against people of color. Using the law to seek restitution for families and survivors or police rape and torture, Moore situates the Garner case within a historical pattern that shapes to NYPD aggressions and harassments. Singular, for Moore, is "stop and frisk." NYC residents brought a lawsuit that alleged that the police street encounters with mostly people of color engaged in racial profiling. The 2013 ten-week federal trial on stop-and-frisk ended with a judgment (not a settlement) against the NYPD. The court ruled that for years "as a matter of policy and practice . . . the police department had engaged in a policy of racial profiling."

Moore links these routine, racist procedures to Eric Garner's homicide. He notes that the NYPD's "encounter with Eric Garner began as a run-of-the-mill ordinary street encounter. A stop, possibly question, and frisk that turned bad." For Moore it is detrimental to communities and societies if police departments allow officers "to make decisions based upon improper motivations." That is, there was no justification for NYPD stopping or searching Eric Garner on July 17, 2014. Moore asserts that no NYS or US law permitted stopping, searching, and arresting Eric Garner because there was no credible report or evidence that he was violating the law—not any felony, common law, or penal law misdemeanor set by New York. Moore suggests that the public might be ill-informed about such encounters, thinking that such an engagement with police would be quick, routine, and not intrusive. He corrects that misperception: "Well, we see in the Eric Garner case, how intrusive it could be."

Central here is not just the procedure but the white nationalist animus that turns such encounters into warfare that intimidates and terrorizes Black and Brown communities: "From about 2008 to 2012, there were four million documented stops and frisks on the streets of New York, 90 percent of which were directed at people of color, and 90 percent of which led to no further investigative activity. In other words . . . the police were wrong 90 percent of the time."[7]

For Moore, the "struggle for racial equality" and against racist policing means that we have to ask: "what remedy works?" The attorney is not going to provide the answer as "revolutionary struggle." Attorneys work within the legal framework. So, it would be more accurate to ask what remedies, in the plural, work. What is our function and capacity to care for ourselves and each other without dependency on the law whose enforcers dishonor and hunt us?

Moore's legal representation of the estate of Eric Garner led the family to receive $6.9 million in 2019. Officer Pantaleo was fired in 2020. Yet, in his litigation, Moore described that the medical examiner determined that Eric Garner was killed by multiple NYPD officers. The video footage identified the death as the result of a combination of

7. Jonathan Moore, "International Commission of Inquiry – Hearing on the case of Eric Garner – January 18, 2021," https://inquirycommission.org/video-and-transcript-eric-garner-hearing-monday-january-18-international-commission-of-inquiry/.

neck and chest compression through an attack by *at least two* officers: one "had his arm around Garner's neck [and] laid on top of his back, pushing Garner's face into the ground." Holding Garner while he struggled to breath would only be possible, according to Moore, with "several officers being on top of him." Pantaleo was the only one fired, that means the other killers of Garner are still employed or collecting pensions courtesy of the public and taxpayers. *No police officer faced disciplinary charges* for killing Eric Garner after a bogus stop-and-frisk that never should have happened.

Although Moore observes that for over six years, Gwen Carr "has been struggling mightily . . . [to] hold all those responsible for her son's death accountable," he does not note that accountability only comes with power and ability to respond to predatory power with discipline. For example, the Rochester pastor reminds us of one approach: "If you kill us, we will kill your economy."

Moore tells us that Garner's death is not "an aberration," but one in a "long series of police killings of people of color, throughout the '80s and '90s, and into this current century."[8] Yet, we already know that. We also already know what he emphasizes in his testimony: that the remedy for police reform remains elusive and the search for remedy "very arduous." Moore makes a grim assessment of justice through litigation. "It's been like pulling teeth." His legal confession is that we need new strategies because the current strategies of working with "the system" bring us more death and dishonor. "Non-reformist reforms" do not work to our advantage, they work for the state structures which encompass policing. Before the election of the Black mayor and former NYPD Eric Adams, who states that he will bring back "stop-and-frisk," was the first Black woman NYPD commissioner Keechant Sewell, who protects, or does not have the capacity of disciplining or firing predatory police.

Jonathan Moore, the human rights litigator, notes the evidence of contradictions and cycles without a dialectic that spirals lateral or vertical to better explore our options for escaping captivity:

> I have to say, after almost over six years, I'm not sure how far we've gotten, or whether we've really changed or are beginning to put

---

8. Moore, "International Commission of Inquiry – Hearing on the case of Eric Garner."

mechanisms in place that would change the culture of the police department. Although the number of stops has gone down over that period of time, the percentage of people being stopped is still the same in terms of the racial breakdown, which suggests that officers are still making decisions based on race more than any other factor.[9]

Despite the 3,000-plus complaints of police malfeasance and brutality, Moore notes the "zero substantiated complaints by the police department," which civil rights attorneys bring to the court's attention to improve judicial oversight. But the courts fail the citizenry. Moore reflects that it is "difficult to see how you can really effect this change through the courts."

For Moore, bringing misconduct cases to court is essential, but a caveat exists, it will take mobilization, movement, marronage, and war resistance to challenge police predators. Moore argues that essentially community involvement will pressure the state structure; lawsuits are not enough (the taxpayers not the police unions fund monetized death payments). If the community rises up—I would use the word "rebels"—Moore seems confident that as with the case of George Floyd, anger in the community becomes a catalyst for change. He offers the National Lawyers Guild slogan "justice is a constant struggle." In some ways, that echoes the slogan "freedom is a constant struggle." Positioning what might become T-shirt slogans or platitudes into sophisticated or astute strategies is not quite clear. Moore as an attorney is bold and skillful in delivering care through litigation and advocacy "for significant change in policing." We can appreciate his candor when he acknowledges "we realize how much further we have to go."[10]

JUDGES PETER HERBERT AND MAX BOQWANA OFFER AN INTERNATIONAL PERSPECTIVE

Political activist and Judge Peter Herbert asserted that "everywhere people of African descent, live, work, or try to survive, whether it be France, whether it be Australia, whether it be Brazil, the same form of brutality. . . is it really possible to look at the court or the justice sys-

---

9. Moore, "International Commission of Inquiry – Hearing on the case of Eric Garner."
10. Moore, "International Commission of Inquiry – Hearing on the case of Eric Garner."

tem in isolation without looking at the social status of African people, not only in the diaspora, but as they are in the United States, to form a solution?" Moore agreed that racist "violence against people of African descent is not just isolated to this country or to any one country." But he maintains that stronger international mechanisms and forums can address the crisis. Max Boqwana follows up with a philosophical query concerning violence:

> Africans and the Black people everywhere else in the world come from a history of being non-human. That's the history of slavery where people were part of the property. And you get to a place like the United States of America, where the entire political framework of the country is also based on lies. That here is a country that was founded by white tribes. And it had no people. So even today, anybody therefore, that is not white is being seen as an outsider. And it's in that context that the police are dealing with both outsiders, and I dare say nonhumans. Should we not put that in the entire education system of the country, because I think inasmuch as we're talking about police brutality, I think in other sectors of society, there's a similar discrimination against the people of color. Do you think that education is important in this regard? And, what you call sensitivity training? Shouldn't that be part of the law schools as well?[11]

For Moore, "defund the police" reflects a powerful slogan that won't likely "lead to a meaningful reform, because people obviously, in every society see a need for some kind of law enforcement" for protection. The attorney sees "that the police have become an instrument of state control of mostly people of color and poor people." Thus, the task becomes to "reimagine how the police perform their responsibilities," as they interact with "so-called people with emotional difficulties or mental health histories." Moore argues that the NYPD homicide of Eric Garner represents "a total failure of the disciplinary process." Five to six officers were involved in Garner's death; none faced disciplinary charges. Pantaleo remains the only one charged; yet, he also remained a police officer for five years at full pay and with bonuses before his termination.

---

11. Max Boqwana, "International Commission of Inquiry – Hearing on the case of Eric Garner – January 18, 2021," https://inquirycommission.org/video-and-transcript-eric-garner-hearing-monday-january-18-international-commission-of-inquiry/.

State and federal governments could have prosecuted the NYPD but refused. This happened in democratic and republican administrations. Both administrations refused to investigate and charge police predators with criminal prosecution. Thus, Moore asserts that there is "absolute failure of the disciplinary system" partly because the police usurped the community's involvement in disciplining police forces. Decisions are left up to the department (or as noted earlier to City Hall). Police and capital and government control the terrain. Civilian review boards make recommendations, but police departments and commissioners decide outcomes. Police commissioners will not antagonize police unions nor will mayors. Since civilian review boards cannot enforce discipline and their recommendations are usually mild and still ignored, *civilian authority does not exist over militarized police departments.*

Police unions protect predatory police. Moore notes that police "unions" are not "labor advocates, like teachers' unions. . . [as] arbiters of predatory violence and they do not work for public safety but for the security of their forces, including those guilty of but not convicted of crimes." The NYPD's approximately 35,000 cops shielded by protective unions hold disproportionate powers. With autonomy and impunity, they determine labor contracts and the outcome of misconduct complaints. Moore highlights a possible remedy—which I read as Captive Maternal agency—invest in community organizing in order to counter the powerful and their corruption.

When Judge Peter Herbert asks about the US, from a global perspective, shielding "a highly militarized police force," Moore acknowledges the hyperviolence of the United States: "we invade a country and use all this military armor and . . . bring it all back and give it to the police departments." Thus, armaments and force are prioritized. Contrasting US police with police forces in the Global South, retrained into a new constitutional police service, Jurist Max Boqwana distinguishes between "police service" and "police force" to assert that in the Global South police are better trained to exhibit "responsibility to serve the community rather than to mete out force. . . it's not really about law and order, but it's about safety and security, which is a different philosophical outlook." Here, law and order is identified with force, and "safety and security" with caretaking. Boqwana asks Moore if US police culture would become less violent "If we convince the police that they are joining a police service, where the responsibility is to ensure safety and security?" Moore responds that the "militarization of the police has gone on basically unchecked for too many years" to persuade police that this is not a warzone.

In US militarized culture, according to Moore, there is a "blue wall of silence, officers protect each other." Moore then adds that "we have a horrible history of racism . . . beginning with slavery, and then with Jim Crow and now with . . . the rise of white supremacy." Linking NYPD violence with political violence, Moore asserts that it's neither a mistake nor a coincidence "that a number of those folks who assaulted the Capitol building on January 6, [2021] a couple of weeks ago, were former military and law enforcement officers, or even current law enforcement officers. That's not surprising to us, those of us who have been working in this area [of litigating for civil rights against police violence] for many years."

Boqwana poses his final query concerning "the proportion of similar violence against white civilians" and "people of color." Moore returns back to "stop and frisk." In 2022, former NYPD captain Eric Adams was elected as the second Black mayor in NYC history. Adams publicly promoted his plans to restore stop and frisk, plainclothes policing in low-income neighborhoods, and other repressive tactics to NYC policing. Progressives argued that in the 2022 elections, Adams (who had campaigned on destroying the Democratic Socialists of America [DSA]) used tactics of fear mongering through crime reports to assist conservatives and republican voters to prevail at the polls in NYC. As noted in the opening chapters, Adams appointed Keechant Sewell as the first Black female NYPD commissioner only to curtail her institutional power and autonomy. The NYC mayor also hired an administrator for Rikers Island jail that curtailed the rights of the incarcerated, and refused to curtail the violence of the guards, or restructure and diminish the draconian conditions for the incarcerated.[12] Hence, the mayor sought and seeks to place a firewall between the citizenry and the police and prison guards, not in order to control

---

12. "NYPD Commissioner Sewell Announces New Executive Designations and Appointments," New York City Police Department, January 20, 2022, https://www.nyc.gov/site/nypd/news/p00035/nypd-commissioner-sewell-new-executive-designations-appointments.

violence, but in order to shield police and prison guards from being accountable for their violence.

Figure 5: The January 1, 2022, swearing-in ceremony of NYPD Commissioner Keechant Sewell by Mayor Eric Adams, before a mural of Black radicals persecuted by police forces, including: Malcolm X, Nat Turner, Angela Davis, Huey Newton, Paulo Freire, and Assata Shakur. Image: Matthew Chayes.

HISTORICAL AND CONTEMPORARY RACISM

In Moore's final statement on "stop and frisk," he bookends the symbiosis between anti-Black violence and police violence, with the latter being protected by legalism and union payrolls. Moore notes that of the four million people stopped over several years, 90 percent were Black or Latinx/Hispanic. In addition, 90 percent of the cases led to no further charges. Blacks were stopped at a higher rate than whites (and Latinx/Hispanics), but whites had a higher percentage than Blacks of possessing contraband. Police focus on BIPOC is not rational or productive policing. The higher incidences of contraband, usually drugs, but Moore mentions guns, are found on whites.

Moore argues that the fundamental problem is US historical and contemporary racism. He focuses largely on the phenomenon of anti-Blackness to assert the transparent hatred and hunting of Blacks: "[U]ntil we begin to understand that truth, we can never move beyond what we have now to a true system of accountability." The New Testament states: "The truth will set you free." (John 8:32). Captive Maternal abolitionist Frederick Douglass notes in his 1852 "What, to the Slave, is the Fourth of July?" The character of the nation's laws that should protect, instead corrupt governance, policing, and banking: "You boast of your love of liberty, your superior civilization, and your pure Christianity, while the whole political power of the nation (as embodied in the two great political parties) is solemnly pledged to support and perpetuate . . . enslavement."[13] The abolitionist and/or Captive Maternal at all stages—if not stagnant—will confront the reality that law does not through structure protect or ensure them justice, particularly if they are not wealthy or white.

CONCLUSION

Everyone will not be able to save themselves or save their communities. If we are to explore the meanings of the mandate to "train" our families, we would have to engage with international and national political analyses and coalitions. "Train your family" extends beyond the zone of the personal family. There is the spiritual family and the political family to which we devote our time, energy, skills, and discipline. Marronage offers a buffer or sanctuary for training, meditating, evaluating our choices, and caretaking. Any buffer against predatory police, poverty, stress, and anti-Blackness is a reprieve and an opportunity to breathe, nap, sleep, dream, meditate, or strategize. Freedom schools, Agape-driven churches, temples, mosques, and media are training sites. Land, labor, and love collectively shared, can suture self/com-

13. Frederick Douglass, "What, to the Slave, is the Fourth of July?" 1852, https://www.black-past.org/african-american-history/speeches-african-american-history/1852-frederick-douglass-what-slave-fourth-july/.

munal protections on every metric: physical, spiritual, intellectual, psychological, and sexual. Every Captive Maternal, consciously or unconsciously, trains to develop defenses against predatory aggressions as a form of self-worth and self-love.

CHAPTER 10

WAR RESISTANCE: *WE CHARGE GENOCIDE* AND *RETURN TO THE SOURCE*

CHARGING GENOCIDE AND PETITIONING GLOBAL COMMUNITIES

During the Cold War era, historical examples of radical Captive Maternal agency include: in 1951, the Black-led Civil Rights Congress' *We Charge Genocide: The Crime of Government against the Negro People*, the 1960 creation of the Student Nonviolent Coordinating Committee (SNCC), the 1964 formation of the Organization of Afro-American Unity by Malcolm X, the 1966 emergence of the Black Panther Party for Self Defense, and the 1971 Attica rebellion following George Jackson's assassination in San Quentin. All of these formations were antiracist, anti-imperial, and anticolonial. Black communities and their allies combined their focus on resistance with caretaking. Delivering care in the form of expansion and defense of voting rights, integration (noting Derrick Bell's warning of "interest convergence"), medical care, competent education and food supplies, freedom from lynching, and racial terror were all resistance to decay, death, and dishonor. Revolutionary Panthers, who were and are Captive Maternals, realized that all forms of Black care on the marronage stage of autonomous communities—from free food, education, medical care to self-defense—would be persecuted by the state, police, and prisons.

In international struggles for justice, to what degrees are governmental bodies protecting communities? US domestic and foreign policies are not misaligned. Organizing is local and transnational (as is the working class and billionaire clubs). A firewall against predatory policing would radiate beyond Staten Island, New York City, New York State, the Northeast, the US, North America, and the Americas into global politics. The US, specifically, the NYPD, has trained police forces around the globe, including in Brazil where political assassinations and police terror against Black favelas is the norm.[1] Its police have been militarized through training of Israeli police that occupy Palestinian lands. Policing is militarism. Racism and anti-Blackness, as well as political repression, break bones on a daily basis. There is always resistance. The 1951 *We Charge Genocide* treatise reminds us of political possibilities:

> It is our hope, and we fervently believe that it was the hope and aspiration of every Black American whose voice was silenced forever through premature death at the hands of racist-minded hooligans or Klan terrorists, that the truth recorded here will be made known to the world; that it will speak with a tongue of fire loosening an unquenchable moral crusade, the universal response to which will sound the death knell of all racist theories.
> —*We Charge Genocide*, 1951[2]

The document remains relevant seventy years after its publication and dissemination throughout the globe as a condemnation of anti-Black human rights violations and subjugations. Today, cell phone footage of the police killings of Eric Garner and George Floyd circulate throughout the world in ways in which *We Charge Genocide* could not. Still, the document has value and utility.

In November 2014, young activists from Chicago, aligning themselves with the 1951 *We Charge Genocide* petition, met with the Committee Against Torture in Geneva, to discuss the Chicago police tor-

---

1. With the largest Black population outside the African continent, Brazil leads the world with police killings of [Black] civilians largely due to its paramilitary forces or "death squads." See Joy James and Jaime Amparo Alves, "States of Security, Democracy's Sanctuary, and Captive Maternals in Brazil and the United States," *Souls: A Critical Journal of Black Politics, Culture, and Society* 20, no. 4 (2018), 345–367.
2. Patterson, *We Charge Genocide*.

ture ring that had forced over one hundred, mostly Black men, into false confessions and imprisonments.[3] *We Charge Genocide*, despite its lack of content about the analyses shaped by feminism and queer theory, is referenced in contemporary tribunals on international struggles for liberation and basic protocols for human rights.

Although originally conceived or portrayed in the post-World War II era as an impartial, international body safeguarding human rights, the United Nations (UN) adheres to dictates by the United States. The UN is situated on pricey midtown Manhattan real estate (subcommittees in the UN are more willing to challenge the imperial violence). *We Charge Genocide* links the past through the present and to the future. Its proposal for "remedies" borrows from a phrase in Ida B. Wells' 1892 *Southern Horrors*.[4] The Civil Rights Congress, Black communists in the CPUSA, as Black internationalists authored and presented *We Charge Genocide*—signed by William Patterson, Paul Robeson, W. E. B. DuBois, and Claudia Jones—to the UN. The document unequivocally cites the anti-Black violence of the emergent US empire:

> Out of the inhuman black ghettos of American cities, out of the cotton plantations of the South, comes this record of mass slayings on the basis of race, of lives deliberately warped and distorted by the willful creation of conditions making for premature death, poverty and disease. It is a record that calls aloud for condemnation, for an end to these terrible injustices that constitute a daily and ever-increasing violation of the United Nations Convention on the Prevention and Punishment of the Crime of Genocide.[5]

The same charges would be brought to the UN a decade later by Malcolm X upon the founding of the Organization of Afro-American Unity in 1964 in Addis Ababa, Ethiopia. Decades ago, Black interna-

---

3. Noah Berlatsky, "At the United Nations, Chicago Activists Protest Police Brutality," *Atlantic*, November 17, 2014, https://www.theatlantic.com/national/archive/2014/11/we-charge-genocide-movement-chicago-un/382843/.

4. Ida B. Wells, "Southern Horrors: Lynch Law in All Its Phases," February 8, 2005, https://www.gutenberg.org/ebooks/14975.

5. See "Dec. 17, 1951: 'We Charge Genocide' Petition Submitted to United Nations," Zinn Education Project, https://www.zinnedproject.org/news/tdih/we_charge_genocide_petition; "(1951) We Charge Genocide," *BlackPast*, July 15, 2011, https://www.blackpast.org/global-african-history/primary-documents-global-african-history/we-charge-genocide-historic-petition-united-nations-relief-crime-united-states-government-against/.

tionalist activists asserted that the United States promoted racism, capitalism, and imperialism through a violent trajectory of accumulations based in terrorizing Black communities. The documents made legible to the world that US democracy was a prime violator of human rights, and that the global community needed to reign in the powerful violator. The US is often in arrears for funding the UN which is steered by the Security Council (permanent members include China, France, the Russian Federation, the United Kingdom, and the United States). Critical analysts assert that the UN is an extension of the US and that the UN has never countered US egregious crimes against humanity. Hence, community formations for war resistance within the local, state, national, and international realms become essential. How does *We Charge Genocide* provide a legacy that issues more than moral condemnations?[6] International and national organizations find the document to be a stable foundation for a shared language to resist predatory powers and navigate international bodies that might be able to shift into agency that extends beyond the limits of liberalism and legalism.

On December 6, 2022, the United Nations Working Group on Experts of People of African Descent (UN WGEPAD) filed an amicus brief on behalf of Mumia Abu-Jamal. The brief calls the Abu-Jamal case "emblematic of the problems of racial discrimination faced by people of African descent living in the diaspora." Over thirty countries are under US unilateral—thus illegal—sanctions unauthorized by the United Nations. The UN consists of 193 countries linked by treaties and the constantly violated 1945 UN Charter. Yet, as noted in

---

6. In 2016, #chicopwatch pushed *We Charge Genocide* analyses forward to the greater public when it organized in June 2014: Noting that they were inspired by the 1951 *We Charge Genocide* petition to the UN to document the violence and torture to which young Chicagoans of color (in particular Black youth) were subjected. They mobilized after the Chicago Police Department killed Dominique (Damo) Franklin Jr and created in 2014 "We Charge Genocide" (WCG), an organization raised $20,000 to send eight young activists to Geneva in November 2014 to attend hearings held by the United Nations Committee Against Torture. They cite their accomplishments on their website: http://wechargegenocide.org/one-year-of-we-charge-genocide/; data transparency in stops and frisks through the youth-led #ChiStops campaign; their report about the failures of community policing (http://wechargegenocide.org/press-release-community-policing-is-not-the-answer-countercaps-report/); and "raised awareness about how much of Chicago's operational budget is consumed by policing through the Chicago for the People campaign (http://www.chicago4thepeople.com)." Other endeavors included supporting mobilizations against police violence, http://wechargegenocide.org/sunsetting-we-charge-genocide/.

We Charge Genocide, it cannot stem systematic attacks of people of African descent residing within the United States. The United States has the largest per capita of imprisoned beings in any nation—two million people, and its police kill 1,000 people a year.[7]

According to Julia Wright, after the disturbing footage of the 2020 Minneapolis police murder of George Floyd was made public, all fifty-four African state members of the UN requested a UN investigation into US domestic law enforcement. This led to the landmark July 2021 Report on Racial Justice and Equality in Law Enforcement by the Human Rights High Commissioner. The letter initiated by Burkina Faso is considered by Wright to indicate the emergence and expansion of Pan-African or a United African public opinion. Abu-Jamal sent a letter of thanks to the supportive African states and allies, writing that their attempts "gave hope to those living on the brink in US ghettos and prisons, on death rows, and beyond." The Global South recognizes and responds to police murder, and political imprisonment as well as mass incarceration within a democracy in which, as Mumia Abu-Jamal notes, "police narratives still held [hold] sway" and dominate courts.[8]

After nearly two years of negotiating with the UN Human Rights Council, according to Wright, Abu-Jamal advocates in the US and the WGEPAD went "to the roots of the case . . . [recognizing] that racism is a crime against humanity that cannot be time barred . . . state and court decisions should be continuously reinterrogated in the light of the slavery-old harms of systemic racism, that evidence of racial bias, even decades old, has no expiry date, and that Mumia's case is the tip

7. Campaign to Bring Mumia Home / Love Not Phear Campaign Press Conference, "United Nations Steps in with Amicus Brief in Mumia Abu-Jamal Case" (with Johanna Fernandez, Julia Wright, Wendell Griffen, Vijay Prashad, Linn Washington, Jr.), December 13, 2022, https://www.youtube.com/watch?v=Xh38IKVc_oc.

8. Campaign to Bring Mumia Home / Love Not Phear Campaign Press Conference, "United Nations Steps in with Amicus Brief in Mumia Abu-Jamal Case." Wright observed during the press conference: "In October 2021, I was invited to the UN to speak on mass incarceration. I had three minutes. Our prison work is about time, the prisoners do time, their prognosis gives them no time, while the courts drag out the time of their appeals, and when we stand to speak of them, we must triage because we have no time. . . . I had to triage who would I speak of, of Mumia's heart condition or Maroon? I spoke of Maroon because he was dying [Russell Maroon Schultz died December 17, 2021] . . . elderly comorbid prisoners, primarily the political ones, are subjected to a death by incarceration that is torture."

of a very dangerous white supremacist iceberg."[9] The UN WGEPAD amicus brief asserts that "presumed victims of racial discrimination" need not prove that they were targeted by discriminatory intent. Instead, the US is obligated to investigate and then provide a remedy or "remediate discriminatory effects." Citing international human rights law as their framework, UN WGEPAD argued that the state is obligated "to confront and address ongoing racially discriminatory effects." This would include predatory or racially driven police violence and arrests. It does not matter how old the case is or if the discrimination existed for decades, according to UN WGEPAD. Actually, in the context of the US, it would be *centuries* of discriminatory harm.

To hold the US accountable means that Captive Maternal unions would have to connect care with material and economic strategies against predatory policing. Hence, they would engage political economies and consumerism, and offer protections to political prisoners and radical organizations. The marrow and foundation for new bones in an international and entangled world will be based upon the organizing and protective zones offered to the working class, the impoverished, the hunted, and the rebels.

STAGES OF DEVELOPMENT

Martin Luther King, Jr. is celebrated in popular or commercial culture in ways that distort our struggles for life and dignity and against poverty, dishonor, premature and violent death. So, too is Malcolm X. Both went through dramatic transformations. Malcolm's transition from an orphan to "petty criminal," to prisoner, to leader in the Nation of Islam, to a revolutionary intellectual and organizer who impacted the globe, is often more elevated when we discuss metamorphosis in Black radical trajectories and traditions. However, despite the images and narratives, the culture captured and popularized Rev. King, as he went through a deep and massive transformation to arrive at the same destination as Malcolm X in their joint condemnations of racism, colonialism, imperialism, and capitalism. At times popular

---

9. Campaign to Bring Mumia Home / Love Not Phear Campaign Press Conference, "United Nations Steps in with Amicus Brief in Mumia Abu-Jamal Case."

culture sells distorted memories of our objective history and legacy in war resistance. Martin and Malcolm led liberation movements focused on Agape. Both were assassinated—Malcolm X in 1965 and Martin Luther King in 1968. When most people think of love and the "beloved community," they think of King. However, Malcolm was just as deeply committed of a revolutionary. Both sacrificed their lives for being staunch war resisters on all terrains—local, national, and international.

Since King is the more familiar male Captive Maternal, this reflection will focus on his transitions through varied stages. Along with his wife Coretta Scott King, Rev. King moved into tenement slums in Chicago and regularly met with gang leaders. He moved toward segregated communities that would never be integrated through migration into white suburbs or schools. King not only comprehended the lives of the impoverished and persecuted, he felt and then joined, communities that embraced or held those lives. King did not brand or promote "freedom dreams." He encouraged and modeled mass movements to stabilize through marronage and march into war resistance. He understood the internal political structures in the US, its lethal and legal/extralegal police forces such as the FBI and CIA

Black and white people distanced from King once they realized that his embrace of Agape was pushing him deeper into the stages of Captive Maternal Agency. During the Montgomery Bus Boycott in Alabama—launched when Rosa Parks (thinking about Emmett Till) refused to relinquish her seat on a segregated bus in 1955—the Black middle classes, and white liberals were eager to have King in their midst. His PhD in theology from a white, middle-class institution, Boston University, made him a desirable face for a movement that for some was to be about integration into capitalism. As King became politicized into compassion and caretaking, those sectors, and the non-profit corporate funders, rapidly distanced from him because he had become a war resister, opposing empire. King's emotionally-rich "I Have a Dream" speech on the Washington Mall in 1963, embodies the nightmare that also constructs the material and spiritual dimensions of our lives.

Obviously, the Kennedy administration largely controlled the event. But they could not control or stop Black socialists from embedding into the August 28th date, the anniversary of self-deputized white nationalists who abducted, tortured, sexually assaulted, and murdered fourteen-year-old Emmett Till, allegedly for whistling at a white woman. Although guilty, the white nationalists (they confessed to the crime in a paid *Like Magazine* issue in 1955), were exonerated in court. As an impacted family member, Mamie Till Mobley made a defiant war resistance gesture that cannot or will not be leveraged today—an open casket funeral for a mutilated teen. Those photos printed in *Jet Magazine* (only a Black publication would have dared to do so) traveled the globe. Today the photographs of Black corpses also circle the globe, but our capacity to stop such visuals by terminating state murders is unclear.

King offers a model that few of us might embrace. Embed oneself into the most vulnerable sectors of our communities, those lacking resources and protections. Move back into our communities or failing that, fund them with energy, commitment, monies, goods, education, freedom schools, rest, and respite centers. Over thirteen painful years, from 1955–1968, King transitioned through the stages of the Captive Maternal. He moved from being a conflicted, but celebrated caretaker—one who had betrayed Fannie Lou Hamer and the Mississippi Freedom Democratic Party in 1964 by attempting to get them to cancel their third-party electoral campaign and return to the Democratic Party and its presidential candidate, Lyndon Johnson and vice-presidential candidate, Hubert Humphrey. King learned though, as we all do, sometimes slowly and often painfully.

In his 1968 speech-sermon, just before his assassination, King presciently spoke about how longevity would be great but not available for him. He promised that "we as a people" would get to the mountain top and there be reunited. Thus, the war resistance prevails. It is not clear how, but ancestors have insights and so we will stay with the mission. For those who want or need hope to transition into marronage and resistance, a reflection on King's oft-cited April 3, 1968 sermon-speech "I've Been to the Mountaintop" offers helpful reminders that structure hope and then transcend it. He recognizes that he would like to live a long life, but that it is not what is going to happen. So, he let's go and surrenders to God's will.

Reverend King is grateful because he painfully climbed the mountain and saw another dimension. He calls it "the Promised Land." Perhaps it is the zone beyond the wars. He says that he might not accompany the community in the journey, and he downplays what he already knows to be true; he will be assassinated, abandoned and betrayed. So, he clarifies that he might not (likely will not) "get there with you." But here's the promise, the people will survive the journey. It might sound a bit like Exodus. So, what? It is the emotional register of a Captive Maternal who surrenders, but not to predatory police powers. Hence, King declares his happiness, his lack of worry and fear of "any man." He has sight into the future. The segment of his offering is the most quoted. This Captive Maternal, the author who has not advanced to King's stages, is drawn to another segment in which King says to the community that is simultaneously mourning, and celebrating with him, because they also have prescient knowledge:

> Another reason that I'm happy to live in this period is that we have been forced to a point where we're going to have to grapple with the problems that men have been trying to grapple with through history, but the demand didn't force them to do it. Survival demands that we grapple with them. Men, for years now, have been talking about war and peace. But now, no longer can they just talk about it. It is no longer a choice between violence and nonviolence in this world; it's nonviolence or nonexistence.[10]

King was working with Black sanitation workers who were being killed at their work sites in Memphis, Tennessee. Memphis is the former home town of Ida B. Wells who was run out of town in 1892 by white lynch mobs. Wells later engineered a British boycott of Memphis cotton to cripple the city's economy—remember what the Black pastor from Rochester said about killing economies if states kill us? Memphis is also the city with a Black woman police commissioner whose (and perhaps complicit white?) officers beat Tyre Nichols to death in 2023 while they were yelling seventy-one contradictory commands that no could have followed, during a random and innocuous traffic stop.

---

10. "'I've Been to the Mountaintop' by Dr. Martin Luther King, Jr.," American Federation of State, County and Municipal Employees (AFSCME), https://www.afscme.org/about/history/mlk/mountaintop.

STUDENTS REFLECT ON LEVERAGING THE UN

In their December 10, 2022 International Human Rights Day interviews of activist alumni for the seminar "Captivity, Betrayal, Community," Kaon Suh and Micaela Foreman interrogate capitalism, imperialism, and anti-Blackness in a coauthored paper that demystified freedom struggles against state violence. Their seminar studied the entwined genocides against Indigenous and African/Black communities in the Americas and in Africa. Observing that "language holds immense power" the students note how academics and authors illuminate war atrocities *or* more often, "sanitize and sometimes even rationalize violence," by smoothing "over the past to tuck it neatly into the genocidal logic of the present." Reflecting upon the twentieth century Black Liberation Movement, the student authors write that "history can be subject to cruel and cynical vivisection . . . [or] invoked and paid homage to—while [radicals are] spending their last years, or days, incarcerated."[11] Students examine political imprisonment, varied death penalties, and state persecution noting that in "retaliation for their candor in *We Charge Genocide*," Civil Rights Congress leader William L. Patterson and coauthors/cosigners "were jailed, had their passports confiscated, were harassed by the FBI" and that artist Paul Robeson, persecuted by the McCarthy zealots and anticommunists, was physically beaten while giving a performance in Peekskill, New York. Some of the leadership in crafting *We Charge Genocide* as a war resistance strategy were forced into the underground.[12]

Observing that the Thirteenth Amendment creates a social and legal chasm that creates a dichotomy between "enslaved rebels" seeking marronage and "citizens" seeking state protections, student authors juxtaposed the cases of Ruchell Magee, currently incarcerated for over sixty years, and his former co-defendant Angela Davis acquitted in 1972:

> Denouncing the entire judicial and prison system as the system of slavery which existed four hundred years ago, at his 1971 trial where

11. "Dhoruba bin Wahad on Assata Shakur, Angela Davis and COINTELPRO," *Black Power Media*, November 3, 2022, https://www.youtube.com/watch?v=qwMISdgoJAs&t=1s.
12. Tony Pecinovsky, "'Black Revolutionary' Explores Life of William Patterson and Global Freedom Fight," *People's World*, November 8, 2013, https://www.peoplesworld.org/article/black-revolutionary-explores-life-of-william-patterson-and-global-freedom-fight/.

he [Magee] was briefly co-defendant of Angela Davis, the said system made Ruchell Magee[13] an example, sentencing him to life in prison. . . . What distinguishes Magee from Davis is that Magee refused to give any semblance of validity to the US's violent, genocidal court system. According to Magee, he argued this stance in court not only for himself, but for others who were oppressed or enslaved by the judicial system.[14]

Magee was acquitted in 1973 facing the same charges as Davis, but his judge did not read the jury's verdict into the court records. The jury convicted Magee of "simple kidnapping" which carries a maximum five-year sentence. (Magee was released from prison on July 21, 2023, after sixty-seven years incarcerated; he was never convicted of a serious crime.). [15]

We Charge Genocide's strategies appear to be consigned to protests. However, they have the capacity to move beyond conventional conferences and petitions. Local and grassroots campaigns, despite contradictions, likely offer the best way forward for grappling with state and police violence, while levying massive boycotts and economic penalties to the corporations who fund predatory policing. Voting can also work if it is strategic and not purely fear-based. The May 2023 conference against the death penalty and predatory policing in Texas was not a conventional conference. It was a gathering and communal formation that would disperse within a few days, but still leave an impact and a template for participants to follow and develop.

RADICAL COMMUNAL INTENT

In May 2023, S.H.A.P.E., a Black progressive cultural center, founded fifty-five years ago in Houston, Texas, hosted "Lethal Violence & the Lone Star State: A Southwest Conference on State Authorized Exe-

13. Kiilu Nyasha, "Ruchell Cinque Magee, sole survivor of the Aug. 7, 1970 Courthouse Slave Rebellion," February 2, 2017, https://sfbayview.com/2017/02/ruchell-cinque-magee-sole-survivor-of-the-aug-7-1970-courthouse-slave-rebellion/.

14. Ruchell Magee was released from prison in July 2023 at the age of 84. See Joy James and Kalonji Changa, "Slave Rebel or Citizen?: Abolitionist Ruchell Cinqué Magee is the country's longest-held political prisoner," *Inquest*, May 2, 2023, https://inquest.org/slave-rebel-or-citizen/.

15. See James and Changa, "Slave Rebel or Citizen?"

cutions." Different from elite academic conferences, this gathering was hosted by HBCU Texas Southern University's Thurgood Marshall School of Law, and was sponsored by grassroots anti-death penalty, and anti-genocide groups such as the Spirit of Mandela Coalition, Pan-African Connection Bookstore and Resource Center, Texas Death Penalty Abolition Movement, and Texas People's Tribunal. The gathering's speakers included Captive Maternals such as Sekou Odinga, Dequi Sadiki, Rodrick Reed, Kindaka Sanders, and Obie Weathers. Lethal Violence's conference program printed the complete last words of Shaka Sankofa:

> We must keep our faith. We must go forward. We recognize that many leaders have died. Malcom X, Martin Luther King, and others who stood up for what was right. They stood up for what was just. We must, you must brothers, that's why I have called you today. You must carry on that condition. What is here is just a lynching that is taking place. But they're going to keep a lynching us for the next 100 years, if you do not carry on that tradition, and that period of resis tance. We will prevail. We may lose this battle, but we will win the war. This death, this lynching will be avenged. It will be avenged, it must be avenged. The people must avenge this murder.

After the first panel which included Black Panther Party and Black Liberation Army veterans, several young Black women raised a query based in academic abolition. They lamented that Panther veterans and liberators of Assata Shakur did not share their "dreams," and so asserted that elders, who they had just met during the panel, had betrayed the youth of today. They had heard BLA member Sekou Odinga, who helped liberate Assata Shakur from prison (without injuries to anyone), say that the youth were the leaders of today because elders had played their part. Indeed, Odinga was captured and sentenced to thirty-three years in prison; activists in the political prisoner movement maintain that his police interrogators tortured him by pulling out his finger and toe nails (additionally Italian citizen Sylvia Baraldini served twenty years in a US prison). The youth did not acknowledge the care-taking and sacrifices offered for decades by revolutionaries, liberating Assata Shakur, who could then publish a memoir studied by youth today. Theory, discipline, and strategic thinking seemed to be put on pause because elders did not say how to wage and win a revolution—and share "freedom dreams."

Three generations debated. In the audience, young Black men critiqued the young Black women for their freedom dreaming-focus, suggesting that they lacked political analysis. A BPP vet criticized BPP/BLA panelists for not asserting that the Panthers were the vanguard for twenty-first century struggles. The academic/nonprofit epicenter had just met the underground and revolutionary hypocenter. Without shared material struggles and relationships, young academic-trained abolitionists asked revolutionary elders if they knew or worked with any youth (the answer was, "Yes they are in our formations and routinely ask to dialogue.").

Historical objectivity and study seemed pushed aside for discourse on dreaming. Recognizing the academic abolition language in play, I asked if "freedom dreams" would be functional care or dysfunctional care for an unhoused mother forced to sell her older child in order to feed the younger one. Perhaps that mother had nightmares and anxiety and dream impairment shaped by the material conditions of degradation and despair. Caretaking and devotion, would be more of a curative for her than faulting her for not aligning with the dreams of left-leaning bourgeoisie. I insisted to the gathering that youth and communities benefit more from our devotion than dream mirroring. There is also a strong possibility that the state and corporation filter or shaped dreams so that they misalign with stages of development that could empower communities to unravel the webs of bureaucratic and militarized state craft. New Bones are fashioned on terrain that often looks like a battlefield. How we even define and speak about our stages and development is uneven and broken because academic abolitionist language is not liberatory.

Students Suh and Foreman note that it is "easier to preemptively lower our voices and submit to the rationalities of the state, no matter how irrational it may be." They maintain that people need to "define our realities before creating new ones" because the political language we have been taught in institutions "is treacherous" and "can be co-opted and used to launder and cipher violence." This process of confused or ineffectual discourse is not accidental: "The incompleteness and vagueness of 'liberatory language' is not unintentional."[16] The collected speeches of revolutionary Captive Maternal Amílcar Cabral offers instruction.

CABRAL'S *RETURN TO THE SOURCE*

"Liberatory language" can be found in the speeches of African freedom fighter Amílcar Cabral.[17] Cabral's assertion that the "lack of clean water, adequate food and shelter" cannot be addressed through policy. If so, we would only need accommodation packages from our colonizers or former enslavers. For Cabral, mission statements without material aid to freedom fighters are designed to meet the preferences of the empire and its beneficiaries. Thus, academia and nonprofits, and the state bureaucracies, mirror the United Nations in many ways.

An International Captive Maternal, freedom fighter, father, and theorist during the anti-colonial war against Portugal, Amílcar Cabral[18] lived long enough to see a liberation movement free three-quarters of the countryside before he was assassinated in 1973. (Allegedly the US/CIA, NATO, and Britain clandestinely supported Portugal—the first European state to invest in, and the last to relinquish, genocidal trafficking of Africans in order to build an economy.) Cabral's injunction to "return to the source" synthesizes abolitionism, anti-imperialism, and communal culture to assert that collective material struggles create and sustain the cultures of liberation movements. This means that our varied analyses and strategies to oppose genocide, femicide, filicide, poverty, war, and environmental devastation, require a convergence in epistemology and praxis. We can expand on Cabral's contributions as a critical lens for liberation struggles.

As Secretary-General of PAIGC, Cabral was an outstanding theorist practitioner in the abolition of imperial warfare. He understood

---

16. See their conversation with Margaret Kimberley of the *Black Agenda Report*, 2020–2023 Williams College "Just Futures" Project. Kaon Suh and Micaela Foreman, hosts, "Margaret Kimberley '80 – Micaela and Kaon," *Captivity, Betrayal and Community* (podcast), December 16, 2020, https://www.podomatic.com/podcasts/jep4/episodes/2022-12-1 6T13_03_37-08_00.

17. Africa Information Service, *Return to the Source: Selected Speeches of Amílcar Cabral* (New York: Monthly Review Press, 1975).

18. Africa Information Service, *Return to the Source*.

both the victimization and the transformative agency of the peasant and working classes. Revolutionary struggle would be shaped by revolutionary culture emanating from the lives of the masses, overly policed and struggling with impoverishment and exploitation. With the allies of Cabral, we see something special: academics and professional intellectuals work to preserve the memory of revolutionary struggle without infiltrating abstractions or political compromises aligned with liberalism or hegemony academia. Academics and intellectuals took up roles within militant formations. They provided speaking platforms for Cabral, comprehending that he and African people were not hapless victims of imperial police powers, but agentic intellectuals and skillful strategists.

After Cabral's CIA-assisted assassination, Africa Information Service (AIS) and presses such as Monthly Review Press, as well as academics and educators, continued to support African, African-Caribbean, and African American freedom movements and preserved speeches and analyses in texts distributed for popular education. (A similar process also occurred with Malcolm X's speeches and analyses as they evolved towards socialism and [Black] revolutionary internationalism.) Such struggles by Malcolm X—supported by Black women such as Fannie Lou Hamer, Rosa Parks, and Maya Angelou—linked his travels throughout the United States to the Africa liberation struggles led by Patrice Lumumba (assassinated in 1961) and Amílcar Cabral. All three leaders were surveilled by and eliminated with the assistance of international police forces such as the CIA.[19] Still, the "source" did not come from those engaged in material struggle against repressive regimes. The co-architects of the source were always vulnerable to the lethal violence of (international) policing.

Return to the Source asserts that in order to be "effective," the UN must provide "simultaneously moral, political and material" support to the resisters in the fields and combat zones who disproportionately shoulder the risks of liberation movements—even after the UN failed to intervene in meaningful and material ways. Cabral stated that he did not appear before the UN Committee "in order to obtain more violent condemnations and resolutions against the Portuguese colonial-

---

19. Malcolm X, "The Ballot or the Bullet" (speech), Detroit, Michigan, April 12, 1964, https://www.youtube.com/watch?v=CRNciryImqg.

ists." Rather, he came to the UN for material aid. However, he left empty handed. Amílcar Cabral was assassinated in 1973 through the joint efforts of the Portuguese, NATO, and the United States. The speeches and communiques of this ancestor live on in *Return to the Source*.

CONCLUSION

Patrice Lumumba was assassinated in the Congo in 1961 with assistance from the CIA and Portugal. Ernesto Che Guevara spoke at the UN declaring that he and revolutionary leaders fighting against colonialism and poverty would be happy to abide by "peaceful coexistence"—a Soviet agreement since the 1950s, not to be antagonistic with the US—if the US/CIA stopped "killing us." Guevara was executed and secretly buried in 1965 by Bolivia military trained by the CIA. All liberation leaders were/are surveilled by and eliminated with the assistance of international police forces.[20] Still, the "source" remained with those engaged in material struggle against repressive regimes. The co-architects of the source were always vulnerable to the lethal violence of (international) policing but were also the architects of culture and resilience.

Amílcar Cabral challenged the international community and its elite representatives and management with a query: "When a fighter had succumbed in our country to police torture, or had been murdered in prison, or burnt alive or machine-gunned by the Portuguese troops, for what cause had [they] given [their] life?" His answer: those who gave their lives for the liberation of their people served the cause of the United Nations because they had sacrificed their lives "in a context of international legality, for the ideals set forth in the [UN] Charter and resolutions . . . ." Motivated by the ideal of their inalienable rights, those seeking a liberation culture would be ruthlessly undermined by the Portuguese government, US, NATO—and the UN that would not, or could not—support Black or Third World liberation in a meaningful way.

---

20. Malcolm X, "The Ballot or the Bullet."

During his last tour of the United States, Cabral sought to connect the struggles of Africans and Black Americans. Recognizing the primacy of international struggle, he asserted:

> I am bringing to you our African brothers and sisters of the United States—the fraternal salutations of our people in assuring you we are very conscious that all in this life concerning you also concerns us. We try to understand your situation in this country . . . . we realize the difficulties you face, the problems you have and your feelings, your revolts, and also your hopes. We think that our fighting for Africa against colonialism and imperialism is a proof of understanding of your problem and also a contribution for the solution of your problems in this continent. Naturally, the inverse is also true.[21]

Centuries of international police violence have devasted countries and colonized cities and continents and disappeared diasporic communities and revolutionary internationalists. Cabral moved through painful stages to evolve as a beloved liberator and revolutionary. Likewise, our communities will do the same, in this lifetime or the ones that follow.

---

21. See Amílcar Cabral, *Return to the Source*, ed. Africa Information Service (New York: Monthly Review, 2023[1973]), 76.

Figure 6: Kalonji Jama Changa (FTP) and Kofi Taharka at the National Black United Front Community House, Houston, TX, May 2023, following the Texas Anti-Death Penalty Conference. The painted sign in the People's Garden honors Sundiata Acoli. Photo by J. James.

CONCLUSION:
PRIORITIZING CARE AND ANCESTORS

Today, social justice leaders and healers formally educated with advanced degrees refuse demeaning, boring, or repetitive jobs to retain their dignity. The well attired rarely eat from garbage cans. Some, with advanced degrees leave professional schools. Those with a (petit) bourgeois education, networks, and public persona accumulations rarely live with the class that dropped out of high school, or never attended. The gig economy of public intellectualism and political avatars is precarious without a financial benefactor such as the one that harassed Zora Neale Hurston. In Atlanta, one can see a Black mother shepherding small children on the street while she wears a size 9 shoe and a size 7 shoe because she cannot afford a matching pair. Another Black mother traffics or sells one child in order to feed the others. Competitors for resources embody not poverty but lack of wealth. One can hustle a concept, project, or pain and no longer belong to the laboring classes based on the acquisition of advanced education and networks. Diverse sectors of underserved or under-resourced peoples cannot be conflated. Which ones should be prioritized for care? Those who present as social leaders with some degree of visibility or those who remain largely unknown in their desperations?

Captive Maternals have limited energy, time, and means—and their own health issues. They often lack protections from those hustling their sacrifices garnered from disciplining themselves to be distributed to those who find discipling demeaning. Care recipients do not engage in reciprocity if they feel that they are entitled to your labor, time, and space. There are specific frailties based on age. Laws prohibit child abuse and elder abuse, although the latter category is often forgotten. For Captive Maternals in the middle, forming the fulcrum to balance the plank of a seesaw in a balancing act will definitely crash if adults in their twenties and thirties, or forties and fifties, demand care as if they were entitled children. Demanding privatized care-as-an entitlement from a Captive Maternal caring for and organizing with others reflects childhood ego. The middle class or affluent require care yet their material needs cannot be conflated with the impoverished whose lives are shaped not by desires for autonomy but by desperation.

Markets rely on personal stories to emphasize victimization in the narratives of those who claim to be virtuous. Stories become more significant than phsycial engagement in movement building, marronage, and war resistance. There is always harm in the family, school, society, and state. Echos from the past become imprinted on the present as if these were reality in the material world. Traumas from childhood recycle and register as hypocenter catastrophes when they are painful as saviors or executioners. Discern between the desperate who have middle-class families and advanced education, yet need a spotlight to appear in the world, and the desperate who walk around as specters abandoned by society with bare literacy and limited or no employable skills in exploitation-based economies. The health of the political body is tethered to the mind. Fred Hampton's "I am a revolutionary" declaration urged calm so that we can focus on structure and material struggle. One doesn't have to emulate Hampton, assassinated in 1969 by the FBI and CPD, but it is useful to recall his advocacy:

> A lot of people get the word revolution mixed up, and they think revolution is a bad word. Revolution is nothing but like having a sore on your body and then you put something on that sore to cure that infection. I'm telling you that we're living in an infectious society right now. I'm telling you that we're living in a sick society right now. I'm telling you that we're living in a sick society and anybody that endorses integrating into a sick society before it's cleaned up is a man who's committing a crime against the people."[1]

The theatrical is tied to political performance and the polarity of a sick society. The Magical Black Negress to be embraced and the Nasty

---

1. "Fred Hampton Speech Transcript on Revolution and Racism," https://www.rev.com/blog/transcripts/fred-hampton-speech-transcript-on-revolution-and-racism.

Black Negress to be obliterated are scripted in a colonizing democracy. Hattie McDaniel's 1939 Oscar for Best Supporting Actress in *Gone with the Wind* was based on her performance of "Mammy," the loyal, giving caretaker of whites. Mo'Nique's 2010 Oscar for Best Supporting Actress was leveraged by her performance as the vicious anti-Madonna "Mary" in *Precious*, who violated her young Black traumatized daughter. Mammy and Mary are two Black women who are *not* your mother. Ethical Captive Maternals are likely to drop the hashtag culture and shoulder the burden and blessing of revolutionary futures. But even if you do not trust any elders, let go of the hungry ghosts and find the holy ghosts or ancestors who function as caretakers in liberation struggles.

Caretaking that confronts predatory violence is the marrow of militancy. In its varied forms, self-defense (as my former seminarian cadre who worked to end domestic/family/intimate violence in the household) directed disproportionately at women and children—is *not* violence. It is self-love. Captive Materials defend (after)lives so that they/we can evolve beyond the triage centers of basic New Bones growth. Break, and mend. Seeking the higher stages that liberate us from all forms of violence, particularly state violence, means confrontations that liberate one from fear of the predator and comprador. Whatever exists beyond war resistance, in the (after)life, the Captive Maternal will retrieve in order to secure freedoms that reclaim our essence from the battlefields.[2]

---

2. Our desperate need for more than emotional care, i.e, concentric circles of security and self-defense require. On July 29, 2023, a group of men demanded that O'Shea Sibley, a professional dancer, stop vogue dancing to Beyoncé with other Black men at a Midwood, Brooklyn, gas station on Coney Island Avenue. The men allegedly stated that the dancing offended their religion as Muslims (they were Russian Christians). Their homophobic and anti-Black slurs commanded shirtless Black men in beach shorts (with no concealed protections) to stop dancing. Verbally confronting antagonists, Sibley died minutes later from a stab wound in the heart, inflicted by a seventeen-year-old white male. The Instagram call for an August 4th "Emergency Action: Justice for O'Shea" gathering at the gas station led to a memorial ball/protest in which the Black queer/trans artistic community shared care, grief, and love. SAI attended the memorial, and in an email reflected on how in the post-George Floyd-era the vogue performance mobilized a protest in which "if one does not dance, the only role left is that of bystander." Relating police and civilian violence, SAI determined Sibley's cause of death as "dancing while being Black and queer." Every form of care is present except for a security apparatus. The vogue protests of nonviolent resistance produce nonviolent performances, yet as a stark departure from the Student Nonviolent Coordinating Committee (SNCC) battles in the face of white nationality terror and murder during the civil rights movement. According to SAI, protest "audiences" armed with camer-

We lose family and community members, clean water and air, fecund soil, and kin-species. Peaceful protestors and political prisoners are murdered by police and troopers, or disappeared into jails and prisons by bureaucracies and bureaus. As noted earlier, in Atlanta, the FBI incarcerated activists and environmentalists on "terrorist" charges after Georgia State Patrol shot a meditating environmental and community protector fifty-seven times. Current and future generations of political prisoners are to be captured and tortured and broken. Yet we mend, from the state's aggressions against us, and the conflicts and attacks by hustlers and compradors.

New Bones growth is uncomfortable when not painful, yet it is shared through connectors between individuals, communities, and ethics that transfer bones into branches of Agape-enriched Aspen. Our underground will burrow toward the hypocenter. Conduits of shared root systems will distinguish performers and attention-seekers from workers and the warriors. Some will be distracted by spectacle and/or x [Twitter], others mutate and clone into terrain that cradles marronage, and maps out strategies of war resistance against predatory policing. Marrow mutates. Abolitionists burrow. Living cultures digging deeper can decipher performance capture from risk-taking, disciplined commitments. New Bones abolition will stabilize communities, forests, food, flowers, and gardens.[3] The mandate exists within our culture(s). Ordinary people within a rapacious democracy resist (self)objectification and capitalist consumption. In *Mind of My Mind*, Octavia Butler asks: "Could a creature who had to look upon ordinary people literally as food and shelter ever understand how strongly those people valued life?"[4]

---

as emerged as documentarians or social media influencers with grants, bylines, cinematic awards, and followers. A communal gathering to respond to hate with performance culture is not insufficient. Using the 1976 film *Network* to illustrate this, Kim Holder references the protagonist stalwart news anchor who breaks down into rebellion in which he yells during a live broadcast—as apartment dwellers scream out their apartment windows—"I'm mad as hell and I'm not going to take this anymore!" We capture the melt down, according to Holder, and then package it for consumption in markets monetizing Black death and grief. The antidote to a poli-trauma commodities market can be found in revolutionary cultures shared in *Return to the Source*.

3. "New York Police Planned Assault on Bronx Protestors," Human Rights Watch, September 30, 2020, https://www.hrw.org/news/2020/09/30/us-new-york-police-planned-assault-bronx-protesters.

4. Octavia Butler, *Mind of My Mind* (New York: Grand Central Publishing, 1994).

Honor ancestors and avoid hungry ghosts. Return to the sources of spiritual, emotional, and material sustenance that connect and discipline us. Providing (self)protections and security, we resist to pour a foundation solidified in political-will love. This reflection on abolition and Captive Maternal agency began with Lucille Clifton's poem "new bones." It ends with an excerpt from the poem "My mama's love and her mother's hold: Lie, Mama, Lie" by then nineteen-year-old Isaiah Blake, whose gift to me on Mother's Day, May 12, 2019, unveiled an ouroboros Captive Maternal:

> Mama. . . You threw me
> Deep into the ground
> Sent me backwards spinning
> Three thousand years
> into the roots of old
> Okra, old yam, old watermelon,
> And Bloody red beets. . . .
> I got love for the captive maternal. . . .

FURTHER RESOURCES

For further information, including a compiliation of Erica Garner's tweets and other activist media communications, scan the QR code below.

INDEX

ABOUT THE AUTHOR

Political philosopher **Joy James** is the Ebenezer Fitch Professor of Humanities at Williams College. James is author of *Resisting State Violence* (1996); *Transcending the Talented Tenth* (1997); *Shadowboxing: Representations of Black Feminist Politics* (1999); *Seeking the Beloved Community* (2012); *In Pursuit of Revolutionary Love* (2023); *Contextualizing Angela Davis* (2024). She is the editor of *The Angela Y. Davis Reader* (1998); *States of Confinement* (2000); *Imprisoned Intellectuals* (2003); *The New Abolitionists* (2005); *Warfare in the American Homeland* (2008); and coeditor of *The Black Feminist Reader*.

Publishing on US politics and political theory, feminism, policing and abolition, political prisoners, diasporic anti-Black racism, her writing appears in *Inquest; The Black Scholar; Parapraxis; SOULS; LOGOS; New York Times; American Philosophical Association*; and *Truthout*. James studies the Captive Maternal as framed within her 2016 article "The Womb of Western Theory: Trauma, Time Theft and the Captive Maternal," and creates social justice archives through platforms such as the Harriet Tubman Literary Circle at University of Texas, Austin.

ABOUT COMMON NOTIONS

Common Notions is a publishing house and programming platform that fosters new formulations of living autonomy. We aim to circulate timely reflections, clear critiques, and inspiring strategies that amplify movements for social justice.

Our publications trace a constellation of critical and visionary meditations on the organization of freedom. By any media necessary, we seek to nourish the imagination and generalize common notions about the creation of other worlds beyond state and capital. Inspired by various traditions of autonomism and liberation—in the US and internationally, historical and emerging from contemporary movements—our publications provide resources for a collective reading of struggles past, present, and to come.

Common Notions regularly collaborates with political collectives, militant authors, radical presses, and maverick artists around the world.

www.commonnotions.org
info@commonnotions.org

BECOME A COMMON NOTIONS
MONTHLY SUSTAINER

These are decisive times ripe with challenges and possibility, heart-ache, and beautiful inspiration. More than ever, we need timely reflections, clear critiques, and inspiring strategies that can help movements for social justice grow and transform society.

Help us amplify those words, deeds, and dreams that our liberation movements, and our worlds, so urgently need.

Movements are sustained by people like you, whose fugitive words, deeds, and dreams bend against the world of domination and exploitation.

For collective imagination, dedicated practices of love and study, and organized acts of freedom.
By any media necessary.
With your love and support.

Monthly sustainer subscriptions start at $15.

commonnotions.org/sustain

MORE FROM COMMON NOTIONS

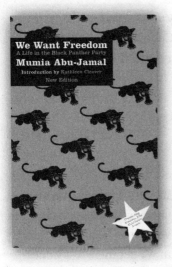

We Want Freedom: A Life in the Black Panther Party (New Edition)
Mumia Abu-Jamal

978-1-942173-04-5
$20.00
336 pages

Mumia Abu Jamal, America's most famous political prisoner, is internationally known for his radio broadcasts and books emerging "Live from Death Row." In his youth Mumia Abu-Jamal helped found the Philadelphia branch of the Black Panther Party, wrote for the national newspaper, and began his life-long work of exposing the violence of the state as it manifests in entrenched poverty, endemic racism, and unending police brutality. In We Want Freedom, Mumia combines his memories of day-to-day life in the Party with analysis of the history of Black liberation struggles. The result is a vivid and compelling picture of the Black Panther Party and its legacy.

Applying his poetic voice and unsparing critical gaze, Mumia examines one of the most revolutionary and most misrepresented groups in the US. As the calls that Black Lives Matter continue to grow louder, Mumia connects the historic dots in this revised/updated edition, observing that the Panthers had legal observers to monitor the police and demanded the "immediate end to police brutality and the murder of Black people." By focusing on the men and women who were the Party, as much as on the leadership; by locating the Black Panthers in a struggle centuries old—and in the personal memories of a young man—Mumia Abu-Jamal helps us to understand freedom.

MORE FROM COMMON NOTIONS
& ABOLITION COLLECTIVE

Spirituality and Abolition
Abolition Collective
Edited by Ashon Crawley and Roberto Sirvent

978-1-942173-72-4
$20.00
224 pages

Abolition can be a spiritual practice, a spiritual journey, and a spiritual commitment. What does abolition entail and how can we get there as a collective and improvisational project? To posit the spirituality of abolition is to consider the ways historical and contemporary movements against slavery; prisons; the wage system; animal and earth exploitation; racialized, gendered, and sexualized violence; and the death penalty necessitate epistemologies that have been foreclosed through violent force by Western philosophical and theological thought. It is also to claim that the material conditions that will produce abolition are necessarily Black, Indigenous, queer and trans, feminist, and also about disabled and other non-conforming bodies in force and verve.

Spirituality and Abolition asks: what can prison abolition teach us about spiritual practice, spiritual journey, spiritual commitment? And, what can these things underscore about the struggle for abolition as a desired manifestation of material change in the worlds we currently inhabit? Collecting writings, poetry, and art from thinkers, organizers, and incarcerated people, the editors trace the importance of faith and spirit in our ongoing struggle towards abolitionist horizons.

Making Abolitionist Worlds:
Proposals for a World on Fire
Abolition Collective

978-1-942173-17-5
$20.00
272 pages

Making Abolitionist Worlds gathers key insights and interventions from today's international abolitionist movement to pose the question: what does an abolitionist world look like? The Abolition Collective investigates the core challenges to social justice and the liberatory potential of social movements today from a range of personal, political, and analytical points of view, underscoring the urgency of an abolitionist politics that places prisons at the center of its critique and actions.

In addition to centering and amplifying the continual struggles of incarcerated people who are actively working to transform prisons from the inside, *Making Abolitionist Worlds* animates the idea of abolitionist democracy and demands a radical re-imagining of the meaning and practice of democracy. Abolition Collective brings us to an Israeli prison for a Palestinian feminist reflection on incarceration within settler colonialism; to antipolice protest movements in Hong Kong and elsewhere; to the growing culture of "aggrieved whiteness," to the punitive landscapes of political prisoners to the mass deportations and detentions along the U.S. southern border. *Making Abolitionist Worlds* shows us that the paths forged today for a world in formation are rooted in antiracism, decolonization, anticapitalism, abolitionist feminism, and queer liberation.

MORE FROM COMMON NOTIONS
& ABOLITION COLLECTIVE

Abolishing Carceral Society
Abolition Collective

978-1-942173-08-3
$20.00
256 pages

Beyond border walls and prison cells—carceral society is everywhere. In a time of mass incarceration, immigrant detention and deportation, rising forms of racialized, gendered, and sexualized violence, and deep ecological and economic crises, abolitionists everywhere seek to understand and radically dismantle the interlocking institutions of oppression and transform the world in which we find ourselves. These oppressions have many different names and histories and so, to make the impossible possible, abolition articulates a range of languages and experiences between (and within) different systems of oppression in society today.

Abolishing Carceral Society presents the bold voices and inspiring visions of today's revolutionary abolitionist movements struggling against capitalism, patriarchy, colonialism, ecological crisis, prisons, and borders. The Abolition Collective renews and boldly extends the tradition of "abolition-democracy" espoused by figures like W.E.B. Du Bois, Angela Davis, and Joel Olson. Through study and publishing, the Abolition Collective supports militant research, recognizing that the most transformative scholarship is happening both in the movements themselves and in the communities with whom they organize. *Abolishing Carceral Society* features a range of creative styles and approaches from activists, artists, and scholars to create spaces for collective experimentation with the urgent questions of our time.